S0-CFN-404

From Erica Back
for my Birthday 1994

SEASHELLS
OF
THE
NORTHERN
HEMISPHERE

SEASHELLS OF THE NORTHERN HEMISPHERE

R. TUCKER ABBOTT

LONGMEADOW PRESS

Published by Longmeadow Press. 201 High Ridge Road.
Stamford, CT 06904.

EDITOR Diana Steedman
DESIGNER David Hunter
EDITORIAL DIRECTOR Pippa Rubinstein

ISBN: 0-681-45382-6

Printed in Italy

First Longmeadow Press Edition

0 9 8 7 6 5 4 3 2 1

Contents

Introduction..9

    Geographical Distribution   10
    The Ecology of Molluscs   10
    Molluscan Marine Provinces   10
    Map of Marine Provinces   12
    Classification and Scientific Names 14
    How Molluscs Reproduce   16
    How Molluscs Feed   18
    Collecting Shells   20

The Univalves (CLASS GASTROPODA)................................24

Terrestrial Snails (SUBCLASS PULMONATA)..............103

Tusk Shells (CLASS SCAPHOPODA)..............................106

Chitons (CLASS POLYPLACOPHORA)...........................110

The Bivalves (CLASS BIVALVIA)....................................116

Glossary..184

Bibliography...188

Index..189

Acknowledgments...191

Introduction

To our great grandparents conchology was a pleasant and inspirational pastime that taught them about newly discovered shells from far-away, exotic seas. Then the bounties of nature were for the taking, but not so today. With man's burgeoning populations, and the great destruction and pollution of our shorelines, a more serious science of malacology has arisen to help combat oil spills, toxic drainage and other radical disturbances to the world's ecology. What affects Alaska or the North Sea has its long-term consequences in Labrador or Japan.

While conchology consists of the study of only the hard shells, the more advanced science of malacology deals with the biology, ecology and anatomy of the molluscan soft parts that produce the shells. The rates of normal growth, the environmental limits for survival, the nature of reproduction and the factor influencing the replacement of depleted populations is information that environmentalists must use in solving extreme cases of man's pollution. The extent and condition of various colonies of molluscs are delicate monitors of water conditions and may predict the chances of the return to a normal, healthy habitat.

The phylum Mollusca, includes seashells, squid and octopuses, as well as terrestrial and freshwater snails and clams, and outnumbers all the vertebrates in number of kinds of species. The estimated 80,000 species of molluscs are a dominant part of marine life, being one of the main sources of food for fish, birds and man. Along our sandy or rocky shores their populations are a barometer of the health of our seas.

This book illustrates the most frequently encountered of the several hundreds of kinds of molluscs found in three major regions of the Pacific and Atlantic: the north-eastern Pacific from the Aleutian Islands and Alaska, south to Oregon; the north-western Atlantic from Labrador to approximately Virginia; and the north-eastern Atlantic from Scandinavia to Portugal. Most of the shallow-water shells are quite distinct in each of these provinces, although further north most shells are common to both Arctic Canada, Siberia and northern Scandinavia.

Geographical Distribution

The Arctic Ocean and the warmer boreal seas that border it in the northern hemisphere, are a natural path for the interchange of circumpolar species, but the further south one goes, the more separate and distinct become the faunas in these warmer waters that are isolated by continental masses. While the life cycle of many snails and clams includes free-swimming, veliger stages that permit far-flung distributions, there are also many molluscs that lay stationary egg capsules or give birth to live, crawling young. This creates isolated populations and eventually leads to subspecies unique to small isolated places.

The Ecology of Molluscs

Water temperature, substrate and wave action are the three primary factors influencing the nature of molluscan populations. Shorelines in Arctic and boreal regions are largely destitute of shells because of the grinding effect of seasonal ice cover. Offshore and under the ice there is a fairly rich fauna. In more temperate waters, protected back bays and tidepools along rocky coasts teem with many forms of marine life, although the number of species is relatively low.

Molluscs are never as evident as birds and fish, mainly because of their small size, poor locomotive abilities and nocturnal inclinations. Knowing the habits and habitat preferences of the various species makes finding them much easier. Some periwinkles and dogwinkles are hidden under festoons of rock-clinging algae; other snails are found only among clusters of barnacles and mussels; and the mud-loving nassa snails abound on intertidal flats. An old floating log when broken apart may reveal several species of wood-boring bivalves, and clinging to the underside of some sea stars and sea-urchins may be found tiny parasitic snails and clams.

Molluscan Marine Provinces

The Eastern Pacific or western part of North America is bounded by the Arctic Sea where about 110 species can only be obtained by dredging from a boat or investigating with winter scuba gear. Southward, in the Aleutian subprovince, the collecting improves and many species common to northern Japan and southern Alaska are readily obtained in shallow water. Below this is the Oregonian Province, one of the richest areas in the world for numbers of molluscan specimens. The temperate waters from northern British Columbia to Oregon and the northern sections of California are rich in rock-dwelling limpets, dogwinkles and mussels. Puget Sound, for example, can boast of having over 500 species of univalve snails and 200 different bivalves.

On the eastern side of North America, the inhospitable shores of Hudson Bay, Labrador, Greenland and northern Iceland are relatively barren, although offshore waters support a respectable community of polar species. The Acadian subprovince extending from Newfoundland and the Maritime Provinces south to Cape Cod is fairly rich in shallow-water and shore species. There is a vast variation in habitats, from the extensive, intertidal mud flats of the Bay of Fundy to the gravel bottoms of the Georges Banks and to the

A wide variety of habitats support molluscan life.

sandy beaches of Cape Cod. New England supports about 800 species of marine molluscs, although the majority of these are in offshore waters.

Western Europe, or the Eastern Atlantic, is also a mixture of major faunal elements. The conditions in northern Scandinavia and the Shetland Islands are as severe as those in northern Alaska. But the Celtic Province, encompassing the British Isles, the Baltic Sea and France, is much richer and, indeed, has some elements that have invaded from the warmer Mediterranean Province, especially around northern Portugal. Occasionally, warmer-water pelagic species are wafted on to the southern shores of England. Common to most of these provinces in the Northern Hemisphere are many species of pelagic squids and tiny pteropod gastropods, all of which serve as an important source of food for fish and whales. Many shell-less sea-slugs, or nudibranchs, are common to England and New England. On the deep slopes of the continents, at several hundred metres in depth, there are many species of molluscs that have a circumpolar distribution because of the similar dark, cold conditions around the globe at those high latitudes.

A rich intertidal fauna of snails and clams await the collector at low-tide.

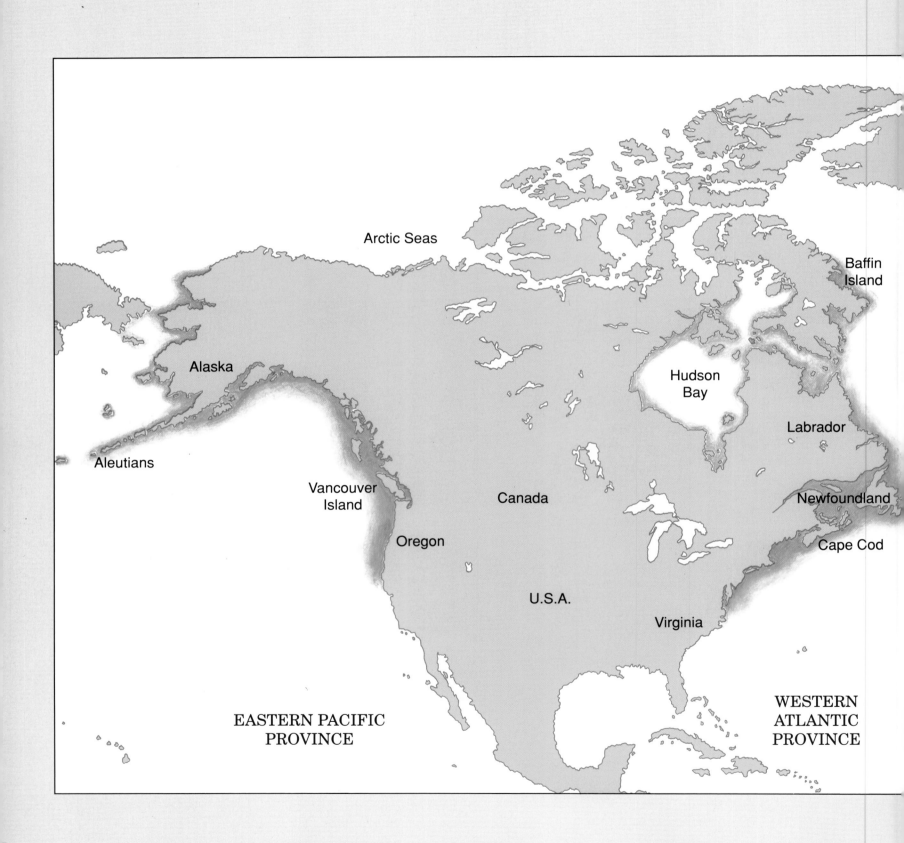

Arctic Seas

Baffin Island

Alaska

Hudson Bay

Labrador

Aleutians

Vancouver Island

Canada

Newfoundland

Oregon

Cape Cod

U.S.A.

Virginia

EASTERN PACIFIC PROVINCE

WESTERN ATLANTIC PROVINCE

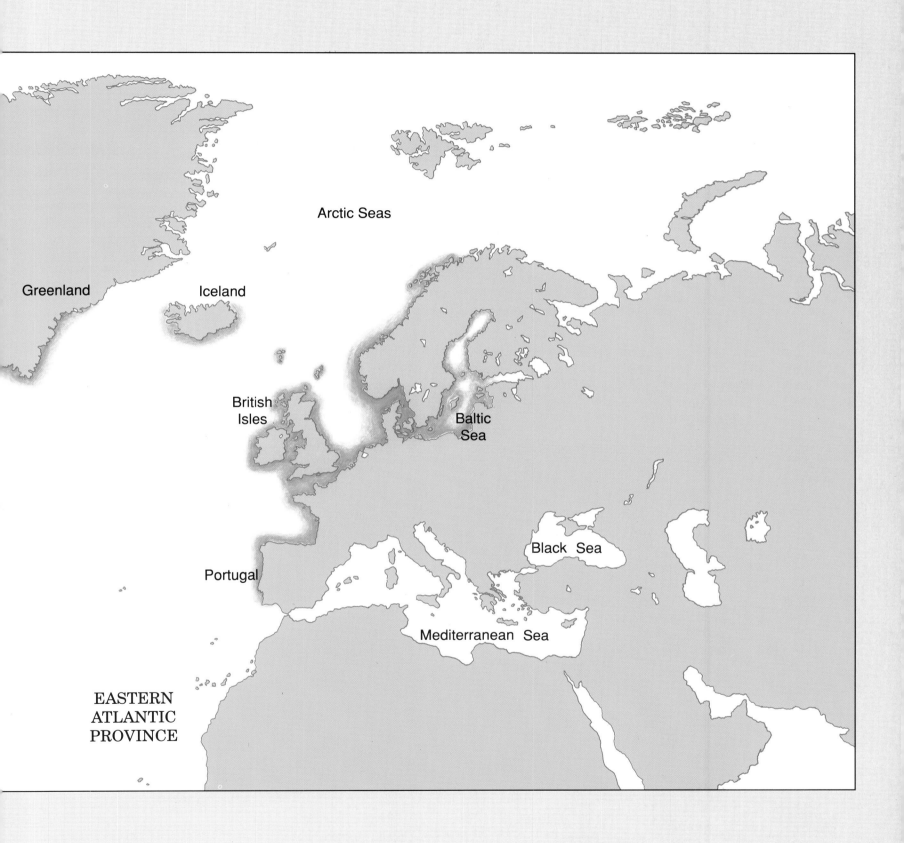

Greenland

Arctic Seas

Iceland

British
Isles

Baltic
Sea

Portugal

Black Sea

Mediterranean Sea

EASTERN
ATLANTIC
PROVINCE

Classification

As with other large groups of living organisms, the molluscs are arranged in taxonomic categories in order to facilitate classification and identification. Six major classes of living molluscs are recognized within the phylum, Mollusca:

1) Class **Gastropoda** contains the univalves, conchs, whelks and periwinkles, and has about 50,000 species, many living throughout the world's seas, but others are limited to freshwater lakes and rivers, and some exist only on land. They have a single, coiled or cap-shaped shell, although some, like the land slugs and the marine nudibranchs, lack a shell altogether. Most have a set of radular teeth, well-developed tentacles and a pair of eyes. Many produce an operculum, or trapdoor, for the purpose of sealing the opening of the shell.

2) Class **Bivalvia** contains the bivalves, or so-called pelecypods, clams, oysters and scallops. Most of the 10,000 species live in the ocean, but many are inhabitants of lakes, ponds and rivers. The two shelly valves that protect the soft parts are hinged together by a series of small teeth. The valves are kept together by one or two adductor muscles. Bivalves are either attached to a hard suface, as in the case of oysters, or may move freely through the sand by means of a fleshy, swollen foot. There are no radular teeth in this class, feeding taking place by filtering incoming water.

3) Class **Cephalopoda** includes several hundred species of squids, octopuses and the Chambered Nautilus. Locomotion is by walking with suckered arms or by jet propulsion of water through the siphon. They have a parrot-like beak and a set of strong radular teeth. The class is limited to salt water.

Arranging a shell collection in taxonomic order can be a useful and pleasurable project.

4) Class **Amphineura** or the coat-of-mail shells are rock-dwelling marine molluscs, having shelly plates encircled by a leathery girdle. The underside has a large flat foot and a head without tentacles or eyes. There are well-developed radular teeth. Most of the 600 known species are vegetarian, although a few feed on shrimp. Many are shore dwellers, but over 100 live in very deep water.

5) Class **Scaphopoda**, or the Tusk Shells, have simple, tube-like shells open at both ends, the larger one having the foot and numerous, tentacle-like filaments, the captacula. Water is drawn in at the narrow end which protrudes above the surface of the sandy bottom. Most of the 300 species live in deep water of the world's seas.

6) Class **Monoplacophora**, or gastroverms, consist of less than a dozen known marine species whose shells resemble limpets. The internal organs are arranged in pairs in separate segments. There are no eyes or tentacles. All are found at great depths. These are not included in this book.

Below the level of class are small groupings such as orders, families, genera and finally, species. With such an arrangement, based upon shell characters and internal anatomy of the soft parts, closely related species are clustered together in a natural classification. An example of a complete classification of the Hooded Puncturella, *Puncturella (Cranopsis) cucullata* (Gould, 1846) is given below:

Category	Ending used	Molluscan example	Author and date
Phylum	varies	Mollusca	Cuvier, 1797
Class	varies	Gastropoda	Cuvier, 1797
Subclass	-ia	Prosobranchia	Milne-Edwards,1848
Order	-a	Archaeogastropoda	Thiele, 1925
Suborder	-ina	Pleurotomariina	Cox & Knight, 1960
Superfamily	-oidea	Fissurelloidea	Fleming, 1822
Family	-idae	Fissurellidae	Fleming, 1822
Subfamily	-inae	Emarginulinae	Gray, 1834
Genus	varies	*Puncturella*	Lowe, 1827
Subgenus	varies	*Cranopsis*	A. Adams, 1860
species	varies	*cucullata*	(Gould, 1846)

Scientific Names

The scientific name of a shell consists of four basic parts: genus, species, author and date, as for example: *Patella vulgata* Linnaeus, 1758. The genus name, *Patella*, is always capitalized and printed in italics. The species name, *vulgata*, is not capitalized. Following these two Latin names are the name of the person who first described the species and the date of publication. The author and date are a quick bibliographic reference when searching for the original description. Very often, later research makes it necessary to place the species in a genus different from the one that was originally used. To indicate that this has happened, parentheses are placed around the author and date. The Hooded Puncturella was originally placed in the genus *Rimula*. It is now known as *Puncturella cucullata* (Gould, 1846). If a subgenus is to be used, it is put in parentheses between the genus and species name, i.e. *Puncturella (Cranopsis) cucullata* (Gould, 1846).

How Molluscs Reproduce

The creation of new generations of marine molluscs varies from one group to another, some having separate sexes, while others are hermaphrodites with both male and female reproductive organs in each individual. It is not uncommon for some bivalves to change from male to female within one season or to alternate their sexes every other year. In most snails, such as the periwinkles and whelks, the male bears a short, prong-like penis on the right side of the head. The female has an open tube, the oviduct, on the side of her body where sperm may be temporarily stored and down which pass fertilized eggs. In the case of hermaphrodites, two snails interchange sperm by means of an extrudible penis. Self-fertilization is very rare, but possible.

Once the eggs are ejected by the female, there are many modes of protecting the developing larvae and young. The primitive abalones, limpets and trochoid snails simply release their floating eggs freely into the water. Other snails, like the *Lacuna* periwinkles, may encase their microscopic eggs in jelly-like masses or place them, as in the case of the *Buccinum* whelks, in small leathery jackets or capsules. Hatching may occur from three to six weeks. Characteristically, most developing eggs pass through a trochophore larval stage and finally into a veliger stage in which the embryonic shell is formed and in which there are oar-like flaps covered with minute cilia. The latter facilitate swimming, so that veligers in some species may travel for several kilometres before settling to the bottom and transforming into miniature adults.

In the case of some whelks, such as *Buccinum* and *Busycon*, the young become fully developed within the protective capsule, and, when ready to travel on their own, escape by eating their way through a weakened escape hatch. A few species of periwinkles brood their young within the oviduct of the female. Some snails, like the

At top left the fleshy penis of the male slipper shell is seen attached to the top of the female's shell.

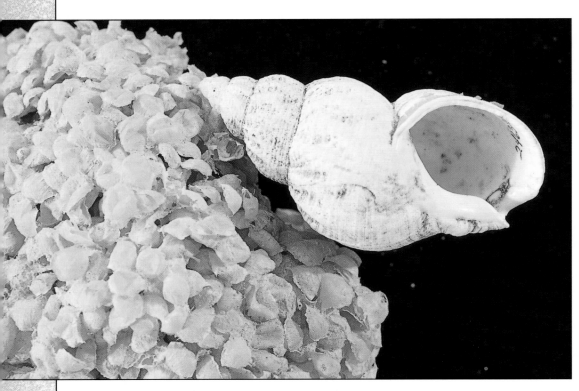

The common whelks lay masses of leathery capsules, each containing many young. Development and hatching takes several months.

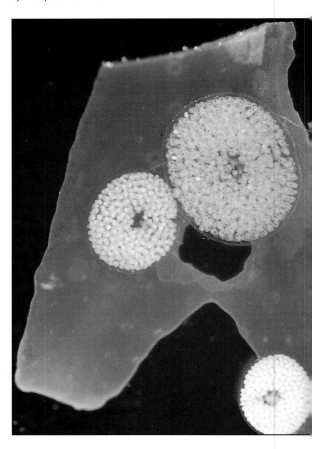

Small Lacuna *snails lay their egg masses on seaweed. The pink mass is about to hatch its tiny young.*

trivias, bury their eggs in holes eaten out from the surface of sponges and tunicates. The naticid moon snails create collar-like, sandy capsules in which they bury as many as a hundred minute eggs.

Once a snail is fending for itself, further growth depends upon the supply of food and the optimum required water temperature. Most growth takes place in the first one or two years, with sexual maturity occurring by the second or third year. In many kinds of gastropods sexual maturity is accompanied by the thickening or flaring of the outer lip of the shell. A prime example is the thin, sharp lip of an immature Pelican's Foot Snail which become thickened and bears large spines as soon as adulthood is attained.

The vast majority of bivalve eggs are shed in large numbers freely into the water, usually at the same time that sperm from neighbouring male clams are also released. The Blue Mussel, *Mytilus*, may spawn as many as 12 million eggs in a season. The floating eggs develop into planktonic larvae which may travel long distances in the ocean currents until they finally settle to the bottom. If larval oysters land in soft mud they are likely to perish, but if they settle on a shell or rock they will develop into young oysters, called 'spat'. Within a year or so they grow to adulthood. A few kinds of bivalves brood their developing young within the internal folds of their mother's gills before they are released as miniature, fully-shelled young.

In squid and octopus the sexes are separate. The sperm is transferred from the male to the female in sperm packets by a specially developed arm, called the hectocotylus. Eggs are usually laid in long, sausage-shaped jelly masses that are attached to rocky bottoms or the sides of protective caves. In the *Sepia* cuttlefish, the eggs are quite large and are laid like black grapes to the sides of rocks. The female octopus usually guards and broods her eggs, while the Paper Nautilus, *Argonauta*, carries her tiny eggs in a parchment-like, cup-shaped 'shell' created by two of her flat-ended arms.

A side view of the female Lacuna *snail.*

Beds of Mytilus *mussels exposed at low-tide. Myriads of carnivorous and parasitic snails hide in the clusters.*

How Molluscs Feed

During the gradual evolution and spread of molluscs to all oceans and to all types of habitats they chose a wide variety of foods. Many molluscs are carnivorous, others vegetarians and a surprising number are parasitic upon other marine organisms.

Because gastropods are mobile they have had a wider choice of food than their bivalve relatives. Most snails possess a feeding organ armed with a set of radular teeth which are used to bore through other shells or to scrape away at both flesh and vegetable matter. The Nassa Mud Snails are scavengers with a well-developed sense of taste or 'smell' for dead fish, molluscs and crustaceans. Top-shells prefer to rasp on hydroids and sponges, while naticid moon snails attack living clams. Limpets are constantly grazing at night on rock surfaces covered with algae and diatoms.

Several groups of snails are parasitic. The tiny pyramidellid snails are commonly found attached to the mantle edges of oysters where they suck at the blood of their hosts. A few gastropods are parasitic upon living fish and some are even found burrowed within holothurians or in the spines of sea-urchins.

*Dog-winkles (*Nucella lapillus*) feeding on barnacles.*

Queen Scallop. The shell valves are separated, revealing a fringing mantle which bears tentacles and well-developed eyes.

Bivalves, whether permanently attached to the hard bottom, like the oysters, or whether like the clams and cockles are buried just below the surface of the sandy bottom, have little recourse other than to extract what food they need by filtering in seawater. Diatoms, single-celled algae and minute floating scraps of food are passed over the mucus-covered gills and passed by waving cilia to the mouth of the bivalve. A few bivalves, such as the *Nucula* nut clams, are carnivorous and are capable of entrapping and engulfing minute copepods with their long, fleshy palps.

The swiftly swimming squid customarily feed in chase of schools of small fish. The more slowly moving octopus seeks out living snails and clams and carries them to its lair where it later bores a hole in its victim and injects an anethesia.

Molluscs are carnivorous, vegetarian, or parasitic. Most possess a feeding organ used to bore through other shells or scrape at flesh or vegetable matter.

Collecting Shells

While modest collecting of live specimens has less effect than nature's normal pruning by predation, aging and natural ecological changes, today there are more and more naturalists who prefer to hunt with camera or observe molluscs at close range in aquariums. But even well-executed surveys and censuses must be backed by a sampling of correctly identified specimens. Building a personal, well-documented shell collection is a pleasure and a useful project. This guide can only skim the surface of the molluscan world of the northern hemisphere, and therefore serves as a bridge to the more complete works listed in our bibliography.

Shells with soft parts may be cleaned by boiling them in water for five minutes or placing them in a plastic, open bag in the microwave oven set on high for 2 minutes. The best preservative for very small shells or large soft parts is 70% grain alcohol. Formalin, unless well-buffered, will etch and eventually dissolve calcium carbonate shells. Geographical and ecological data should be recorded in a catalogue and be repeated on good label paper to accompany the india-ink-numbered shells. Arrange the collection in phylogenetic order, as is presented in this book and most shell guides.

Cleaned shells should be catalogued and numbered, then stored in uniform paper trays that fit into wooden drawers.

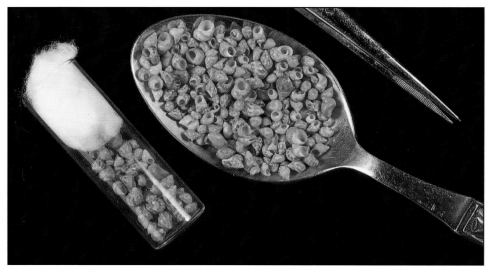

Minute Pheasant Shells may be kept in glass vials with a numbered slip .

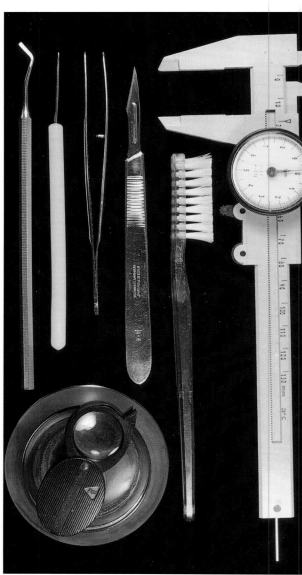

A shell collector's study tools.

Mudflats were made for digging. Always follow the tide out. Night-time is extremely productive.

THE
UNIVALVES

The Univalves
(CLASS GASTROPODA)

The largest class of molluscs is the univalves, or gastropods, which includes snails, periwinkles, whelks and conchs. Most have a single, coiled shell, although some, like limpets and slipper-shells, have an open, cap-shaped shell. Others, like the nudibranch sea-slugs and the garden slugs, produce no shell. Of approximately 80,000 known living species of gastropods there are probably 50,000 ocean dwellers, 25,000 terrestrial, air-breathing snails, and about 5000 or more inhabitants of freshwater ponds, lakes and rivers.

Like other classes, the gastropods have a fleshy cape, or mantle, endowed with numerous glands that secrete calcium carbonate and various pigments to form a hard protective shell. All molluscs, other than the bivalve class, possess a feeding organ, the *radula*, which is made up of a rasping band of numerous microscopic, hard teeth.

The gastropods are unique in having an embryonic stage in which the entire animal undergoes 'torsion', a 90 degree twisting of the posterior half towards the front. The anus now faces forward within the mantle cavity. In some cases, as in the limpets, the animals become secondarily 'untorted', do not have a coiled shell and the anus faces the rear.

Gastropods are diversified in habits and structure. By adapting to new environments they have become further divided into three large subdivisions, or subclasses:

1) The subclass **Prosobranchia** includes most of the marine snails including the limpets, periwinkles, whelks and many other groups, most of which have a horny or shelly operculum and bear two tentacles and eyes on the head. A row of fine gills is attached to the roof of the mantle cavity. A few families have become terrestrial air-breathers with oxygen being absorbed into the tissues of the roof of the mantle cavity. The majority of the species have separate sexes.

The prosobranchs originated from two quite different stocks, one of them being the primitive order **Archaeogastropoda** that includes the vegetarian limpets, top-shells, turbans and pheasant shells. The radulae consist of many rows of numerous similar teeth. The remainder of the snails, such as the murex snails, whelks and cones belong to the advanced order, **Caenogastropoda**. They have much fewer, larger and specialized radular teeth. Most are carnivorous.

2) The subclass **Opisthobranchia** are the marine sea-slugs and nudibranchs, most of which have assumed an external bilateral symmetry and lost their shells. All are hermaphroditic. Usually, the plume-like gills are located externally.

3) The subclass **Pulmonata** includes the land-dwelling garden and tree snails, the slugs and a few odd groups, such as the *Siphonaria* limpets and the *Melampus* swamp snails that have returned to the sea. Breathing takes place through a small pore leading to an internal lung. The head bears two pairs of tentacles, in the case of the land snails, and the radular teeth are very small and numerous. Both sexes are in every hermaphroditic individual.

Abalones; Ormers
(Family Haliotidae)

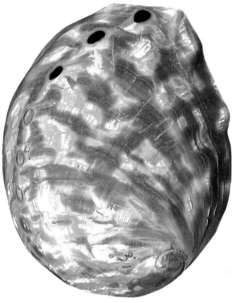

**Red Abalone
polished
10 in (26 cm)**

Worldwide in distribution, the several dozen species of abalones, or ormers as they are called in Europe, are a favourite food, especially in Japan, western United States and southern Australia. Many hundreds of thousands of pounds of abalone meat are harvested annually throughout the world, but because of over-fishing there are now laws limiting the size of individual abalones, the depth at which they may be caught and the season of harvesting. The mariculture of abalones in artificial habitats is being undertaken in western United States and Australia. Attempts to farm the European Ormer are in their experimental stages. Only the foot is used as food, and because of its toughness it must be pounded before cooking. Most meats are marketed in a fresh condition or frozen.

The low shell with a large expanded last whorl is characterized by a vivid, iridescent, mother-of-pearl interior and by a series of small, round open holes that help in water circulation. All species live on rocks where encrusting algae are their main source of food. The iridescent shells are a by-product used in shellcraft and the jewelry trade, either cut, polished or crushed.

The European Ormer feeds mainly on delicate red algae and marine plant detritus. Most live from the low tide mark down to a depth of a few feet, but there are a few, very small, deep-sea species. The animals are capable of a rapid, gliding motion and in the face of attacking octopods, crabs and otters, are capable of clamping down very firmly to the substrate. Some species are capable of crawling over a rock surface at the rate of 15 or 18 feet (4-5 m) per minute. There is no operculum in the adult stage. The free floating eggs are fertilized externally by the sperm.

The sole genus *Haliotis* is represented by seven species in Western United States, but none in New England and only one in north-western Europe.

Red Abalone,
Haliotis rufescens Swainson, 1822. Oval, rather flattened. Outer surface rough, dull brick-red with a narrow, red border around the inner edge of the shell. Interior is bright iridescent blue and green, with a large central muscle scar. Usually only three or four holes are open. Its main range is from Oregon to central California.

When polished, the exterior is a bright, glossy red and white. This is a heavily collected, commercial species with a legal minimum size for sportsmen of 7 inches (18 cm) and the catch limited to five specimens per person per day. Small specimens may occur intertidally, but large ones live from 30–130 ft (10–40 m).

**Black Abalone
6 in (15 cm)**

Black Abalone,
Haliotis cracherodii Leach, 1814. Shape usually oval, fairly deep, with a smooth outer surface, except for coarse growth lines. Exterior bluish to greenish black. Interior pearly white. About eight or nine holes open, but rarely, in freaks they may be absent. This species is uncommon in Oregon, but more common in California where it occurs in crevices in intertidal rocks. The legal capture size is 5 inches (12.5 cm) or more. It feeds on encrusting marine algae. Polished specimens are bright black and white.

Northern Green Abalone
5 in (13 cm)

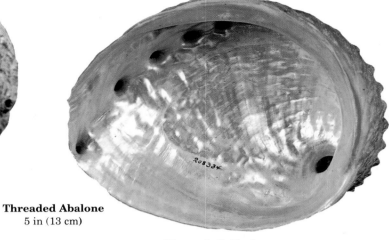

Threaded Abalone
5 in (13 cm)

Northern Green Abalone,
Haliotis walallensis Stearns, 1899.
Oval–elongate, flattened, with
numerous small spiral threads.
Exterior dark, brick-red, mottled with
pale green. Interior a bright
iridescence, with white predominating.
Six or seven holes usually open, and
their edges are not elevated. It is
sometimes called the Flat Abalone. It
lives just below the low-tide line on
rocks down to a depth of about 82 ft
(25 m). Only moderately common from
British Columbia to northern
California.

Threaded Abalone,
Haliotis kamtschatkana subspecies
assimilis Dall, 1878.
This is a southern form of the Japanese
Abalone ranging from Point
Conception, California, to Baja
California. The shell is oval, fairly
deep, with weak corrugations and weak
to strong spiral threads. Four or five
holes are open and have tubular edges.
Outer colour mottled with brick-red,
greenish blue and grey. The specimen
shown here is the holotype from the
Smithsonian Institution. Moderately
common offshore on rocks.

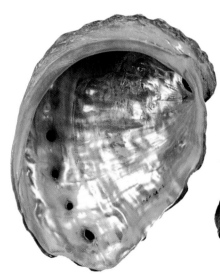

European Ormer
2.5 in (6.5 cm)

Japanese Abalone
4 in (10 cm)

Japanese Abalone,
Haliotis kamtschatkana Jonas, 1845.
Elongate, with a moderately high spire.
Usually four or five holes open which
have raised edges. Exterior of shell is
roughly corrugated, but a few
specimens may have weak, spiral
threads or cords. The soft parts are
mottled tan and greenish, but some are
tinged with orange. Tentacles are green
and slender. Moderately common in its
northern range which is from Oregon to
southern Alaska and Japan. Lives on
subtidal rocks.

European Ormer,
Haliotis tuberculata Linnaeus, 1758.
Shell elongate, with three or four
rapidly expanding whorls. Exterior
rough, with growth lines and fine spiral
threads. Dark reddish brown or mottled
in green. About nine or ten holes open.
Interior bright, whitish iridescent.
Tentacles on head are long; eyes bluish.
Uncommon on intertidal rocks in the
Channel Islands, but more common
further south to the Mediterranean in
3–164 ft (1–50 m). A popular, edible
species. In the Mediterranean the
common subspecies *lamellosa* Lamarck,
1822 is very similar but has a rougher
surface with numerous incised lines.

Emarginulas, Puncturellas and Keyhole Limpets

(Family Fissurellidae)

Crass Emarginula
1 in (2.5 cm)

The small, limpet-like, white emarginulas are characterized by a small slit in the front edge of the shell. The larger puncturellas, also limpet-shaped and usually white or grey, have a slot-like opening just at the back of the hooked apex. Within the slot is a cup-like shelf. There are about 60 worldwide, mainly deep-water species. Most are believed to feed on sponges. Occasionally they are brought up in dredges from a habitat of stony bottoms. Of the several dozen species found in the northern hemisphere, those shown below are fairly common in the north-western parts of the American continent.

The keyhole limpets bear an opening in the apex of the shell, shaped like a keyhole, through which waste waters are expelled. Most of these species are vegetarians and many of them live in shallow water or in the intertidal zone where they graze for food at night.

Crass Emarginula,
Emarginula crassa Sowerby, 1813.
One of several, small slit limpets belonging to the family Fissurellidae that live on subtidal rocks throughout the temperate regions. The small white shells are coiled in their young stages, but grow into shield-shaped limpets. The narrow slit on the back edge of the shell serves as an exodus for water and waste products. This one-inch (2.5 cm), white species is distributed from Norway and Iceland to Ireland and Scotland. Sculpture of fine reticulations with about 50 fine radiating threads. Fairly common, especially in the north, under stones in subtidal regions to depths of 656 ft (200 m).

EMARGINULAS

Sicilian Emarginula,
Emarginula sicula Gray, 1825.
Shell small; colour whitish to cream. Base subcircular. Anterior slope convex, posterior slope straight. Apex elevated and at the posterior fourth of the shell. Nuclear whorls minute. Anal slit in shell narrow and straight-sided. Sculpture of 26 strong radial ribs between which may be weaker, secondary riblets. Concentric threads form minute beads where they cross the radial ribs. Margin of shell crenulated. Dredged offshore down to 1640 ft (500 m). Ranges from the Channel Islands to the Mediterranean; also in southern Florida and the West Indies. Uncommon.

Sicilian Emarginula
0.6 in (1.5 cm)

PUNCTURELLAS

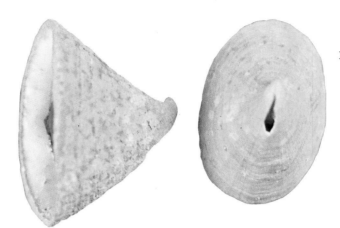

Noah's Puncturella
0.5 in (1 cm)

Noah's Puncturella,
Puncturella noachina (Linnaeus, 1758).
Shell small, limpet-shaped, conical, laterally compressed, with an elliptical base. There are 21 to 26 primary radial ribs between each of which are added a smaller, secondary rib farther down. Margin crenulate. There is a tiny slit just anterior to the hooked apex, and internally it is bordered by a funnel-shaped cup on each side of which is a minute triangular pit. Colour white, internally glossy. A circumpolar species found in Alaska and south to off Cape Cod, Massachusetts, as well as north-western Europe. Common; subtidal among rocks to very deep water.

Hooded Puncturella
1 in (2.5 cm)

Helmet Puncturella
0.7 in (2 cm)

Helmet Puncturella
Puncturella galeata (Gould, 1846).
Shell solid, fairly high, oval in outline with the larger, posterior half being slightly wider. Apex hooks towards the narrower, shorter end. Slit short and narrow. Ribs numerous, small and of irregular strengths. Edge of shell smoothish. Exterior grey to whitish; interior glossy white. The interior shelf behind the slit is reinforced by a second straight shelf. Lives in rocky and muddy areas from 100–500 ft (30–150 m). Moderately common from the Aleutian Islands to off northern California.

Hooded Puncturella,
Puncturella cucullata (Gould, 1846)
A strong, fairly high shell with a small, elevated apex which is hooked over towards the front end. Behind it is a small, elongate slit penetrating through the shell. Internally the short slit is separated from the apex by a calcareous, convex shelf. Exterior of shell with 14 to 23 major radiating ribs with one to five smaller ones between. Colour dull grey externally; inside glossy white. Edge of shell crenulated. Fairly common from low-tide mark to 656 ft (200 m) from Alaska to northern California.

KEYHOLE LIMPETS

Volcano Limpet
1 in (2.5 cm)

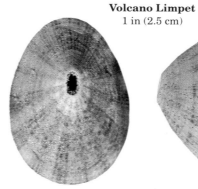

Volcano Limpet,
Fissurella volcano Reeve, 1849.
Elongate-oval, fairly high shell with a single, oblong hole at the central apex. In this genus there is a swollen ridge or callus bordering the 'keyhole' on the inner side. Sculpture of numerous, rather large, but low and rounded, radial ribs of varying sizes. Base of shell slightly crenulated and with colour blotches. Exterior grey, with pinkish mauve, radial rays. Interior glossy white, with a pink line around the callus surrounding the hole. Common on intertidal rocky rubble; uncommon in Oregon, but more common further south to California.

Cloudy Keyhole Limpet
1 in (2.5 cm)

Italian Keyhole Limpet
1.5 in (4 cm)

Cloudy Keyhole Limpet,
Fissurella nubecula (Linnaeus, 1758).
Ovate-elongate, fairly high and solid. Exterior with numerous unequal radial riblets; grey with a dozen rays of dull-purple. Keyhole oblong, parallel-sided. Interior white and green tinted. The internal callus around the keyhole is white or green and bounded by a brown line. This is a southern Mediterranean species that lives as far north as Portugal and southern France. Fairly common on subtidal rocks where it feeds on minute algae.

Graecian Keyhole Limpet
0.8 in (2 cm)

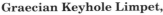

Graecian Keyhole Limpet,
Diodora graeca (Linnaeus, 1758).
Shell oval, a little narrower in front. Keyhole is small, oval and located near the front end. Exterior with numerous elevated, radiating ribs, alternately larger and smaller, with concentric thread intersecting to form small square pits. Colour dull yellow brown, sometimes rayed with darker brown. Interior white, its margin strongly denticulate. Callus around the keyhole is squared off and minutely excavated behind. Mantle edge of the animal projects through the keyhole to form a short siphon. Foot with 30 to 35 minute tentacles. Feeds on sponges. Moderately common subtidally to 820 ft (250 m) on rocks. Southern coasts of the British Isles to the Mediterranean.

Italian Keyhole Limpet,
Diodora italica (Defrance, 1820).
Shell ovate, narrower in front, rather depressed; sides are slightly convex near the edge of the shell, but concave or straight near the small keyhole opening. Exterior with numerous slightly rounded radial riblets of unequal size, crossed by very fine concentric threads. Colour greyish yellow or solid grey; sometimes with darker purplish rays. Interior glossy white, with a concentric bluish band. Border finely denticulate. Callus surrounding the interior of the keyhole is truncate at the posterior, narrower end. Moderately common from Portugal to the Mediterranean on subtidal rocks.

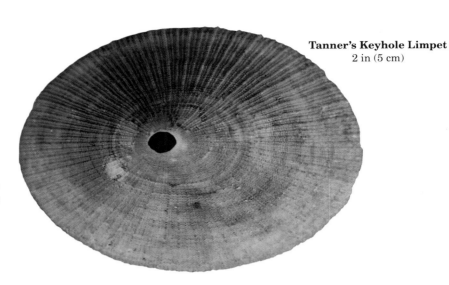

Tanner's Keyhole Limpet
2 in (5 cm)

Tanner's Keyhole Limpet,
Diodora tanneri Verrill, 1883.
Fairly large, rather thin-shelled,
conical and with straight sides. Base
broadly ovate. Apex in front of the
middle, pierced by a circular orifice.
Sculpture of numerous, very fine, close-
set radial ribs which are crossed by fine
concentric threads to form tiny nodules
or scales. Colour greyish white.
Internal callus around the keyhole is
truncate behind. A deep-water species
found off Delaware to Georgia and in
the West Indies. Uncommonly dredged.

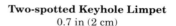

Rough Keyhole Limpet
1.5 in (4 cm)

Two-spotted Keyhole Limpet
0.7 in (2 cm)

Rough Keyhole Limpet,
Diodora aspera (Rathke, 1833).
Shell ovate, slightly narrower in the
front; moderately elevated. The flat-
sided keyhole is almost round and
located slightly towards the front.
Exterior of rough, radial and numerous
weaker concentric threads. Colour
greyish white with about 12 to 18
irregularly sized, purplish-blue radial
colour bands. Interior bluish white;
callus around the keyhole is truncate at
the front end. Commonly found
attached to rocks from the low-tide
mark to several feet (metres) in depth.
Feeds on bryozoans and may cling to
kelp weed stalks. Ranges from Cook's
Inlet, Alaska, southwards to southern
California.

Two-spotted Keyhole Limpet,
Megatebennus bimaculatus (Dall,
1871).
Elongate-oblong, low, with the ends
turned up slightly. Large apical keyhole
is elongate-oblong, located at the centre
of the shell. Numerous radial and
concentric threads give the exterior a
cancellate sculpturing. Brownish to
grey with a wide, darker ray on each
side. Interior glossy white. Animal is
several times the size of the shell and
coloured with reds, yellows and white.
Common under stones at low-tide mark
and deeper. Ranges from Alaska to
southern California.

European True Limpets
(Family Patellidae)

Several unrelated families produce limpet-shaped shells, but the true limpets are represented by the common, rock-dwelling genus *Patella* in Europe and South Africa. They differ from the similar-looking Acmaeidae of the Americas in lacking leaf-like gill plumes and in having only a gill cordon. No operculum present. Patellids are usually shallow-water rock-dwellers whose shells are greatly influenced by the environment. They are very common in Western Europe but absent in the cooler waters of North America.

Limpets begin life as males but after a year and upon reaching about one-inch (25 mm) in size they all change to females. Most are vegetarians and make short nightly forays to scrape away at algae or kelp fronds. They usually return to their original locations in the morning. The estimated lifespan is about 15 years. Individuals can clamp to a rock surface with surprising strength, and can remain exposed to air for many hours.

Blue-rayed Limpet
0.5 in (1 cm)

Blue-rayed Limpet,
Helcion pellucidum (Linnaeus, 1758). Belonging to the family, Patellidae, this common European species lives on the kelp weed, *Laminaria*. Cap-shaped, sometimes elevated, with no keyhole or marginal slit. Surface smooth, shiny, horn-coloured with narrow, bright-blue rays. Rarely, red rays appear near the margins. Apex location varies with age and the surface upon which the animal grows. No operculum is present. The white body has a large head with two tentacles, each bearing an eye at the base. Mantle edge has minute tentacles. This species breeds in winter and spring, the planktonic young settling on fucoid seaweeds, and later moving to kelp. Common subtidally from Norway to Portugal.

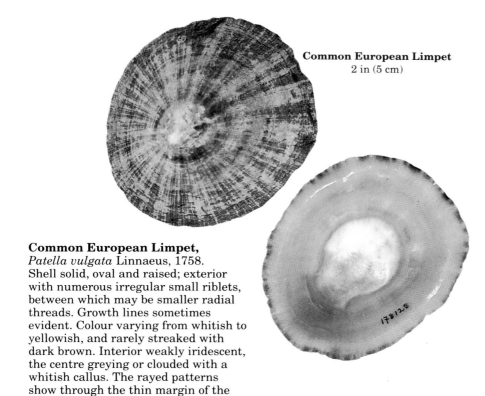

Common European Limpet
2 in (5 cm)

Common European Limpet,
Patella vulgata Linnaeus, 1758. Shell solid, oval and raised; exterior with numerous irregular small riblets, between which may be smaller radial threads. Growth lines sometimes evident. Colour varying from whitish to yellowish, and rarely streaked with dark brown. Interior weakly iridescent, the centre greying or clouded with a whitish callus. The rayed patterns show through the thin margin of the shell. No operculum present. A common, edible, rock-dwelling species living from Norway to the Mediterranean.

Rustic Limpet
1 in (2.5 cm)

European China Limpet,
Patella aspera Röding, 1798.
Similar to the Common European
Limpet, but is more elongate. Exterior
has strong, sharper ribs, resulting in a
serrated edge to the shell. Interior
porcellaneous white, with a head scar
of pale orange. The apex is closer to the
front of the shell. The animal is cream
to yellowish with an apricot-yellow sole
of the foot. Lives in rough, more
exposed parts of the shoreline. Common
from the southern British Isles to
southern France.

European China Limpet
1.5 in (4 cm)

Rustic Limpet,
Patella rustica Linnaeus, 1758.
Shell small, solid, ovate, tall-conical,
with the apex slightly anterior to the
middle. Sculpture of numerous closely
spaced, narrow, uneven, granulose
radial riblets. Exterior pale yellowish
brown to greyish, often with the
granules on the ribs being black in
colour. Interior has broad brown or
bluish-black rays on a silvery
background. Head scar white with a
yellow border. A common intertidal
species ranging from south-west France
to the Adriatic Sea.

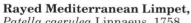

**Rayed Mediterranean
Limpet**
2 in (5 cm)

**Ribbed Mediterranean
Limpet**
2 in (5 cm)

Rayed Mediterranean Limpet,
Patella caerulea Linnaeus, 1758.
Shell thin, depressed, usually distinctly
six- or seven-angled because of the
broadly rounded primary ribs that
project at the margin. Surface crowded
with secondary radial riblets, mostly
imbricated by concentric growth lines.
Colour whitish or buff externally, the
interior silvery white, radially lined or
banded in blue. A common rock-
dwelling southern European species,
also occurring in Portugal, the Azores
and the Canary Islands.

Ribbed Mediterranean Limpet,
Patella ferrucginea (Gmelin, 1791).
Very solid, ovate, conical, with the apex
subcentral, coarsely sculptured with
numerous strong radial ribs that are
made rough by concentric growth lines.
Margin strongly corrugated. Exterior
colour dull ashen and stained with
brown. This fairly common southern
species is found on intertidal rocks
from the Aegean Sea to Spain and
North Africa.

American Limpets
(Families Acmaeidae and Lottiidae)

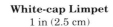

White-cap Limpet
1 in (2.5 cm)

The western coast of North America abounds with a variety of limpets, many formerly placed in the genus *Collisella* (now *Lottia*). Essentially cold-water dwellers, only a few representatives are found in New England and north-western Europe.

The family Acmaeidae includes the single, white-shelled limpet of the Pacific coast of North America and a few blind, small deep-sea pectinodont limpets. The remaining 19 species of *Lottia* and *Tectura* belong to the family Lottiidae. All are rock-dwellers and are major components of the intertidal zones and the beds of giant kelps. There is one set of gills in the front mantle cavity. The foot lacks an operculum and the epipodial tentacles. Eggs are laid in spring and early summer in a mucus sheet on seaweeds or rocks. Some species are capable of homing back to their original resting places.

White-cap Limpet,
Acmaea mitra Rathke, 1833.
Shell white or greyish white, solid, conic in shape with an almost circular base. Apex pointed and near the centre. Often covered with small knobby nullipore growths. Interior white. Edge of shell smooth. Rarely pink-rayed. Fairly common at the low-tide mark where they feed upon coralline algae. Most abundant in its northern range from the Aleutian Islands, but uncommon as far south as southern California.

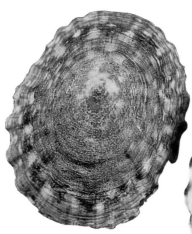

Shield Limpet
1.2 in (3 cm)

File Limpet
1.2 in (3 cm)

Shield Limpet,
Lottia pelta (Rathke, 1833).
Shell strong, base elliptical in outline, with a moderately high apex situated almost near the centre. Exterior has about 25 very weak radial riblets. Concentric growth thread very weak. Edge of shell slightly waved. Colour cream-grey with strong black radial, often intertwining stripes. Interior usually faint bluish white, with or without a dark-brown head blotch. Inner border edged with alternating black and cream bars. A common intertidal rock-dweller from Alaska to Mexico. Formerly in the genus *Collisella*, a synonym of *Lottia*.

File Limpet,
Lottia limatula (Carpenter, 1864).
Base elliptical to almost round; low to quite flat. Characterized by radial rows of small beads which form tiny riblets. Exterior greenish black. Interior glossy white with a bluish tint. Patches of brown on white interior surface may be faint or absent. Edge of shell usually with a solid, black-brown, narrow colour band. A common intertidal, rock species occurring from Puget Sound, Washington, south to southern California.

PACIFIC AND ATLANTIC LIMPETS

Fingered Limpet,
Lottia digitalis (Rathke, 1833).
Elliptical to ovate in outline; with a moderately high apex minutely hooked forward and placed one third back from the front edge. Has 15 to 25 moderately well-developed, coarse radial ribs which give the shell a wavy border. Colour greyish with tiny, distinct mottlings of white dots and blackish streaks and lines. Interior white with a faint bluish tint and with a large, usually even, head patch of dark brown in the centre. Inner edge of shell with a solid or broken narrow band of black-brown. A common species preferring vertical rock surfaces where action is severe. Rarely, a white form is attached to goose barnacles. A homing species ranging from the Aleutians to California.

Fingered Limpet
1 in (2.5 cm)

Unstable Limpet
1 in (2.5 cm)

Unstable Limpet,
Lottia instabilis (Gould, 1846).
A small, solid, all-brown species living on the stems of large kelp weeds. Shell heavy, oblong, with a high spire, and with its sides compressed. Lower edge curved so that the shell may fit evenly against its kelp stem substrate. Exterior smoothish, a dull light-brown. Interior whitish with a faint brown stain in the centre and with a narrow, solid border of brown. Moderately common from Alaska to southern California.

Seaweed Limpet
0.6 in (1.5 cm)

Seaweed Limpet,
Discurria insessa (Hinds, 1842).
A small, solid shell, with a high spire and compressed parallel sides. Twice as long as wide. Exterior is a uniform, greasy light-brown. Abundant on the stalks and holdfasts of the large kelps, such as *Egregia*. Occurs along the Pacific coast from Alaska to Baja California. A similar-looking small species, the Black Limpet, *Lottia asmi* (Middendorff, 1849) is solid black inside and out, and is found attached to several kinds of *Tegula* snails from Alaska to Baja California.

Mask Limpet
1.2 in (3 cm)

Mask Limpet,
Tectura persona (Rathke, 1833).
Oval-elongate, smoothish, with a fairly high apex pointing forward and one third the way back from the front edge. Exterior smoothish with a fine pattern of white squares and triangles on a dark grey background. Interior bluish white to blackish blue. This species is very common from northern California to Alaska where it lives between tides on rocks where strong waves flush the shaded rock crevices. It feeds mostly during low-tide at night.

Rough Pacific Limpet
1 in (2.5 cm)

Rough Pacific Limpet,
Tectura scabra (Gould, 1846).
Elliptical in outline, with a fairly low apex located one third back from the front end. The 15 to 25 strong, coarse radiating ribs make the edge wavy. Coloured a dirty grey-green. Interior glossy, whitish and irregularly stained in the centre with brown. Edge of the shell between the serrations stained with purplish brown. A common species found clinging to gently sloping rock surfaces high above the water-line but within reach of the ocean spray. It is a southern species ranging from Oregon to Baja California.

Pacific Plate Limpet,
Tectura scutum (Rathke, 1833).
Shell fairly large, almost round in
outline, quite flat, with the apex
towards the centre of the shell.
Smoothish, except for very fine radial
riblets, best in young specimens.
Exterior greenish grey, with slate-gray
radial bands or mottlings. Interior
bluish white with faint or darkish-
brown head scar. Inner edge with
alternating, small bars of blackish
brown and bluish white. A rock-dweller
along the coasts of Alaska to Oregon
where it is common; in California it is
rare.

A similar species, *Tectura tessulata*
(Müller, 1776) from the British Isles is
only half-inch (15 mm) narrower at the
front end and has chocolate-brown
radial patterns. It is locally called the
Tortoiseshell Limpet and is common in
rocky tidepools.

Pacific Plate Limpet
1.5 in (4 cm)

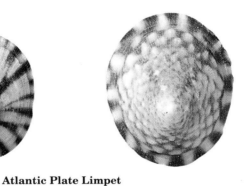

Fenestrate Limpet
1.2 in (3 cm)

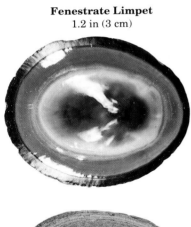

Atlantic Plate Limpet
1 in (2.5 cm)

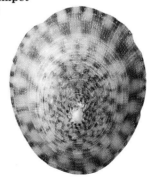

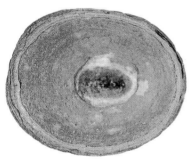
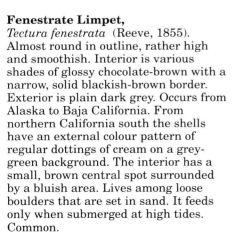

Fenestrate Limpet,
Tectura fenestrata (Reeve, 1855).
Almost round in outline, rather high
and smoothish. Interior is various
shades of glossy chocolate-brown with a
narrow, solid blackish-brown border.
Exterior is plain dark grey. Occurs from
Alaska to Baja California. From
northern California south the shells
have an external colour pattern of
regular dottings of cream on a grey-
green background. The interior has a
small, brown central spot surrounded
by a bluish area. Lives among loose
boulders that are set in sand. It feeds
only when submerged at high tides.
Common.

Atlantic Plate Limpet,
Tectura testudinalis (Müller, 1776).
Shell strong, oval in outline, low to
moderately high with the apex nearly
at the centre of the shell. Smoothish,
except for a few coarse growth lines and
numerous, very fine axial threads.
Interior bluish white with a dark- to
light-brown centre and short radial
brown bars at the edge. Exterior dull
cream-grey with irregular axial bars
and streaks of brown. A common
littoral, rock-dwelling species from
Arctic Seas to Long Island, New York.
A thin, elongate, heavily mottled
ecological variant form *alvea* (Conrad,
1831), lives on eelgrass blades.

The Trochoid Snails
(Family Trochidae)

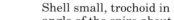

Greenland Margarite
0.5 in (1 cm)

This is a very diversified snail family of many genera and species found in most parts of the world from intertidal habitats to very deep water. Most have an iridescent, mother-of-pearl finish inside the top-shaped shell. The operculum is circular, of many whorls and corneous. All are vegetarians or feed on sponges and hydroids. Sperm and eggs are usually shed freely into the open sea, or sometimes are laid in jelly-like strands.

In Arctic seas, the small Margarite and Solarelle snails are common bottom-dwellers that serve as a main source of food for many small fish.

Greenland Margarite,
Margarites groenlandicus (Gmelin, 1791).
Shell small, trochoid in shape, with the angle of the spire about 110°. Whorls strongly rounded, aperture round, umbilicus wide and deep. Outer lip and columella very thin. Base smooth; top of whorls glassy smooth. Suture is finely impressed. Colour glossy cream. Interior of aperture pearly. Jelly-like masses containing eggs are laid on seaweeds. The young emerge as miniature adults. Common on sandy and rock bottoms from 32–984 ft (10–300 m) from the Arctic Seas to Maine and to the British Isles.

Northern Rosy Margarite
0.5 in (1 cm)

Baird's Spiny Margarite
2 in (5 cm)

Sordid Margarite
0.8 in (2 cm)

Northern Rosy Margarite,
Margarites costalis (Gould, 1841).
Shell a little wider than high and with five evenly and well-rounded whorls. Narrowly and deeply umbilicate. Angle of spire about 90°. Next to last whorl with two to four unequal, raised spiral cords. Base with eight to ten threads. Upper three whorls strongly carinate. Columella and outer lip thin, sharp, the latter finely crenulate. Colour rosy to greyish cream. White within the smooth umbilicus. Aperture pearly rose. Commonly dredged on rocky bottoms from 64–393 ft (20–120 m) from Greenland to Cape Cod, Massachusetts; and from the Bering Strait to Port Etches, Alaska.

Sordid Margarite,
Margarites sordidus (Hancock, 1846).
Shell very similar to *M. costalis*, but usually larger, with more rounded whorls, with finer spiral, uneven threads, and with numerous very fine, slanting, axial threads. Suture more strongly indented, below which are crowded, short, slanting riblets. Base rounded and the umbilicus deep. This species is found in Arctic waters around the world.

Baird's Spiny Margarite,
Lischkeia bairdii (Dall, 1889).
Fairly large and fragile, with no umbilicus. Shell whitish with a thin, glossy, yellowish-green periostracum. Interior of aperture pearly white. Rare in collections but locally common in deep water from the Bering Sea to off Chile.

Regular Spiny Margarite,
Lischkeia regularis (Verrill and Smith, 1880).
Similar to *L. ottoi*, but the umbilicus is almost closed. The whorls are more rounded and well-beaded by three or four prominent spiral rows of tiny, sharp beads. The base has five spiral threads bearing minute beads. Colour greyish, dull white. Interior of aperture pearly white. Fairly common offshore from Nova Scotia to off New York.

Regular Spiny Margarite
0.7 in (2 cm)

Adams' Spiny Margarite
1.5 in (4 cm)

Adams' Spiny Margarite,
Lischkeia cidaris (Carpenter, 1864).
Shell moderately fragile, sculptured with three or four spiral rows of fairly large beads. Suture deeply indented. Base has seven or eight smaller, weakly beaded spiral cords. Outer lip thin and wavy. Exterior greyish tan. Operculum thin, translucent brown, multispiral. Moderately common offshore from Alaska to southern California.

Obscure Solarelle,
Solariella obscura (Couthouy, 1838).
Shell small; whorls strongly shouldered by one or two large, feebly beaded, spiral cords above the periphery. Base smoothish, except for microscopic spiral scratches. Umbilicus narrow and bordered by an angular rim. Colour greyish to pinkish tan, often eroded to reveal a pearly-golden colour. Aperture pearly white. Some specimens may have weak riblets below the strongest spiral cord on the periphery of the whorls. Commonly dredged from 20–2624 ft (6–800 m) from the Arctic Seas to Virginia and from Alaska to Washington; also Norway.

Obscure Solarelle
0.4 in (1 cm)

Otto's Spiny Margarite,
Lischkeia ottoi (Philippi, 1844).
Shell small, lightweight, as wide as long. Outer lip thin and sharp. The round narrow umbilicus is partially covered by the top of the slanting, smooth columella. Exterior pearly white. Sculpture of whorls in the spire with three evenly spaced, spiral rows of prickly beads. Suture wavy. Base of shell with four or five spiral threads which bear very small beads. Nuclear whorls with axial riblets. Commonly dredged offshore in deep water from Nova Scotia to off North Carolina and from Norway to off France.

Otto's Spiny Margarite
0.7 in (2 cm)

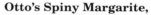

Lovely Pacific Solarelle
0.7 in (2 cm)

Lovely Pacific Solarelle,
Solariella permabilis Carpenter, 1864.
Shell small, as long as wide, solid, semi-glossy. Aperture circular, pearly within and ridged. Umbilicus fairly wide, round, very deep and bordered by a strong, beaded cord. Seven whorls, shouldered just below the suture by a flat shelf. Lower two-thirds of the whorl with numerous weak spiral cords that are smoothish in the last whorl, but are crossed by numerous axial riblets in the earlier whorls. Colour tan with light-mauve streaks and mottlings. Moderately common on rocky rubble bottoms from 328–1968 ft (100–600 m). Japan and Alaska south to off California.

Puppet Margarite,
Margarites pupillus (Gould, 1849).
Trochoid in shape; spire moderately high. Five or six whorls, the upper ones with five or six smoothish, small, spiral threads between or over which are microscopic, axial, slanting threads. Umbilicus narrow and deep. Columella smooth, rounded and gently curving. Exterior a dull chalky-white to yellowish grey. Aperture rosy to greenish pearl. Apex usually eroded away. A common littoral species from Alaska to Oregon; somewhat common in warmer waters south to San Diego, California.

Puppet Margarite
0.4 in (1 cm)

Calliostoma Top-shells
(Subfamily Calliostominae)

The hundreds of species of top-shaped shells generally found in cool or deep water are usually placed in the subfamily Calliostominae. The handsome shells are finely beaded, sometimes iridescent and may or may not have an umbilicus. The operculum is chitinous, thin, with many whorls and completely seals the aperture of the shell.

Calliostoma top-shells feed on detritus adhering to algae. Their jaws are very weak. The radular teeth are numerous, feathery, with about three dozen teeth in each row. The sexes are separate. The females lay a gelatinous ribbon, several inches (centimetres) long and about one-quarter inch (4 mm) wide. The yellow, embedded eggs develop within their capsules and emerge in a few weeks as crawling young.

Northern Top-shell
0.5 in (1 cm)

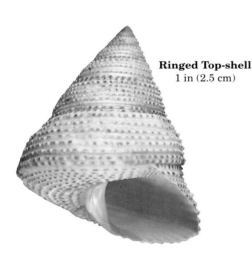

Ringed Top-shell
1 in (2.5 cm)

Baird's Top-shell,
1 in (2.5 cm)

Ringed Top-shell,
Calliostoma annulatum (Lightfoot, 1786).
An unusually beautiful shell, trochoid in shape, with a flattish spire with an angle of about 70°. Lightweight, golden yellow in background colour with a mauve band at the periphery of the whorls. Has numerous spiral rows of tiny, distinct beads, usually five to eight rows in the spire whorls. Nucleus pink. Columella short, iridescent white with a purplish base. Interior of aperture pearly. No umbilicus. Outer lip sharp and finely crenulated. Operculum corneous, circular and light yellow. Adults common on giant kelp, but the young are usually on nearby bottom rocks. Ranges from southern Alaska to northern Baja California.

Baird's Top-shell,
Calliostoma bairdii Verrill and Smith, 1880.
Shell solid, with straight sides and an apical angle of about 70°. Base rather flat, periphery of the last whorl strongly angular. Sculpture of six or seven spiral rows of small, neat beads with those on the topmost row being the largest. Suture difficult to find. No umbilicus. Brownish cream with faint maculations of iridescent reddish colour. Moderately common offshore from New England to north-eastern Florida.

Northern Top-shell,
Calliostoma occidentale (Mighels and Adams, 1842).
Shell small, trochoid, glistening iridescent-white. Whorls convex and with three or four strong spiral cords, the lower ones smooth, the uppermost neatly beaded. No umbilicus. Outer lip fragile, slightly crenulated. Interior pearly white. Spire straight-sided, sometimes with a reddish tinge. The nuclear whorls are minutely reticulated. The soft parts are cream with purplish-brown mottlings. This species lives offshore and feeds on alcyonarians and hydroids. Common from Nova Scotia to off New Jersey; Scandinavia and Iceland to the northern British Isles.

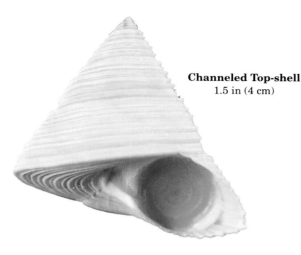

Channeled Top-shell
1.5 in (4 cm)

Western Ribbed Top-shell
0.8 in (2 cm)

Channeled Top-shell,
Calliostoma canaliculatum (Lightfoot, 1786).
Shell lightweight, spire sharp and with straight sides. Periphery of last whorl rather sharp and angular. Base of shell almost flat. The numerous sharp spiral cords are slightly beaded and make the suture between whorls difficult to distinguish. Nuclear whorls white. Interior of aperture iridescent white and with many spiral lirae. Operculum circular, corneous and yellow. Fairly common on kelps. Ranges from Alaska to southern California.

Western Ribbed Top-shell,
Calliostoma ligatum (Gould, 1849).
Shell solid and rather heavy, with well-rounded whorls. Six to eight strong, smooth spiral, light-brown cords on a background of dark chocolate. Rarely flushed with mauve. No umbilicus. Aperture pearly white. A very common littoral species from Alaska to northern California, but rare southwards.

European Painted Top-shell
1 in (2.5 cm)

Variable Top-shell
1 in (2.5 cm)

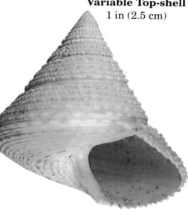

Horn Top-shell
1 in (2.5 cm)

European Painted Top-shell,
Calliostoma zizyphinus (Linnaeus, 1758).
Solid, trochoid in shape, with a flat-sided apex at an angle of about 70°. Periphery on last whorl well rounded. Whorls with three to five spiral, smooth cords, the largest being just above the suture. Colour pale yellow with streaks and blotches of darker tan. Columella short, white. Umbilicus indented slightly. Shape of shell variable, and a rare, pure-white colour form exists. Moderately common among small stones and weeds from the low tide mark down to 984 ft (300 m). Ranges from Norway to the Mediterranean.

Variable Top-shell,
Calliostoma variegatum (Carpenter, 1864).
Shell solid, its spire slightly concave and the indented sutures quite prominent. Periphery of the last whorl well rounded. Five or six beaded cords on the above whorls. Nucleus pinkish. Colour light tan with speckles of reddish brown. Uncommonly dredged offshore down to 656 ft (200 m). Ranges from Alaska to southern California.

Horn Top-shell,
Calliostoma conulum (Linnaeus, 1758).
Shell elevated-conical, higher and narrower than the European Painted Top-shell. Flesh coloured with alternating blotches of whitish and brown below the suture and on the sharp periphery of the last whorl. Surface highly polished. Early post-nuclear whorls in the apex are densely granulated. Columella knobbed at the base and pearly. A shallow-water species fairly common in the Mediterranean and extending to Portugal, the Azores and the Canary Islands.

**European Granular
Top-shell**
1 in (2.5 cm)

Black Tegula
1.5 in (4 cm)

Black Tegula,
Tegula funebralis (A. Adams, 1855).
Heavy, solid, dark purple-black in
colour; smoothish, but with a narrow,
puckered band just below the suture.
Weak spiral cords rarely evident;
coarse growth lines present in large,
more elongate specimens. Base
rounded. Umbilicus closed or merely a
slight dimple. Columella pearly, with
two small nodules at the base. The
head and tentacles are entirely black.
The sole of the foot of males is usually
light cream in colour, that of the
females usually brownish. A very
common littoral, rock-dwelling species
ranging from Vancouver, Canada to
southern California.

European Granular Top-shell,
Calliostoma granulatum (Born, 1778).
Spire pointed, slightly concave.
Periphery of the last whorl rather
sharp and bounded by a fairly large,
smooth spiral cord. Whorls above have
six or seven smaller, beaded spiral
threads. Suture minutely indented.
Base of shell with a dozen faint spiral
threads and coloured cream with
numerous reddish-brown spots.
Columella short, white and wide at the
centre. Soft parts cream with brown
specklings. Tentacles slender, white
and with a dark central line.
Uncommon from 23–984 ft (7–300 m)
on rough, stony bottoms. Ranges from
the southern British Isles to the Azores
and Mediterranean.

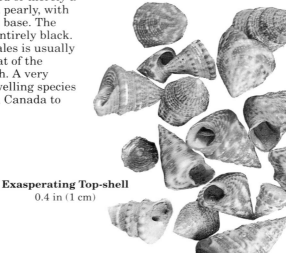

Gualteri's Top-shell
0.5 in (1 cm)

Exasperating Top-shell
0.4 in (1 cm)

Magical Gibbula
1.2 in (3 cm)

Exasperating Top-shell,
Jujubinus exasperatus (Pennant, 1777).
Shell small, solid, pyramidal with a
high spire and flat sides. Sculpture of
three or four large, rounded, coarsely
beaded cords. Periphery of the last
whorl made angular by the largest
spiral cord. Base with six flattish,
smooth cords. Umbilicus absent.
Columella white, with a small bulge in
the middle. Colour of variable
maculations of reds, browns and tans.
Lives on *Zostera* marine plants. Fairly
common from southern England south
into the Mediterranean.

Magical Gibbula,
Gibbula magus (Linnaeus, 1758).
Shell solid, low-spired, with shouldered
whorls bearing coarse nodules just
below the suture. Last whorl keeled
and smooth. Umbilicus small. Base
with fine spiral lines. Last whorl with
irregular, slanting axial swellings.
Columella thin, white, with a bulge in
the centre. Colour variable browns and
reddish maculations. Main tentacles
with a longitudinal black line.
Epipodial tentacles sulphur yellow. A
subtidal species in southern British
Isles and south into the Mediterranean.

Gualteri's Top-shell,
Calliostoma gualterianum (Philippi,
1848).
Shell conical-elevated (without an
umbilicus), polished, solid, yellowish
brown or olive clouded with dark
brown, the earlier whorls coloured
bluish black. Spiral cut lines and faint
beads on the early whorls, the rest
smooth. Aperture smooth and nacreous
within. Colours variable, and rarely all
purple. A common shallow-water
species ranging from Portugal south
into the Mediterranean.

Ashen Gibbula
0.8 in (2 cm)

Brown Tegula
1.5 in (4 cm)

Ashen Gibbula,
Gibbula cineraria (Linnaeus, 1758).
Shell solid, somewhat dome-shaped
with a slightly convex spire and blunt
apex. Sculpture of numerous low,
slightly nodulose, spiral ridges crossed
by fine growth lines. Umbilicus narrow
but deep. Colour yellowish with
numerous broken, slanting streaks of
brownish purple. A very common
intertidal species on rocky shores
among weeds and under stones.
Throughout the British Isles and from
Iceland to Portugal.

Brown Tegula,
Tegula brunnea Philippi, 1848
Shell solid, tubinate, with a dimple-like
depression on the closed umbilicus.
Columella with one small tooth near
the base. Colour light chestnut-brown.
Common low-tide mark. Ranges from
Oregon to southern California.

Umbilicate Gibbula
0.8 in (2 cm)

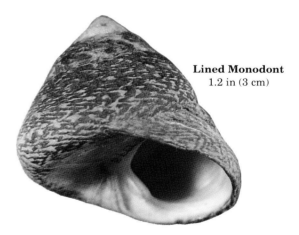

Lined Monodont
1.2 in (3 cm)

Umbilicate Gibbula,
Gibbula umbilicalis (da Costa, 1778).
Shell solid, somewhat globular, with a
convex, rounded spire and flat apex.
Surface smoothish, except for fine
incised lines and eight to ten grooves
on the base. Umbilicus fairly large and
deep. Colour heavily maculated with
speckles of reddish brown on a cream
background, sometimes with axial,
slanting flames of red brown. A
common intertidal species found among
weeds and stones in tidepools. Ranges
from the southern British Isles to the
Mediterranean.

Lined Monodont,
Monodonta lineata (da Costa, 1778).
Shell globose, large, heavy, with
somewhat rounded whorls. Surface
smoothish to rough with low, weak,
spiral ridges. Irregular growth lines
are frequent. Colour dark grey with a
fine mottled pattern and a large white
area surrounding the indented
umbilical area. Columella with a
swollen, small tooth near the base. The
animal is greyish green with numerous
black lines. A fairly common rockpool-
dweller feeding on vegetable detritus
and soft algae. Ranges from the
southern British Isles to Portugal.

Articulate Monodont,
Monodonta articulata Lamarck, 1822.
Shell solid, trochoid in shape, with a
rounded spire. Umbilicus absent.
Surface rough. Colour grey-green or
dirty white, with numerous spiral
bands of alternating squares of white
and reddish brown. Some specimens
are conspicuously spirally grooved,
some quite smooth. Interior of aperture
opalescent. A common southern littoral
snail ranging from southern France
and Portugal to the Mediterranean.

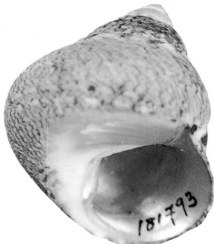

Turbinate Monodont
1.5 in (4 cm)

Turbinate Monodont,
Monodonta turbinata (Born, 1778)
Shell conical, solid, thick-shelled,
whitish, tinged with greenish grey and
with numerous squarish blotches of
purplish brown. Sculpture of several
spiral incised lines. Aperture oblique,
pearly and iridescent within. Base of
columella flattened, opaque-white on
the outside, pearly on the inner side.
Operculum chitinous, multispiral.
Common in shallow rocky areas.
Ranges from Portugal to the
Mediterranean Sea and the Canary
Islands.

Turban Snails
(Family Turbinidae)

This is a very large and diversified family of tropical snails characterized by a round shelly operculum that completely seals the aperture. All species are believed to be vegetarians. Very few representatives of the family live in cold water. Large turban shells from Southeast Asia are used in jewelry, carvings and inlay work because of the nacreous nature of the shells.

Red Turban
2.5 in (6.5 cm)

Rugose Turban
2 in (5 cm)

Rugose Turban,
Astraea rugosa (Linnaeus, 1758). Shell solid, heavy, with a strongly fimbriated surface. Whorls with three rows of short spines, those on the uppermost cord being the largest and being open in front. Base with five or six spiral ridges. Aperture round, smooth and white. Operculum shelly, smooth, brownish and with an irregular depression near the centre. A common shallow-water species ranging from Portugal to the Mediterranean and to the Azores.

Red Turban,
Astraea gibberosa (Dillwyn, 1817). Shell solid, heavy, squat, coloured brick-red to reddish brown. Characterized by five or six strong spiral cords on a flattish base. Operculum thick and shelly, greenish on the inner surface, enamel-white and smooth on the outside. Moderately common in shallow water among rocks from southern British Columbia to Mexico.
 The similar, more southern species, the Wavy Turban, *Astraea undosa* (Wood, 1828), has a brown fuzzy periostracum, and its operculum has three strong prickly ridges. Common from California to Mexico.

Carpenter's Dwarf Turban
0.8 in (2 cm)

Carpenter's Dwarf Turban,
Homalopoma carpenteri (Pilsbry, 1888). Shell small, solid and globose. Colour pinkish to brownish red. Last whorl and the base with 15 to 20 evenly sized, smooth spiral cords. Base of pearly columella with two or three exceedingly weak nodules. Operculum shelly, oval, thick, its exterior having a thick paucispiral whorl. Underside of operculum convex with multispiral, chitinous whorls. A very common species frequently washed ashore from Alaska to Baja California.

Pheasant Shells
(Family Phasianellidae)

The colourful pheasant shells are distributed worldwide in shallow, tropical and temperate seas. While some are large and conspicuous, such as those in Australasian seas, the majority are less than a half-inch (1 cm) in length. The shell is entirely porcelaneous, not nacreous as in the related trochids and turbinids. The operculum is calcareous, usually white and with only a few whorls. Most of the species are herbivorous. The sexes are separate, but there is no penis in the males. Eggs are shed singly into the sea.

Baby Pheasant Shell 0.5 in (1 cm)

Beautiful Pheasant Shell 0.7 in (2 cm)

Baby Pheasant Shell,
Tricolia pullus (Linnaeus, 1758).
Shell small, elongate-ovate, solid, semi-translucent, with fairly deep sutures. Colour bright reddish, yellowish or white with axial flames of red or brown and with a scattering of red dots and oblique lines. There are many colour varieties of this fairly common, shallow-water species which ranges from the southern British Isles to the Adriatic Sea and to the Azores.

Beautiful Pheasant Shell,
Tricolia speciosa (Mühlfeld, 1824).
Shell small, elongate, thin, glossy, white with alternating red and white flames below the suture and several spiral rows of white dots and with oblique descending lines of pink or yellow. Top of the columella with a thick white callus. Operculum calcareous and white. A locally common, shallow-water species of the Mediterranean and Portugal.

Periwinkles
(Family Littorinidae)

Throughout most parts of the world the small periwinkles appear in large numbers along rocky shores between tide marks or on wharf pilings and mangrove trees. They feed on vegetable detritus and living algae. The sexes are separate, with the males bearing a prong-like penis on the back of the head. Eggs are either shed as single, floating capsules or are buried in small, jelly-like masses. The operculum is chitinous and with few whorls.

Marsh Periwinkle
1 in (2.5 cm)

Common Periwinkle
1 in (2.5 cm)

Common Periwinkle,
Littorina littorea (Linnaeus, 1758).
Shell globular, solid, with a coarse exterior and a strong, thin outer lip. Columella arched, smooth and white. Sculpture of faint spiral lines. Colour drab grey, sometimes with fine, spiral streaks of white. This species is common on intertidal rocks. It ranges from Greenland and Norway to the Mediterranean; and from northern Canada to Delaware.

Marsh Periwinkle,
Littorina irrorata (Say, 1822).
Thick-shelled, with numerous regularly formed, spiral grooves. Outer lip slightly flaring and with tiny grooves on the inside. Colour greyish, with tiny, short streaks of reddish brown on the spiral ridges. Aperture yellowish. Columella reddish brown. Commonly found in large numbers among the sedges of brackish water marshes. Ranges from New York to central Florida and to Texas.

Northern Yellow Periwinkle
0.5 in (1 cm)

Northern Yellow Periwinkle,
Littorina obtusata (Linnaeus, 1758).
Small, globular, solid, with a low spire and smoothish exterior. Colour variable but usually a uniform bright brownish yellow or orange-yellow. Rarely with a white or brown spiral band. Columella whitish. Operculum yellowish or brownish. A common rocky coast species, usually hidden under clumps of overhanging seaweeds upon which it lays its jelly-like egg masses. Found from southern Labrador to New Jersey; Norway to the Mediterranean.

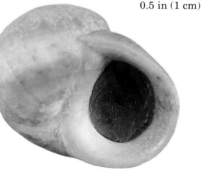

Northern Rough Periwinkle,
Littorina saxatilis (Olivi, 1792).
Shell solid, with a pointed spire, rather distinctly rounded whorls and an impressed suture. Surface smoothish, except for numerous indistinct spiral threads which are usually sharply sloping in cross-section. Typical form grey with a darker tessellate pattern and a dark aperture. The form (or another species) *rudis* Maton, 1797, lacks the tessellate pattern, has a broader lower columella and the aperture is light coloured. Females give birth to live, shelled young. A moderately common, high intertidal, rock species. It lives in the Arctic Seas south to New Jersey; south to Puget Sound, Washington; and south from Norway to France.

Northern Rough Periwinkle
0.5 in (1 cm)

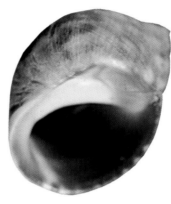

Eroded Periwinkle
0.7 in (2 cm)

Checkered Periwinkle
0.5 in (1 cm)

Sitka Periwinkle
0.5 in (1 cm)

Eroded Periwinkle,
Littorina keenae Rosewater, 1978.
Shell small, with a pointed spire, usually badly eroded. Colour greyish brown with bluish white spots and flecks. There is a flattened, eroded area on the body whorl alongside the whitish columella. Interior of aperture chocolate brown with a white spiral band at the bottom. An abundant species on rocky shore flats in the splash zone. Found from Puget Sound, Washington, to Mexico. Formerly called *Littorina planaxis* Philippi.

Checkered Periwinkle,
Littorina scutulata Gould, 1849.
Shell small, somewhat elongate, with a pointed spire. The columella is not as broad as that in the Eroded Periwinkle. Surface smooth, semi-glossy. Colour light to dark reddish-brown, and often with fairly large irregular spots and blotches of bluish white. Common in the upper intertidal zone. Distributed from Kodiak Island, Alaska, south to the north-western part of Baja California, Mexico.

Sitka Periwinkle,
Littorina sitkana Philippi, 1846.
Shell solid, ovate, characterized by about a dozen strong spiral cords on the body whorl. Columella whitish. Colour dark grey to rusty brown, sometimes with two or three wide spiral bands of whitish. A common rocky-shore species occurring from Alaska to British Columbia; uncommon further south to Oregon.

Lacuna Periwinkles
(Family Lacunidae)

These small, rather fragile, smooth snails are related to the coastal periwinkles, but are generally found offshore. They live among seaweeds and sometimes attach their jelly egg masses to giant kelps. The shells are characterized by a shelf-like columella and a chink-like umbilicus. The operculum is thin, chitinous, with only a few whorls. There are about a dozen species in the northern hemisphere.

Common Northern Lacuna
0.3 in (7 mm)

Variegated Lacuna
0.4 in (61 cm)

Variegated Lacuna,
Lacuna variegata Carpenter, 1864
Shell small, slightly higher than wide, solid, with evenly rounded smoothish whorls. Umbilical slot narrow, long and bounded by a sharp ridge on each side. Outer lip sharp and simple. Colour light brown, but sometimes with darker mottlings or oblique bands of darker brown. Moderately common in eelgrass along the shallow shores from Alaska to northern California.

Common Northern Lacuna,
Lacuna vincta (Montagu, 1803).
Fairly thin, but strong, translucent shell. Columella shelf-like; with a deep, elongate umbilical chink. Outer lip fragile. Exterior smooth, except for microscopic, spiral scratches. Colour light tan to brown with the spire tinted purplish rose. Commonly with three or four narrow brown bands. Common from low water to 164 ft (50 m). An Arctic species found from Alaska to California; and in the North Atlantic south to off Rhode Island and north-west Europe.

Rissoid Snails
(Family Rissoidae)

This family contains many hundreds of extremely small snails which have been divided into numerous genera. Advanced monographs are necessary for their accurate identification. Four species are included here merely to demonstrate how small these common, algae-dwelling snails may be.

Pointed Cingula
0.125 in (3 mm)

Striate Cingula
0.125 in (3 mm)

Striate Cingula,
Cingula semistriata (Montagu, 1803).
Extremely small, less than quarter-inch (1.5–2 mm) in length, elongate, with five to six whorls. Exterior with crowded, microscopic, squarish spiral threads and with about a dozen weak axial riblets per early whorl, usually on the upper third of the whorl. Colour whitish to rusty brown. Abundant from low water mark to 328 ft (100 m), usually among weeds and stones. Ranges from southern Norway and the British Isles to the Mediterranean.

Pointed Cingula,
Cingula aculeus Gould, 1841.
Extremely small, less than quarter-inch (2.5 mm) in length, elongate, with about five whorls, no umbilicus. Whorls rounded. Suture well impressed. Aperture ovate with a slightly flaring lip. Colour light to rusty brown. Spiral sculpture of numerous microscopic spiral incised lines. Below the suture are numerous short axial riblets. Common in shallow brackish water in weeds. Found from Nova Scotia to New Jersey; Scandinavia and northern British Isles. Belongs to the subgenus *Onoba*.

Parchment Rissoa
0.3 in (7 mm)

Bug Alvania
0.25 in (6 mm)

Bug Alvania,
Alvania cimex (Linnaeus, 1758).
Shell very small, quarter-inch (3–5 mm), oval-squat, with numerous spiral rows of tiny beads connected by fine axial threads, giving a cancellate appearance. Outer lip thick, with several fine teeth within. Colour whitish with two or three broad spiral bands of brown. Feeds on detritus. Common locally in shallow water from France south into the Mediterranean.

Parchment Rissoa,
Rissostomia membranacea (J. Adams, 1800).
Shell very small, elongate-turreted, usually with about a dozen axial rounded ribs per whorl. Aperture ovate with a slightly flaring outer lip. Colour usually white or yellowish. Quite variable in shape, those from brackish water being slender, semi-transparent and smooth. Those from ocean water are fatter with heavier ribbing. A shallow-water snail associated with eelgrass. Ranges form Norway to the Canary Islands and the Baltic Sea.

Purple Sea Snails
(Family Janthinidae)

Elongate Purple Sea-snail
1 in (2.5 cm)

The Purple Sea Snails are a small family of pelagic snails usually inhabiting the surface of warm seas, but sometimes drifting into colder waters. The four species of the Caribbean sometimes stray north to southern New England and even the shores of the British Isles. The shell is very thin, but strong; there is no operculum. A float of bubbles is created by the animal, and in some species the egg capsules are attached to the underside. The snails feed on the small, pelagic coelenterates, *Porpita* and *Velella*.

Elongate Purple Sea-snail,
Janthina globosa Swainson, 1822
All rose-purple, with rounded whorls and a projecting lower columella. Worldwide warm seas; rare in England.

Pallid Sea-snail
1 in (2.5 cm)

Common Purple Sea-snail
1 in (2.5 cm)

Common Purple Sea-snail,
Janthina janthina (Linnaeus, 1758).
Whorls angular, two-toned with purplish white on the apex side and deep violet on the umbilical side. Base of columella not extended. Rarely cast ashore in southern New England and the British Isles. It is found in tropical seas in most parts of the world.

Pallid Sea-snail
Janthina pallida (Thompson, 1840)
Shell thin but strong, globular. Base of aperture rounded and without the slight projection seen in *globosa*. Colour whitish violet throughout and not very glossy. Attaches up to 400 minute elongate egg capsules to its foot. A warm-water pelagic species sometimes carried into the North Atlantic by currents.

Dwarf Purple Sea-snail 0.4 in (1 cm)

Dwarf Purple Sea-snail
Janthina exigua Lamarck, 1816
Shell small and fragile. Outer lip with a prominent notch. Colour light violet, banded at the suture. Moderately common in warm seas. The smallest member of the genus. Rarely carried north into cooler waters by currents.

Turret-shells
(Family Turritellidae)

The elongate, narrow, many-whorled turret-shells are mostly warm-water, mud-dwellers with only a few species occurring in cold waters. A number of small species in the genera, *Tachyrhynchus* and *Turritella*, live in deep water. The operculum is thin, chitinous, circular, with many whorls and often with bristles along the edge.

Eroded Turret-shell
1 in (2.5 cm)

Common Turret-shell
1 in (2.5 cm)

Eroded Turret-shell,
Tachyrhynchus erosus (Couthouy, 1838).
Elongate, eight to ten whorls which have five or six flat-topped spiral cords. No umbilicus. Aperture round; columella smooth. Colour chalky cream with a polished tan periostracum. Common from 45–460 ft (14–140 m) on mud bottoms. Arctic Seas to off Massachusetts and also south to British Columbia.

Common Turret-shell,
Turritella communis (Risso, 1829).
Elongate about fifteen whorls; spire usually eroded. Spiral cords small and numerous. Brownish yellow with the base tinged with lilac. Abundant in muddy, shallow waters from Norway to North Africa.

Wentletraps
(Family Epitoniidae)

The wentletraps are a popular group of shells noted for their pure-white shells bearing numerous sharp axial ribs. The aperture is always round and fitted with a black or brown chitinous operculum. The white animal feeds on sea anemones and when disturbed may give off a purple fluid. The sexes are separate. Females lay eggs in small jelly packets that are covered with sand and strung together much like a necklace. The family has numerous genera, with shells that are smooth, reticulated or with sharp ribs. There are several hundred known species, most without an umbilicus.

Northern White Wentletrap
1 in (2.5 cm)

Wroblewski's Wentletrap
1 in (2.5 cm)

Costate Wentletrap
1.2 in (3 cm)

Northern White Wentletrap,
Acirsa borealis (Lyell, 1842).
Elongate, chalky white to yellowish; surface has very weak, axial riblets, and numerous spiral cut lines, sometimes filled with thin periostracum. Two nuclear whorls are smooth. Edge of outer lip thin. Uncommon from just offshore down to 328 ft (100 m). Aleutian Islands to Greenland and south to Massachusetts.

Wroblewski's Wentletrap,
Opalia wroblewskii (Mörch, 1876).
Elongate, solid, always looks beach worn. Greyish white, but often stained purple from its own dye. Has six to eight low, pronounced, wide axial ribs. Base of shell bounded by a strong, smooth, low spiral cord. Fairly common from 3–328 ft (1–100 m) from Alaska to southern California.

Costate Wentletrap,
Acirsa costulata (Mighels and Adams, 1842)
Very similar to *A. borealis* and is sometimes considered a synonym. It is much more elongate, the spire angle is much less, the base of the whorls have a weak carina, the surface is smoother and yellowish. Uncommon offshore in New England waters.

Money Wentletrap
1 in (2.5 cm)

Greenland Wentletrap
1.2 in (3 cm)

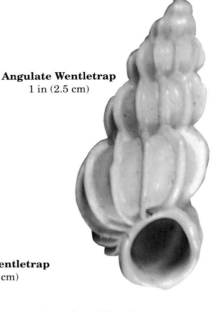

Angulate Wentletrap
1 in (2.5 cm)

Money Wentletrap,
Epitonium indianorum (Carpenter, 1864).
Slender, with about ten well-rounded whorls with a deeply indented suture. Each whorl has 14 or 15 sharp axial ribs which are slightly bent backwards. Tops of the ribs are slightly pointed. Fairly common offshore on gravel bottoms associated with sea anemones. In shallow water from Alaska to British Columbia, but in deeper water further south to Baja California, Mexico.

Greenland Wentletrap,
Epitonium greenlandicum (Perry, 1811).
Solid, elongate, chalky grey, with nine to 12 ridge-like, sometimes broad, ribs per whorl. Spiral sculpture is prominent, with nine spiral cords on the base of the shell. Operculum dark brown. Common offshore on gravel bottoms from 64–853 ft (20–260 m). Ranges from Alaska to British Columbia and from Greenland to Long Island, New York.

Angulate Wentletrap,
Epitonium angulatum (Say, 1830).
Moderately stout, strong and pure white. Eight whorls with about nine or ten strong but thin axial ribs which are very slightly reflected backwards and which are usually angulated at the shoulder. The ribs are usually lined up one below the other. Outer lip thickened and reflected. One of the commonest shallow-water, sand-dwelling wentletraps ranging from New York to Florida and to Texas.

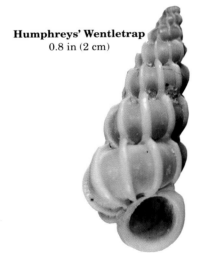

Humphreys' Wentletrap
0.8 in (2 cm)

Many-ribbed Wentletrap
0.5 in (1 cm)

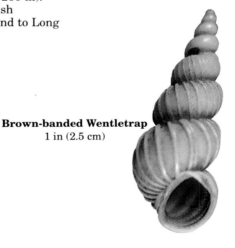

Brown-banded Wentletrap
1 in (2.5 cm)

Humphreys' Wentletrap,
Epitonium humphreysi (Kiener, 1838).
Fairly slender, thick-shelled, dull-white and with a deep suture. The nine or ten convex whorls each have eight or nine ribs that are slightly angled at the shoulder. Outer lip round and thickened. Common from sandy shores to 328 ft (100 m). Extends from Cape Cod, Massachusetts to Florida and to Texas.

Many-ribbed Wentletrap,
Epitonium multistriatum (Say, 1826).
Small, lightweight, elongate, no umbilicus; pure-white; axial blades numerous, crowded (16 to 19 on the last whorl). No basal ridge. Spiral sculpture of numerous cut lines, not crossing the blades. Three or four nuclear whorls are tiny. Uncommon offshore down to 720 ft (220 m) from Massachusetts to Texas and Florida.

Brown-banded Wentletrap,
Epitonium rupicola (Kurtz, 1860).
Moderately stout, whitish to yellowish with two brownish spiral bands on either side of the deep suture. Twelve to 18 weak or strong riblets on each whorl. A former, thickened varix is sometimes present on the whorl above. Base of shell with a single fine spiral cord. Common from low water to about 128 ft (40 m). Ranges from Cape Cod to Florida and to Texas.

Couthouy's Wentletrap
0.5 in (1 cm)

Common European Wentletrap
1.5 in (4 cm)

Turton's Wentletrap
1.5 in (4 cm)

Couthouy's Wentletrap,
Epitonium novangliae (Couthouy, 1838).
Small, umbilicate, somewhat elongate. Later whorls attached only by the costae (nine to 16 on the body whorl). Colour white, sometimes with light-brown banding. Shoulder of blades may have a fine hook. Surface reticulated between costae. No basal ridge. A southern species found from Virginia to Brazil just offshore.

Common European Wentletrap,
Epitonium clathrus (Linnaeus, 1758).
Elongate, strong; whorls barely meeting but linked and braced by eight or nine strong axial ribs. Behind the thick round outer lip there is a swollen varix. Colour greyish yellow, with the ribs spotted with brown spiral lines. Animal white with purplish-black specks. The head lacks a snout. The tentacles are long and slender with an eye at the base of each. The animals are consecutive hermaphrodites, changing sex each season. Common from intertidal sand flats to 228 ft (70 m). Norway to the Mediterranean and Black Sea.

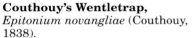

Trevelyn's Wentletrap
0.8 in (2 cm)

Trevely's Wentletrap,
Epitonium trevelyanum (Johnston, 1841).
Shell white, moderately elongate, with about 14 ribs per whorl, the tops being thickened, triangular and flattened. Suture very deep. Spiral lines sometimes present, as well as a peripheral brown, spiral band. Uncommon offshore on sandy bottoms 16–64 ft (5–20 m) deep from Norway to Portugal.

Turton's Wentletrap,
Epitonium turtonis (Turton, 1819).
Similar to *E. clathrus*, but the whorls are more flat-sided, with 12 to 15 ribs per whorl, and the top of the ribs reflected and flattened against the sutures. It is usually more darkly coloured. Spaces between ribs have fine spiral scratches. Moderately common on sandy bottoms from 16–64 ft (5–20 m). Ranges from Norway to Portugal.

Hairy-shells
(Family Trichotropidae)

Members of this cold-water family are characterized by the very hairy periostracal layer covering the outer shell. They have a turbinate shell with a short pointed spire and a fairly large aperture. The operculum is chitinous and with few whorls. In some species, one-year-old snails are males, but turn into females in the second year, and die after laying their gelatinous egg capsules.

Two-keeled Hairy-shell
1.5 in (4 cm)

Grey Hairy-shell
1 in (2.5 cm)

Two-keeled Hairy-shell,
Trichotropis bicarinatus (Sowerby, 1825).
Shell as wide as tall, with a sharp apex, and about four whorls which have two strong spiral cords at the periphery. The columella is wide and flattened. The delicate periostracum is brown and very spinose on the shoulders of the whorls. Moderately common offshore. Occurs in Arctic Seas to the Queen Charlotte Islands, British Columbia; and Labrador and Newfoundland.

Grey Hairy-shell,
Trichotropis insignis Middendorff, 1849.
Similar to *T. bicarinatus* but less than one inch (2.5 cm), a heavier shell, weakly carinate, with numerous uneven spiral threads, and a thin greyish periostracum. Uncommon offshore from Alaska to northern Japan.

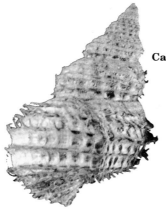

Cancellate Hairy-shell
0.8 in (2 cm)

Cancellate Hairy-shell,
Trichotropis cancellatus (Hinds, 1843).
With five or six rounded whorls bearing between sutures four or five strong spiral cords, between which there may be small axial riblets which produce a cancellate sculpture. Spire high. Periostracum thick, brown, with bristles over the region of the cords. A common shallow-water species from the Bering Sea to off Oregon.

Cap Limpets and Chinese Hats

(Families Capulidae and Crepidulidae)

Cap limpets begin life as small, coiled shells, but upon settling on a stone or bivalve shell, they grow into a cap-shaped limpet. The proboscis, which is formed from the forefoot, is permanently extended from the mouth and used to gather food or the pseudofeces of its bivalve host. The eggs are brooded under the foot and hatch into tiny, spiny, echinospiral, free-swimming larvae.

The chinese hats, or cup-and-saucer shells, are related to the slipper shells but have an extra shelf or cup within the main shell. They lack an operculum and are ciliary feeders, trapping floating food particles on a mucus sheet on the gills.

Pacific Chinese Hat
1 in (2.5 cm)

Fool's Cap Limpet
1.5 in (4 cm)

European Chinese Hat
0.6 in (1.5 cm)

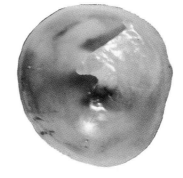

Fool's Cap Limpet,
Capulus ungaricus (Linnaeus, 1767). Cap-shaped, with a small hooked apex. Shell strong, yellowish white, with an ashy-brown, shaggy periostracum. Irregularly sculptured with coarse threads. Animal yellowish, the mantle reddish and bordered by an orange fringe. Uncommon on stones and bivalve shells offshore. Ranges from Greenland to off north-east Florida; and from Norway and Iceland to Portugal.

European Chinese Hat,
Calyptraea chinensis (Linnaeus, 1758). Similar to the Pacific Chinese Hat; exterior with concentric, pustulose growth rings. Colour yellowish white; soft parts yellowish. Common subtidally on other shells and on stones. Ranges from the British Isles to Portugal.

Pacific Chinese Hat,
Calyptraea fastigiata (Gould, 1856). Outline of the base of the thin, strong shell is circular and the apex is at the centre of the shell. Internal cup has a twisted columella ending attached to the edge of the main shell. Colour white to grey. Moderately common offshore, attached to other shells and to stones. Ranges from Alaska to California.

Worm Shells
(Family Vermetidae)

Resembling 'worm tubes' these snails are attached to rocks in colonies. With or without an operculum. Because the snails cannot move in search of food, they extend thin, sticky mucus threads into the water at night in order to entrap passing edible particles.

Scaled Worm-shell
(tube diameter: 0.5 in (1 cm)

Scaled Worm-shell,
Serpuloides squamigerus (Carpenter, 1856).
Grows in large, twisted masses on wharf pilings or attached to rocks below the low waterline. Shelly tubes are circular, about half-inch (1 cm) in diameter. Sculpture of numerous scaled longitudinal cords. Colour grey to pinkish. No operculum present. Common from California to Peru.

Slipper-shells
(Family Crepidulidae)

The curious cup inside the cup-and-saucer shells and the broad shelf within the slipper shells are for the protection of the soft digestive gland of the animal. Most species adhere permanently to other dead shells, with the smaller males usually attached to the larger females. Males customarily turn into females after the second or third year. Eggs, laid in soft capsules, are attached to the substrate under the shell and are brooded until the free-swimming larval stages emerge.

Pacific Half-slipper
0.7 in (2 cm)

Striate Cup-and-saucer
1 in (2.5 cm)

Striate Cup-and-saucer,
Crucibulum striatum Say, 1824. Cap-shaped; base circular, with the slightly twisted, smooth apex near the centre of the shell. Interior shelly cap two-thirds free from attachment. Exterior grey and with small, wavy radial cords. Commonly dredged offshore from 20–656 ft (6–200 m). Found in the Maritime Provinces of Canada to off Florida.

Pacific Half-slipper,
Crepipatella lingulata (Gould, 1846). Shell small, with an almost circular base; apex near edge of shell. Interior tannish mauve with a small cup attached along one side only. Exterior wrinkled and brownish. Common on living snail shells. Ranges from the Bering Sea to Panama.

European White Slipper-shell,
Crepidula unguiformis Lamarck, 1822. Shell pure-white, solid, usually quite flat or concave if attached to the interior aperture of a large gastropod shell. Apex at the end with small, glossy nuclear whorls. Inner shelf about half the length of the entire shell, glossy-white and slightly concave. Exterior dull white to dirty grey. Commonly found on large dead shells. This is a southern species ranging from southern France and Portugal to the Mediterranean.

Hooked Slipper-shell,
Crepidula adunca Sowerby, 1825. Highly arched, with a sharp, hooked apex. Laterally compressed, giving a triangular appearance from the sides. Colour dark brown with lighter rays and spots. Interior brown. Commonly found on small shells. Ranges from British Columbia to southern California.

Hooked Slipper-shell
1 in (2.5 cm)

European White Slipper-shell
1 in (2.5 cm)

White Hoof-shell
0.5 in (1 cm)

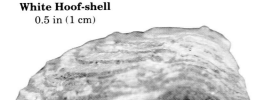

**Common Atlantic
Slipper-shell**
1.5 in (4 cm)

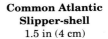

Eastern White Slipper-shell
1.2 in (3 cm)

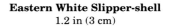

White Hoof-shell,
Hipponix antiquatus (Linnaeus, 1767).
Small, heavy for its size, cap-shaped,
with a poorly developed spire. Nuclear
whorls minute, spiral and glassy-white.
There is a horseshoe-shaped muscle
scar inside the shell. Exterior with
prominent, rugose ribs crossed by
incised lines. Periostracum thin, light
yellow. Sometimes with strong, smooth
circular cords. No operculum. Found
intertidally under stones or on other
shells from British Columbia to Peru;
and from Florida to Brazil. This genus
belongs to the family Hipponicidae.

Common Atlantic Slipper-shell,
Crepidula fornicata (Linnaeus, 1758).
Shelly deck extends over the rear half
of the inside of the arched shell. The
deck is usually slightly concave and
white to buff; its edge is strongly
sinuate or waved in two places.
Exterior dirty white to tan, sometimes
with brown blotches and lines. Variable
in shape. They may be strongly
corrugated if living on a ribbed scallop.
Individuals usually stack up on top of
one another, the lowest one being a
female, the others males. This common
shallow-water species has been
introduced to north-western America
and western Europe. Its normal range
is from the Maritime Provinces of
Canada to Texas.

Convex Slipper-shell
0.5 in (1 cm)

**Western White
Slipper-shell**
1.2 in (3 cm)

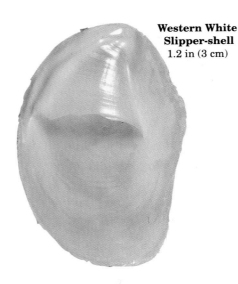

Eastern White Slipper-shell,
Crepidula plana Say, 1822.
Shell thin but strong; pure-white. Very
flat, sometimes convex or concave
depending upon the shape of the
substrate. The glossy-white shelf is
smooth and somewhat convex. The
apex is rarely turned to one side.
Several specimens customarily
congregate on dead shells or horseshoe
crabs, *Limulus*, with the larger ones
being females and the smaller,
surrounding ones being males. When
the female dies or is removed, the
nearest male gradually turns into a
female. The egg capsules are brooded
under the front of the foot of the
female. Slipper-shells are diatom filter
feeders. This very common species
extends from eastern Canada to Texas
and south to Brazil.

Convex Slipper-shell,
Crepidula convexa Say, 1822.
Shell small, usually highly arched and
coloured a dark reddish- to purplish-
brown. Some specimens may be
spotted. The edge of the deck is almost
straight. There is a small muscle scar
inside the main shell on the right side
just under the outer corner of the deck.
Some specimens are thick and heavy,
others quite fragile, the latter type
found attached to other shells. Most
live on other dead shells, but
sometimes they settle on eelgrass
where specimens become long and
narrow. Occurs from Massachusetts to
Texas and the West Indies. Introduced
to California prior to 1899.

Western White Slipper-shell,
Crepidula nummaria Gould, 1846.
Shell elongate, flattened and slightly
concave, with a glossy-white underside
and a large deck which usually has a
weak raised ridge running from the
apical end forward to the leading edge
of the shelf. Exterior whitish, usually
with a thin, yellowish periostracum.
Found in rock crevices and the
apertures of dead shells. Extends along
the entire west coast from Alaska to
Panama, usually in shallow water.

Lamellaria and Velutina Snails

(Families Lamellariidae and Velutinidae)

The lamellarian snails have very thin, fragile shells that are buried in a large slug-like animal. They are associated with shallow-water, compound ascidians upon which they feed and lay their eggs. They are hermaphroditic with all individuals bearing a short, prong-like penis. The colour and ornamentation on the back of the animal mimics nearby sponges and tunicates.

False Arctic Slipper-shell
1 in (2.5 cm)

Transparent Lamellaria
0.5 in (1 cm)

Smooth Velutina
0.7 in (2 cm)

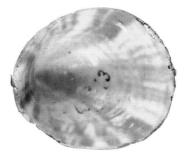

Transparent Lamellaria,
Lamellaria perspicua (Linnaeus, 1758). Shell fragile, smooth, transparent, almost without growth lines, and with two whorls. Nuclear whorl is slightly elevated. Columella slit is open, so that the apex can be seen from below. Parietal wall bears a crescent-shaped thickening. Foot bilabiate in front. Shell covered by the dome-shaped, fused mantle which has a siphonal notch in front. Male has an external penis. Mantle reddish to purplish grey. Operculum absent. Uncommon in rock pools down to 328 ft (100 m). Occurs from Norway and Iceland to the Mediterranean; eastern United States to Florida and to Brazil.

Smooth Velutina,
Velutina velutina (Müller, 1776). Shell very thin, fragile, translucent-amber, and covered with a thick, brownish periostracum which is spirally ridged. Columella arched and narrow. Animal with two long tentacles; foot yellowish and the mantle edge with many white dots. Found in the low-tide area on rocky shores where it feeds on solitary ascidians. This is a circumboreal species extending south to the British Isles, California and to Massachusetts.

False Arctic Slipper-shell,
Capulacmaea commodum (Middendorff, 1851).
A thin-shelled, white, cap-shaped shell covered with a thin brown periostracum. The shell is sometimes strongly rayed and purplish. The low spire is near the anterior end. This cold-water species is in the family Velutinidae, and has a wide distribution in circumpolar waters.

Pelican Foot Shells
(Family Aporrhaidae)

In what was once a widely distributed and diverse family of snails, less than half a dozen now survive in the northern Atlantic. The outer lip of the shell is expanded into the shape of a webbed foot of a bird. They are detritus feeders that live on muddy bottoms. The foot is elongate and bears a long, narrow, chitinous operculum. They lay single egg capsules in summer that hatch into larval veligers.

MacAndrew's Pelican Foot
0.8 in (2 cm)

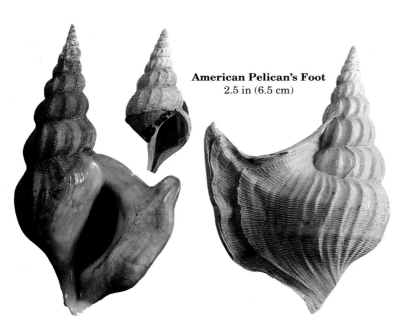

American Pelican's Foot
2.5 in (6.5 cm)

MacAndrew's Pelican Foot,
Aporrhais serresianus (Michaud, 1828). Shell similar to the Common Pelican's Foot, but it is smaller, with thinner, longer, more delicate spines, and with weaker, more numerous axial ribs and knobs. Head of animal red. Deep water from the northern British Isles to Norway. *A. macandreae* Jeffreys, 1867, is a synonym.

Common Pelican's Foot
1.2 in (3 cm)

American Pelican's Foot,
Aporrhais occidentalis Beck, 1836. Spire high, whorls well-rounded and with 15 to 25 curved axial ribs per whorl. Numerous spiral threads present. Outer lip greatly flaring, its edge thickened and the top pointing upwards. Operculum claw-like, with smooth edges. The form *labradorensis* C.W. Johnson, 1930, from off Labrador is smaller, more slender and with up to 29 ribs per whorl. Common from 32-1640 ft(10-500 m) from Arctic Canada to off North Carolina.

Common Pelican's Foot,
Aporrhais pespelecani
  (Linnaeus, 1758).
Spire sharp; the whorls in the spire have about12 axial elongate knobs. On the last whorl there is a second row of rounded knobs. Outer lip expanded above and below, as well as having two or three extensions on the greatly expanded central part. Colour cream tan. Lives partially buried in mud offshore. Abundant from Norway to the Mediterranean.

Trivias
(Family Eratoidae)

Known as members of the 'allied cowries' these small bright shells resemble the true tropical cowries in shape only. Most live in warm seas, but there are three exceptions in western Europe where some of them are popularly called 'groats' or 'nuns'. They have a colourful mantle which extends up over the shell.

Arctic Trivia
0.6 in (1.5 cm)

Nun Trivia
0.8 in (2 cm)

Flea Trivia
0 .3 in (7 mm)

Arctic Trivia,
Trivia arctica (Pulteney, 1799).
Shell globular, solid, resembling the Nun Trivia, but smaller, with fewer ribs, pinkish, and lacking the dorsal spots. This species lives in deeper waters as well as intertidally. Its range extends from Norway to the Mediterranean.

Nun Trivia,
Trivia monacha (da Costa, 1778).
Shell globular, solid, with about 28 strong neat cords running over the rounded top surface. Aperture narrow, with about16 small teeth on the concave columellar side. Colour brownish pink with three diffused, darker spots on the top. Moderately common at low-tide mark. Ranges from the British Isles to the Mediterranean.

Flea Trivia,
Trivia pulex (Link, l807).
Shell small, globular-elongate, pinkish brown, glossy on the top surface and whitish on the apertural side. Ribs very fine and numerous, with about 18 to 20 on the columella. This is an intertidal warm-water species occurring in the Mediterranean, the Azores and north into Portugal.

Cowries and Bonnets
(Families Cypraeidae and Cassidae)

The cowrie family is limited to warm waters, but one species from the Mediterranean reaches north into Portugal. The colourful glossy shell, with its narrow, toothed aperture, is made by the fleshy mantle that extends over the entire shell. There is no operculum.

The bonnets are small representatives of larger, tropical helmet shells of the family Cassidae. The operculum is small and fan-shaped. Bonnets feed on small echinoderms and sand dollars. Only one species is found in British waters.

Agate Cowrie,
Cypraea achatidea Sowerby, 1837. Shell globular-elongate, glossy; upper surface with dense specklings and blotches of rich dark-brown. Underside of shell and outer lip white. Teeth on either side of the narrow aperture are very small, the outer lip bearing about 20 to 25. Uncommon in 3–96 ft (1–30 m). This is a southern species ranging from Portugal to West Africa.

Mediterranean Bonnet
3 in (7.5 cm)

Rugose Bonnet
2.5 in (6.5 cm)

Spiny Bonnet
2.5 in (6.5 cm)

Mediterranean Bonnet,
Phalium granulatum subspecies *undulatum* (Gmelin, 1791). Whorls bearing deep, thin spiral grooves and with six or seven spiral rows of squarish light-brown dots. A southern shallow-water bonnet, common in the Mediterranean and Azores, but rare as far north as Portugal. This species had a wide distribution in Pliocene times, and is now broken into three subspecies, the *undulatum* of Europe, the typical subspecies *granulatum* (Born, 1778) of the West Indies, and the Panamic Bonnet, *centiquadratum* (Valenciennes, 1832) of Pacific Central America.

Rugose Bonnet,
Galeodea rugosa (Linnaeus, 1771). Shell fairly thin but strong. Sculpture of fine spiral threads and with a single row of small round knobs on the shoulder. Aperture glossy white, the inner wall quite wide, and the outer lip bearing a few very small teeth. Umbilicus narrow and chink-like. Lives offshore on mud bottoms. A common variable species of the Mediterranean but extends northwards to the southern parts of the British Isles.

Spiny Bonnet,
Galeodea echinophora (Linnaeus, 1758). Shell solid, with four to six spiral cords on the body whorl bearing about a dozen strong, low, pointed knobs. Between the cords are numerous fine spiral threads. Parietal shield prominent and white. Outer lip smooth white and swollen, with its inner edge bearing a dozen sharp, small prickles. Umbilicus absent. This is a southern species, fairly common in the Mediterranean and usually obtained by dredging offshore.

Moon Snails
(Family Naticidae)

The clam-eating moon snails are worldwide in distribution and are sand-dwellers, usually in shallow water. The operculum completely seals the the aperture and may be soft and chitinous, as in *Neverita*, or may be hard and shelly, as in *Natica*. The females lay a circular, sand-covered collar into which the minute eggs are buried. In England they are called necklace-shells.

Spotted Northern Moon Snail
0.5 in (1 cm)

Drake's Moon Snail,
Neverita draconis (Dall, 1903).
Shell globular, with well-rounded greyish whorls. Umbilicus quite wide and deep. The upper part of the columella has a very small swollen callus. The periostracum in absent on the whorls, but often remaining within the umbilicus. Operculum chitinous, few-whorled and translucent brown. A southern offshore species ranging from Baja California to Oregon.

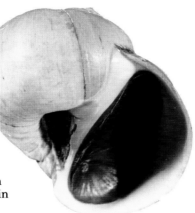

Drake's Moon Snail
2.5 in (6.5 cm)

Spotted Northern Moon Snail,
Lunatia triseriata (Say, 1822).
A small drab, globular shell with a small, deep umbilicus. Usually covered by a dull, thin, tan periostracum. Colour of shell cream, the last whorl bearing three spiral rows of 12 to 14 bluish- or reddish-brown square spots. Common in shallow water to 98 ft (30 m) depth in coarse sand where it drills holes in small tellin clams. Ranges from eastern Canada to off North Carolina.

Shark Eye
2.5 in (6.5 cm)

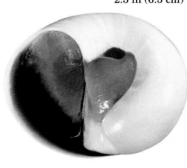

Shark Eye,
Neverita duplicata (Say, 1822).
A slightly flattened, globular, glossy grey shell characterized by a deep umbilicus covered over by a large, button-like brown callus. Columella white. Operculum chitinous, thin and brown. A common shallow-water sand-flat species with a large plough-like forefoot and reduced tentacles. Drills small neat hole in bivalves upon which it feeds. Ranges from Massachusetts to Texas.

Josephine's Moon Snail,
Neverita josephinia Risso, 1826.
Globular, but flattened from above; glossy grey to yellowish brown above and whitish underneath. Aperture chocolate. Umbilicus filled by a brown, flattened callus. A southern Mediterranean sandflat dweller, ranging north into Portugal.

Josephine's Moon Snail
1.5 in (4 cm)

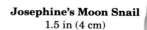

**Common Northern
Moon Snail**
4 in (10 cm)

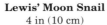

Lewis' Moon Snail
4 in (10 cm)

Common Northern Moon Snail,
Lunatia heros (Say, 1822).
Shell large, globular, relatively thin-shelled but strong. Umbilicus deep, round, not very large, and only slightly covered by a thickening of the columella wall. Colour dirty white to brownish grey. Aperture glossy, tan or with purplish-brown stains. Periostracum thin and brownish. Operculum chitinous, thin and light brown. Egg case has minute eggs embedded in it, is a wide circular ribbon of sand, flexible when wet, but crumbles when dry. A common intertidal species ranging from Nova Scotia, Canada, to off North Carolina.

Lewis' Moon Snail,
Lunatia lewisi (Gould, 1847).
A heavy, globular shell, slightly shouldered a little distance below the suture. Umbilicus deep, round and narrow. Characterized by the brown-stained, rather small button-like callus partially obscuring the top edge of the umbilicus. A very common clam-eating species found in 3–164 ft (1–50 m) of water from British Columbia to southern California.

European Necklace Shell
1.5 in (4 cm)

Guillemin's Moon Snail
1 in (2.5 cm)

European Necklace Shell,
Lunatia catena (da Costa, 1776).
Shell globular, with smooth, well-rounded whorls. Suture distinct. Umbilicus fairly large, deep and rounded. The upper half of the columella is swollen and glossy white. Colour of shell tan with a row of slanting, short, dark-brown streaks just below the suture. Early whorls with a row of tan spots. Operculum chitinous and thin. Sandy egg collars wash ashore in the summer. A common, clam-eating dweller of intertidal sandflats down to a depth of 410 ft (125 m). Ranges from the British Isles to the Mediterranean.

Alder's Moon Snail
0.6 in (1.5 cm)

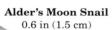

Guillemin's Moon Snail,
Lunatia guillemini (Payraudeau, 1826).
Globular, with a pointed spire; exterior glossy smooth and solid. Umbilicus narrow and deep, bordered by a wide white band. Columella glossy, narrow, tinged with reddish brown. Aperture dark brown. Colour bluish grey with numerous dark-brown intertwining streaks and lines. A common Mediterranean species extending north to the Brittany coast of France.

Alder's Moon Snail,
Lunatia alderi (Forbes, 1838).
Shell small and globular with a short, depressed spire. Exterior glossy smooth. Umbilicus small, deep, partially covered by the brownish, glossy columella. Exterior tan with five spiral rows of chestnut-brown arrow-shaped short streaks. The animal covers the shell with its foot. The forefoot, used for digging, covers the short tentacles and eyes. Lives from the intertidal sandflats to deep offshore waters where it feeds on tellin clams. Ranges from Norway south to the Mediterranean.

Pale Northern Moon Snail,
Lunatia pallida (Broderip and Sowerby, 1829).
Globular, smooth, pure white and covered with a thin, yellowish periostracum. Inner wall of aperture moderately thickened with a white glaze. Umbilicus almost closed. Operculum chitinous and translucent brown. A common, widely dispersed Arctic species found south to California and south to off North Carolina. Present in Scandinavia and rare in the North Sea. Lives on sandy-mud bottoms from 32–6560 ft (10–2000 m).

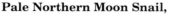

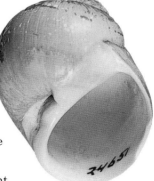

Pale Northern Moon Snail
1.5 in (4 cm)

Dusky Moon Snail
1.2 in (3 cm)

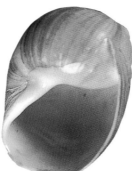

Smith's Moon Snail
1 in (2.5 cm)

Iceland Moon Snail
1.3 in (3 cm)

Dusky Moon Snail,
Lunatia fusca (Blainville, 1825).
Shell small, globular with a low
rounded spire. Colour brown to
chestnut but, when fresh, covered with
a dull, dark periostracum. Columella
glossy, dark brown with the base and
lower aperture white. The columella
is swollen where a spiral, rounded ridge
emerges from the deep umbilicus. The
soft parts are reddish brown. This is a
southern Mediterranean species which
extends northwards into the British
Isles wherever there is shallow water
and a muddy sand bottom.

Smith's Moon Snail,
Bulbus smithi (Brown, 1839).
Shell lightweight, globular, rather
fragile, and with a bright straw-
coloured or golden periostracum
covering the shell whose surface is
minutely reticulated by spiral threads
and growth lines. Aperture very large.
Middle of columella is indented on the
left. Uncommon offshore from Labrador
to the Georges Banks of
Massachusetts.

Iceland Moon Snail,
Amauropsis islandicus (Gmelin, 1791).
Shell globular, somewhat lightweight,
with a strongly channeled suture. The
rounded, smooth whorls are covered
with a thin, yellowish brown
periostracum which flakes off when dry.
Umbilicus absent or only a slight slit.
Columella narrow and glossy white.
Operculum with few whorls, chitinous
and translucent brown and with
microscopic spiral lines. A moderately
common, cold-water moon snail found
just offshore down to 525 ft (160 m). It
is a circumpolar species extending
south to off Virginia and to the North
Sea and Scandinavia.

Purplish Moon Snail
0.7 in (2 cm)

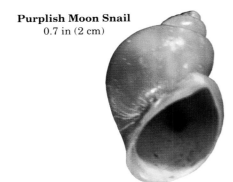

Purplish Moon Snail,
Amauropsis purpurea Dall, 1871.
Very similar to the Iceland Moon Snail
but smaller and with a purplish-green
periostracum and shallower sutural
channels. Possibly only a subspecies
which ranges from Alaska to British
Columbia, Canada. Members of this
genus lay a sandy egg collar in which
are set single, large eggs which hatch
into miniature, crawling snails. They
feed on bivalves.

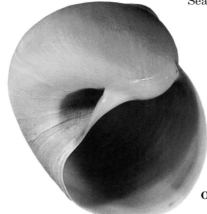

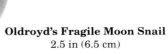

Oldroyd's Fragile Moon Snail
2.5 in (6.5 cm)

Oldroyd's Fragile Moon Snail,
Calinaticina oldroydii (Dall, 1897).
Shell globular, rather thin-shelled, a
little wider than high. Umbilicus wide
and deep, with the upper part obscured
by the expanded upper part of the
white, glossy columella. Spiral lines on
the outer shell are prominent. The
species lives in large colonies offshore
in sandy areas where they feed on
small bivalves and lay sandy egg
collars. Ranges from Oregon to
southern California.

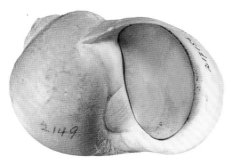

Arctic Natica
1 in (2.5 cm)

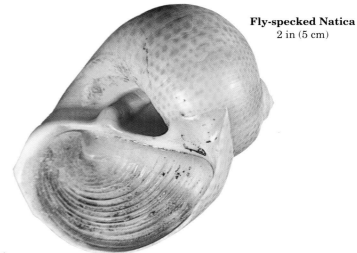

Fly-specked Natica
2 in (5 cm)

Arctic Natica,
*Natica clausa (*Broderip and Sowerby, 1829).
Shell strong, fairly thin-shelled, smooth, yellowish white, with a smooth grey to yellowish-brown periostracum. Whorls evenly well rounded. Umbilicus sealed over by a small, glossy-white, flat callus. Operculum shelly, thin, slightly concave, smooth, white and with only a few whorls. Animal is translucent whitish cream with a large forefoot. This is a common circumpolar species extending through eastern Canada to off North Carolina; south to northern California; and from Scandinavia to off Portugal in deep water.

Fly-specked Natica,
Naticarius sterncusmuscarum (Gmelin, 1791).
Thin- but strong-shelled, smooth, globular, cream coloured with numerous irregularly placed small dots of light brown. Umbilicus fairly large and deep with a large, rounded spiral cord emerging from within and ending at the middle part of the narrow, glossy columella. Operculum shelly, dirty white, with a dozen distinct sharp crowded spiral ridges. Appears in Italian fish markets. A common shallow-water Mediterranean species extending north into Portuguese waters.

Common Baby's Ear
1.5 in (4 cm)

Dillwyn's Natica
0.7 in (2 cm)

Flamed Natica
0.7 in (2 cm)

Dillwyn's Natica,
Naticarius dillwyni (Payraudeau, 1826).
Shell small, depressed globular, solid, glossy tan with white bands bearing obscure, arrowhead, chestnut-brown markings. Periostracum thin and yellowish brown. Umbilicus deep, narrow and partially covered by the glossy end of an umbilical cord. Operculum shelly, ivory coloured, paucispiral and bordered by a deep groove and a raised spiral cord. Found on sand from 13–32 ft (4–10 m), from Portugal south into the Mediterranean.

Flamed Natica,
Naticarius filosus (Philippi, 1845).
Shell small, globular, smooth. Umbilicus nearly covered with a chestnut to violaceous callus. The narrow white band just below the suture has widely spaced slanting brown flames. Just below the periphery of the body whorl is a wide, solid white band. Operculum smooth, calcareous and whitish. A moderately common offshore species found in sand. Ranges throughout the Mediterranean to Portugal and the Madeira Islands.

Common Baby's Ear,
Sinum perspectivum (Say, 1832)
Shell very flat, all-white, with a very large aperture and strongly curved columella. Numerous fine spiral lines on top of the whorls. Periostracum thin, yellowish. Animal fully envelops the shell. Operculum very small. Feeds on small bivalves. Common in south-east United States in shallow, sandy areas, but rare as far north as Maryland and Delaware.

Tritons
(Family Ranellidae)

Most members of the triton family, Ranellidae (formerly Cymatiidae) are large, warm-water dwellers, but one species, the Oregon Triton, has ventured into the cold waters of north-west America. Cold-water forms have a very thick hairy periostracum. They are carnivorous and lay clumps of kernel-shaped egg capsules. The large Triton's Trumpets, *Charonia,* are confined to much warmer waters.

Oregon Triton
3 in (7.5 cm)

Knobbed Triton
7 in (18 cm)

Oregon Triton,
Fusitriton oregonensis (Redfield,1848).
Shell fusiform, with about six whorls, all convex in outline and bearing 16 to 18 axial riblets nodulated by the crossing of smaller spiral pairs of threads. The periostracum is heavy, spiculose, bristle-like and grey brown. Aperture and interior of short siphonal canal are enamel white. There is a single, round white tooth at the top of the inner lip. Operculum chitinous and brown. Common near shore from Alaska to British Columbia; in deeper water south to San Diego.

Knobbed Triton
Charonia lampas (Linnaeus, 1758)
Shell large, solid, with a large last whorl. Aperture flaring. Outer lip white with nine pairs of small white teeth on dark brown, squarish spots. Inner lip whitish with a few low, white, oblique lirae or folds. Colour whitish with chestnut specklings and variagations. Uncommon in shallow water in the Mediterranean and Iberian Peninsula.

Dove-shells
(Family Columbellidae)

The numerous small-shelled dove shells are worldwide in distribution, usually occurring as large colonies in shallow water. Most are tropical, but several dozen, belonging to the genera *Astyris* and *Mitrella*, live in the northern hemisphere. The operculum is small, chitinous and sickle-shaped. The foot is narrow and the fleshy siphonal canal long. They are aggressive carnivores.

Variegated Dove-shell 0.4 in (1 cm)

Variegated Dove-shell,
Astyris tuberosa (Carpenter, 1865).
Shell very small, slender, with a narrow, pointed, flat-sided spire; exterior smooth, usually glossy, tan with light-brown flames and spots. Outer lip thickened and with small teeth within. Common from 6–196 ft (2–60 m) from Alaska to California.

Rosy Northern Dove-shell 0.4 in (1 cm)

Rosy Northern Dove-shell,
Astyris rosacea (Gould, 1841).
Very small, slender, dingy white to rose, with a reddish apex. Smooth, except for microscopic spiral lines. Outer lip sharp, smooth within. A common circumboreal species found offshore in Alaska, Greenland to off New Jersey; and Norway to Portugal.

Lunar Dove-shell 0.2 in (5 mm)

Lunar Dove-shell,
Astyris lunata (Say, 1826).
Shell very small, glossy, smooth, translucent grey and marked with fine, axial zigzag brown to yellow stripes. Base of shell has fine incised lines. Aperture constricted and slightly sinuate. Outer lip has four small teeth on the inside. No prominent varix. Nuclear whorls very small and translucent. A very common shallow-water species associated with weedy areas. Ranges from southern Massachusetts to Texas and to Brazil.

Gould's Dove-shell
0.5 in (1 cm)

Carinate Dove-shell
0.3 in (7 mm)

Gould's Dove-shell,
Nitidella gouldi (Carpenter, 1857).
Shell small, broadly fusiform. Whorls
smoothish and slightly carinate. Spire
almost flat-sided. Base of shell and
exterior of short siphonal canal with
nine fine incised spiral lines. Base of
white columella with a low ridge. Outer
lip simple and sharp, with four or five
weak pustules on the inner rim. Colour
whitish with light-brown maculations.
Periostracum thin and yellowish grey.
Fairly common offshore down to 1968 ft
(600 m). Ranges from Alaska to off
southern California.

Carinate Dove-shell,
Nitidella carinata (Hinds, 1844).
Shell smaller than Gould's Dove-shell,
glossy, more evenly fusiform. Shoulder
of the last whorl strongly swollen.
Exterior of siphonal canal has about a
dozen spiral incised lines. Colour
brightly variegated with orange, white
and brown, and sometimes banded.
Both ends of the aperture are stained
dark brown. This is a common shallow-
water southerly Pacific coast species
ranging from California to Mexico.

Columbian Amphissa
1 in (2.5 cm)

Joseph's Coat Amphissa
0.5 in (1 cm)

Joseph's Coat Amphissa,
Amphissa versicolor Dall, 1871.
Shell elongate to ovate, rather thin-
shelled but strong; with seven glossy
whorls which bear about 15 obliquely
slanting, strong, rounded axial ribs.
Numerous spiral incised lines are
strongest on the base of the body whorl.
Lower columella area has a small
shield. Outer lip thickened within by
about a dozen small white teeth. Colour
pinkish grey with indistinct mottlings of
orange brown. This is a common
intertidal species found as deep as 64 ft
(20 m). Occurs from British Columbia to
off Baja California.

Columbian Amphissa,
Amphissa columbiana Dall, 1916.
Similar to Joseph's Coat Amphissa but
twice as large and with 20 to 24 weaker,
vertical, axial riblets on the last whorl.
There is a low, rounded varix behind the
outer lip. Colour yellow-brown with
indistinct mauve mottlings.
Periostracum thin and yellowish.
Operculum chitinous and brown.
Moderately common in shallow water
from Alaska to Oregon; rarely off the
southern Californian coast.

Murex and Rock Shells

(Family Muricidae)

Nuttall's Thorn Purpura
1.5 in (4 cm)

This is a very diverse and widely distributed family of carnivorous snails, varying from the colourful, tropical murex shells and the famous sources of the Royal Tyrian purple dye to the common oyster drills and *Nucella* dogwinkles. The sexes are separate, and they have a strong set of radular teeth and a tough horny operculum. Eggs are laid in clusters or balls of leathery capsules.

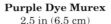

Purple Dye Murex
2.5 in (6.5 cm)

Purple Dye Murex,
Bolinus brandaris (Linnaeus, 1758). Shell with a swollen body whorl, ovate aperture and a long straight siphonal canal. Sculpture of two rows of about six or seven strong, short, straight spines on each whorl. Parietal wall elevated, smooth, glossy orange brown and partially covering the two rows of smaller spines at the base of the last whorl. This was one of the main sources of the purple dye used in ancient Roman times. The species is mainly Mediterranean, but comes as far north as Portugal.

Nuttall's Thorn Purpura,
Cerastostoma nuttalli (Conrad, 1837). Solid, heavy, similar to the Foliated Thorn Purpura, but with less developed varices, and with one prominent, noduled rib between each varix. Spine on outer lip usually long and sharp. Exterior yellowish brown, sometimes spirally banded. Siphonal canal closed along its length. A common littoral species in the southern part of its California to Mexico range. The form with a white band was called *albofasciata* (Dall, 1919). This species feeds mainly on small mussels and barnacles.

Trunculus Murex
2 in (5 cm)

Trunculus Murex,
Hexaplex trunculus (Linnaeus, 1758). Shell broadly fusiform, with a short, broad siphonal canal twisted to the left. Axial ribs and former lips have an open spine at the shoulder. Colour brownish with two or three narrow, spiral bands of whitish. Columella and aperture glossy white. This was also a source of ancient dye. It is common in the Mediterranean, and rare as far north as Portugal.

Foliated Thorn Purpura,
Ceratostoma foliatum (Gmelin, 1791). Solid, heavy shell with three large, thin, foliaceous varices per whorl which are finely fimbriated on the anterior side. Numerous small spiral cords present. Siphonal canal closed along its length, its tip turned up. Base of outer lip has a small, strong spine. Exterior white to light brown. On rocks near shore where it feeds on mussels and barnacles. Found commonly from southern Alaska to northern California.

Foliated Thorn Purpura
2.5 in (6.5 cm)

Festive Murex
1.5 in (4 cm)

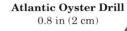

Atlantic Oyster Drill
0.8 in (2 cm)

Festive Murex,
Pteropurpura festiva (Hinds, 1844).
Shell solid, spire high, three varices per whorl. Varix with a thin, fimbriated surface and curled backwards. Exterior brownish cream with numerous fine, dark spiral lines. One very large rounded nodule between varices. A fairly common species from northern California to Mexico.

Atlantic Oyster Drill,
Urosalpinx cinerea (Say, 1822).
Broadly fusiform, without axial varices but having about nine to 11 rounded axial ribs per whorl and with numerous strong spiral cords. Outer lip slightly thickened on the inside and sometimes with two to six small whitish teeth. Coloured dirty grey or yellowish with irregular brown spiral bands. Aperture brown. This common shallow-water species is very destructive to oysters. Females deposit 25 to 28 leathery, vase-shaped capsules, each containing eight to 12 eggs. Ranges from Nova Scotia to north-east Florida. Introduced prior to 1888 to Washington and central California. Later introduced to England.

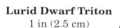

Lurid Dwarf Triton
1 in (2.5 cm)

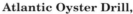

Spindle Dwarf Triton
0.8 in (2 cm)

Lurid Dwarf Triton,
Urosalpinx lurida (Middendorff, 1848).
Fusiform with rounded whorls, elongate spire, and numerous rough, rounded spiral cords crossing eight to ten weak rounded axial ribs. Six to eight small teeth are on the inside of the outer lip. Colour variable, whitish to rusty brown, sometimes banded. Periostracum dark brown and fuzzy. Siphonal canal usually sealed along its length. Very common in rocky intertidal areas from southern Alaska to northern California; rarer to the south.

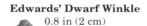

Edwards' Dwarf Winkle
0.8 in (2 cm)

Spindle Dwarf Triton,
Urosalpinx fusulus (Brocchi, 1814).
Shell fusiform; whorls six, slightly shouldered and with nine or ten rounded, axial ribs crossed by numerous spiral cords which form two rows of low tubercles in the whorls in the spire. Siphonal canal fairly long, open along its length. Columella glossy white. Inside of outer lip with four or five strong, short teeth. Suture well indented. Spire pointed; nuclear whorls brown and glassy. Aperture darker within. Operculum chitinous, heavy and brown. Moderately common in rocky shallow areas in the Mediterranean and western Europe.

Edwards' Dwarf Winkle,
Ocinebrina edwardsii (Payraudeau, 1826).
Shell small, broadly fusiform, six whorls, slightly shouldered. Sculpture of about 16 elongate, rounded axial ribs per whorl crossed by numerous fine irregular threads, usually a lighter tan. Columella smooth, stained glossy tan. Inside of swollen outer lip there are six or seven short teeth. Siphonal canal short, closed off on the apertural side. Interior of aperture purplish tan. A shallow-water, hard-bottom species common in the Mediterranean and northwards into Portugal.

Sharp Dwarf Winkle
0.7 in (2 cm)

Spotted Thorn Drupe
1.2 in (3 cm)

Checkered Thorn Drupe
0.5 in (1 cm)

Sharp Dwarf Winkle,
Ocinebrina aciculata (Lamarck, 1822).
Shell small, broadly fusiform, heavily
ornamented with eight to ten slanting,
rounded axial ribs crossed by delicately
fimbriated, spiral threads. Siphonal
canal short, usually closed along its
length. Six or seven elongated teeth are
within the outer lip. Spire pointed.
Colour tan to orange buff. Umbilicus
chink-like. Soft parts red with flecks of
yellow. They probably feed upon small,
intertidal barnacles. Common from
southern British Isles to the
Mediterranean.

Spotted Thorn Drupe
Acanthina spirata (Blainville, 1832).
Low-spired, solid, smoothish, except for
numerous poorly developed spiral
threads. Spine on lower outer lip is
strong, behind which on the base of the
outside of the body whorl is a weak
spiral groove. Whorls slightly
shouldered. Colour bluish grey with
numerous rows of small, red-brown
dots. Aperture within is bluish white.
Rarely, all-yellow form occur. Common
at high-tide mark along rocky shores
and among beds of mussels upon which
they feed. Ranges from Puget Sound,
Washington, to southern California.

Checkered Thorn Drupe,
Acanthina paucilirata (Stearns, 1871).
Shell solid, characterized by about six
spiral rows of small squares of blackish
brown on a cream background. Early
whorls cancellate, later whorls
smoothish except for four or five very
small, smooth, raised spiral threads.
Top of whorls slightly concave. Spine at
base of outer lip small and needle-like.
Aperture dentate, brownish with black
squares on the outer lip. Common
above the mid-tide mark on rocks.
Ranges from California to Mexico.

Crested Dwarf Triton
1 in (2.5 cm)

Thick-lipped Drill
1 in (2.5 cm)

Frilled Dogwinkle
2 in (5 cm)

Crested Dwarf Triton,
Muricopsis cristatus (Brocchi, 1814).
Shell slender and fusiform with a
pointed spire and slightly shouldered
whorls. Low axial rounded ribs are
made knobby because of spiral cords.
Colour brown with two broad spiral
bands of yellowish. Columella pinkish,
glossy and with two indistinct beads
near the bottom. Outer lip thick and
recurved, and with three coarse white
teeth. Siphonal canal fairly long and
open along its length. Intertidal rocky
areas in the Mediterranean to Senegal
and to southern Portugal.

Thick-lipped Drill,
Eupleura caudata (Say, 1822).
Shell fusiform and dorso-ventrally
compressed and with two lateral
varices. Apex pointed; siphonal canal
moderately long, almost closed, coming
to a sharp point below. Last varix large,
rounded and with small nodules. Inside
of outer lip with about six small bead-
like teeth. Whorls with small spiral
cords and strong axial ribs. There are
four to six axial ribs between the last
two varices. An abundant shallow-
water species that feeds by boring into
young oysters. Ranges from south of
Cape Cod to the north half of Florida.

Frilled Dogwinkle,
Nucella lamellosa (Gmelin, 1791).
Solid, with a fairly high spire.
Columella almost vertical and straight,
not flattened. Sculpturing and colour
very variable: white, greyish, cream or
orange, sometimes spirally banded.
Smoothish or with foliated ribs.
Sometimes spinose. A very common
rock-loving species extending from the
Bering Straits, Alaska, to central
California.

Atlantic Dogwinkle
1.5 in (4 cm)

File Dogwinkle,
Nucella lima (Gmelin, 1791).
Broadly fusiform, with a low spire,
rounded whorls with 17 to 20 round-
topped, smooth, crowded spiral cords,
the latter often alternating in size.
Colour whitish or orange brown, rarely
banded. This is a common cold-water,
intertidal species ranging from
northern Japan and Alaska to northern
California.

File Dogwinkle
1.2 in (3 cm)

Atlantic Dogwinkle,
Nucella lapillus (Linnaeus, 1758).
Broadly fusiform; spire usually elevated.
Exterior either smoothish or sculptured
with rounded, spiral ridges which may
be finely fimbriated. Colour usually dull
white, but in many specimens yellowish,
orange or brownish. Rarely with dark-
brown spiral bands. In some areas of
New England there are colonies of
strongly fimbriated specimens. This
abundant species lives on rocky coasts
between tide marks where it feeds upon
barnacles and small mussels. Eggs are
laid in clusters of small, leathery
capsules. The animal gives off a tyrian
purple dye once used as an indelible
laundry marking ink. The species
ranges from southern Labrador to New
York; from Norway to northern
Portugal.

Emarginate Dogwinkle,
Nucella emarginata (Deshayes, 1839).
Has a rather short spire. Aperture
large. Columella strongly arched,
flattened and slightly concave below.
Sculpturing variable, but
characteristically with coarse spiral
cords, usually alternatingly small and
large. Cords often scaled or coarsely
noduled. Exterior dirty grey to rusty
brown, sometimes with darker spiral
bands. Aperture and columella light
brown. A very common rock-dwelling
coastal species ranging from Alaska to
southern California. The species is
quite variable and may have a low or
high spire, and sometimes a smooth,
rounded shoulder.

Emarginate Dogwinkle
1 in (2.5 cm)

Channeled Dogwinkle,
Nucella canaliculata (Duclos, 1832).
Shell solid, elongate-globose, with
about 14 to 16 low, flat-topped, closely
spaced spiral cords on the body whorl.
Suture slightly channeled. Colour
white or orange brown, often spirally
banded. This is a moderately common
intertidal species feeding on mussels
and barnacles in rocky areas. Ranges
from the Aleutian Islands to central
California.

Sting Winkle,
Ocenebra erinacea (Linnaeus, 1758).
Shell broadly fusiform with an
angulate, acute spire. Whorls
shouldered and sculptured by seven or
eight thin, erect, evenly-spaced axial
ribs, crossed by numerous rounded,
finely fimbriated cords. Siphonal canal
closed along its length and fairly long,
with a scarred siphonal fasciole
alongside. Aperture oval. Outer lip
often bounded by a thin, well-developed
varix. Exterior yellowish, often with
brown bandings. Common below low-
tide mark in rocky areas where they
feed on bivalves. In the spring they lay
clusters of urn-shaped egg capsules.
Ranges from southern British Isles to
the Azores and the Mediterranean.

Channeled Dogwinkle
1 in (2.5 cm)

Sting Winkle
2 in (2.5 cm)

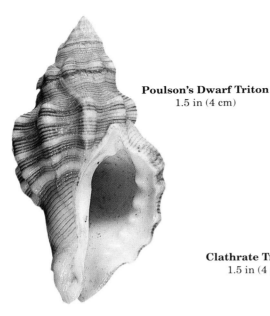

Poulson's Dwarf Triton
1.5 in (4 cm)

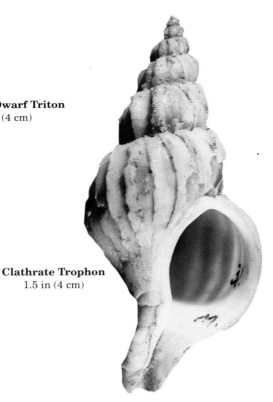

Clathrate Trophon
1.5 in (4 cm)

Poulson's Dwarf Triton,
Ocenebra poulsoni (Carpenter, 1864).
Shell solid, with a semi-gloss finish.
Whorls have eight or nine nodulated,
rounded axial ribs per whorl crossed by
numerous, very fine, incised spiral lines
on the ribs. Siphonal canal narrowly
open. Periostracum thin, greyish or
brownish and smooth. Aperture white.
A very common species on rocks and
wharf pilings, especially in the
southern part of its range, from
California to Mexico.

Clathrate Trophon,
Boreotrophon clathratus (Linnaeus,
1758).
 Shell fusiform, dull white, with a deep
suture which may have a flat area just
below it. Siphonal canal well developed
and open along its side. Whorls with
strong, thin axial ribs which are hollow
in front. In many specimens the tops of
the ribs are rounded, but in others they
may be protruding up into small
projections. Aperture white, and outer
lip slightly flaring. Young specimens
have a fairly long siphonal canal. A
moderately common dweller of mud
bottoms offshore in Arctic Seas. It
extends into the waters of Maine and
Norway.

Carpenter's Dwarf Triton,
Ocenebra interfossa Carpenter, 1864.
Spire half the length of the shell which
is light grey and delicately sculptured.
With eight to 11 axial ribs on the body
whorl crossed by about a dozen strong,
microscopically scaled spiral cords. The
surface is commonly fimbriated axially
between the cords. Siphonal canal
usually closed over. A fairly common
subtidal species also found in several
fathoms of water. It ranges from Alaska
to Mexico.

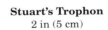

Northwest Pacific Trophon
1 in (2.5 cm)

Stuart's Trophon
2 in (5 cm)

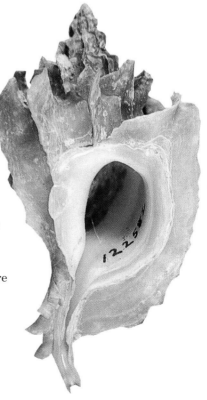

Northwest Pacific Trophon,
Boreotrophon pacificus (Dall, 1902).
Shell white, fusiform, similar to the
Clathrate Trophon, but the length of
the aperture and siphonal canal is
more than half the length of the entire
shell. The well-rounded whorls have 12
to 20 ribs which are slightly shouldered
just below the well-indented suture.
This carnivorous species is fairly
common at the low-tide area in Alaska,
but further south it is found offshore in
deep water.

Stuart's Trophon,
Boreotrophon stuarti (E. A. Smith,
1880).
Broadly fusiform, pure white to yellow
cream and with a waxy texture. Each
of the five or six whorls has nine to 11
strong, thin, lamella-like high-
shouldered ribs. Whorls in the spire are
cancelled by two or three spiral
raised threads. Body whorl with five
very weak spiral, rounded threads.
Uncommon from low tide down to
about 164 ft (50 m). Extends from
Alaska to off San Diego, California.

Alaskan Trophon
1.3 in (3 cm)

Truncate Trophon,
Boreotrophon truncatus (Strom, 1768).
Shell white, fusiform with a sharp
conical spire. Suture deep and bounded
below by a slightly flattened, narrow
gutter. Fifteen to 25 ribs on the last
whorl, strongest at the top and fading
out towards the base of the shell.
Colour yellowish brown. Columella and
aperture glossy white. Outer lip thin
and smooth. No umbilicus. A common
cold-water, circumpolar species
occurring in offshore waters south to
the Georges Banks, Massachusetts;
Alaska; Greenland south to the Bay of
Biscay, France.

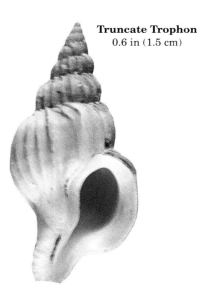

Truncate Trophon
0.6 in (1.5 cm)

Alaskan Trophon,
Boreotrophon alaskanus (Dall, 1902).
Shell cream white, fusiform, with the
whorls almost detached. The suture is
very deep and there is a flat, spiral
gutter adjacent to it. There are about
nine varices per whorl with the tops
extending upwards in the form of open
flutes. Siphonal canal fairly long. This
attractive species ranges from northern
Japan to the Bering Sea in deep water.

Latticed Trophon,
Boreotrophon craticulatus (Fabricius,
1780).
Shell fusiform, of a creamy waxy
consistency with the top of the whorls
shouldered and bearing about ten
delicate, thin, semi-translucent, axial
varices. There are numerous very small
spiral cords that cross the riblets and
give the shell a slightly latticed
appearance. Aperture half the length of
the entire shell and narrowing below
into a fairly short, open siphonal canal.
Nuclear whorls distinct, bulbous and
glassy smooth. *B. fabricii* (Moller, 1842)
is a synonym. It lives in about 196 ft
(60 m) of water from Arctic Canada to
Nova Scotia.

Sandpaper Trophon
1.5 in (4 cm)

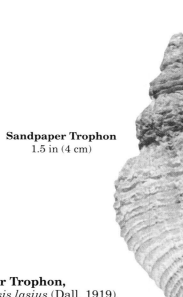

Latticed Trophon
1 in (2.5 cm)

Orpheus Trophon
1 in (2.5 cm)

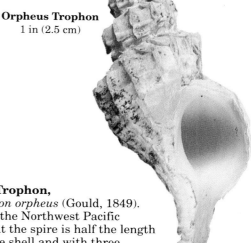

Sandpaper Trophon,
Trophonopsis lasius (Dall, 1919).
Spire half the length of the greyish
white shell. Spiral scaled cords crossing
over rounded ribs give a sandpapery
look to the exterior. Aperture enamel
white. Uncommon offshore from the
Bering Sea to Mexico.

Orpheus Trophon,
Boreotrophon orpheus (Gould, 1849).
Resembles the Northwest Pacific
Trophon but the spire is half the length
of the entire shell and with three
distinct spiral cords showing in the
spire.Twelve to 20 ribs per whorl.
Moderately common offshore from
Alaska to off southern California.

Buccinum Whelks

(Family Buccinidae)

Common Northern Buccinum
3 in (7.5 cm)

This is a family of large, mainly cold-water univalves, known in England as buckies and whelks. Many are found in fish markets. They are largely offshore-dwellers and serve as food for bottom-feeding fish. All have a chitinous, soft, brown operculum. They are carnivorous and sometimes act as scavengers. Eggs are laid in clusters of leathery capsules or singly on stones.

Common Northern Buccinum or **Buckie,**
Buccinum undatum Linnaeus, 1758
The best-known of the northern edible whelks. Shell solid, chalky grey to yellowish brown, with a moderately thick, grey periostracum. Axial ribs slanting, nine to 18 per whorl, low, rounded and extending one quarter- to half-way down the whorl. Spiral cords small, usually about five to eight between sutures. Outer lip usually slightly flaring. Aperture enamel white. Common in shallow water in the lower Arctic Seas as far south as New Jersey and the British Isles.

Totten's Buccinum,
Buccinum totteni Stimpson, 1865.
Thin-shelled, with five or six large, well-rounded, smoothish whorls. Aperture slightly less than half the length of the shell. Colour yellow brown with a thin, straw-coloured periostracum. Spiral sculpture of numerous finely incised striations. Outer lip thin and fragile. Moderately common offshore down to 328 ft (100 m). Ranges from Arctic Canada to Maine; Greenland and Iceland.

Totten's Buccinum
2 in (5 cm)

Plectrum Buccinum
2.5 in (6.5 cm)

Glacial Buccinum
2.5 in (6.5 cm)

Angulate Buccinum
2.5 in (6.5 cm)

Plectrum Buccinum,
Buccinum plectrum Stimpson, 1865.
Shell thin-shelled but strong. Aperture about third the length of the shell. Outer lip thick, smooth and enamel white. Numerous axial, rounded ribs slanting and limited to the upper third of the whorl. Spiral sculpture of numerous crowded, rough threads. Colour greyish to yellowish white. Common offshore in Arctic waters south to Puget Sound; and south to the Gulf of St. Lawrence, Canada.

Glacial Buccinum,
Buccinum glaciale Linnaeus, 1761.
A fairly thick, sturdy shell, but lightweight in comparison to its size. Characterized by its thick, glossy, white, flaring, reflected outer lip, and by the two wavy, strong spiral cords on the periphery of the whorls. Spiral incised lines numerous. Suture narrow and deep. Colour mauve brown. Aperture cream with a purplish flush within. Common from low-tide to several feet. Ranges in the Arctic Seas to Washington State and south to the Gulf of St. Lawrence.

Angulate Buccinum,
Buccinum angulosum Gray, 1839.
Shell solid, similar to the Glacial Buccinum, but with a shorter spire. Aperture half the length of the entire shell. Early whorls smooth. Post nuclear whorls have numerous rounded axial ribs extending from suture to suture. Later whorls with fewer widely spaced, short slanting ribs which are sometimes stained rusty brown. Between the ribs the shell is slightly concave and may bear one or two weak spiral threads. Columella enamel white, slightly twisted below. Outer lip flaring, thickened and smooth. Occurs in the European and Canadian Arctic waters as well as the Bering Straits.

Finmark Buccinum
2.5 in (6.5 cm)

Silky Buccinum,
Buccinum scalariforme Moller, 1842.
Aperture half the length of the entire
shell. Whorls in spire and the upper
two-thirds of the last whorl have
numerous strong, narrow, slanting
axial ribs which are sometimes
intertwining. Outer lip slightly
sinuate, thin and slightly flaring.
Spiral sculpture of microscopic, beaded
threads giving the surface a silky
appearance. Colour light brown but
covered with a dark, thin
periostracum. Common offshore down
to 656 ft (200 m). Arctic Seas to
Washington State; and south to the
Gulf of Maine. *B. tenue* Gray is a
synonym.

Silky Buccinum
2 in (5 cm)

Finmark Buccinum,
Buccinum finmarkianum Verkruzen,
1875.
Shell oblong-ovate, thin-shelled,
smooth, yellowish white with a thin,
yellowish periostracum. Whorls well
rounded. Sculpture sometimes with
very faint spiral threads. Suture neatly
indented. Columella and aperture
enamel white. Outer lip thin, smooth
and slightly flaring below. Operculum
small, almost circular, chitinous and
translucent yellow. An uncommon
species found off Norway.

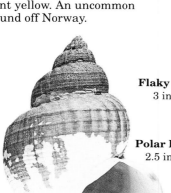

Flaky Buccinum
3 in (7.5 cm)

Flaky Buccinum,
Buccinum hydrophanum Hancock,
1846.
Shell with a tall spire, an aperture
about one-third the length of the entire
shell. Whorls rounded, smoothish
Siphonal fasciole absent. Fine growth
lines may be present. Outer lip thin,
sharp and flaring somewhat below.
Colour pale yellowish-brown.
Operculum chitinous, round, with
concentric lines and the nucleus in the
middle. This carnivorous species lives
from 328–3937 ft (100–1200 m) on
muddy bottoms. It is an Arctic species
ranging across Canada to the Grand
Banks and in Europe south to the
Shetland Islands.

Polar Buccinum
2.5 in (6.5 cm)

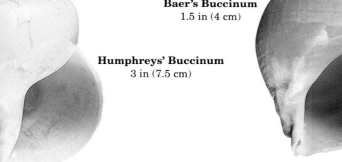

Baer's Buccinum
1.5 in (4 cm)

Humphreys' Buccinum
3 in (7.5 cm)

Polar Buccinum,
Buccinum polare Gray, 1839.
Similar to the Silky Buccinum, but the
shell is more globose, with a lower
spire and broader, more flaring,
sharper, smooth outer lip. Axial riblets
more numerous, much smaller, and
crossed by numerous spiral threads
which form distinct beads and a
latticed effect. Columella and aperture
glossy yellowish-white. Periostracum
thin, light brown. A cold-water
circumpolar species extending
southwards to northern Japan, Alaska
and to Greenland.

Humphreys' Buccinum,
Buccinum humphreysianum Bennett,
1824.
Thin-shelled, broadly oval with
smoothish, well-rounded whorls. Spire
regularly conic, the aperture about half
the length of the entire shell. Siphonal
canal short and wide. Outer lip thin
and fragile. Surface with extremely fine
spiral threads crossed by fine, slanting
growth lines. Periostracum very thin,
yellowish with occasional weak
brownish streaks. An uncommon, deep-
water species found in Arctic Seas in
Japan, Canada and north-western
Europe as far south as off Portugal.

Baer's Buccinum
Buccinum baeri (Middendorff, 1848).
Shell small, ovate-elongate, smoothish,
with an appearance of having been
beach worn. Aperture a little more than
half the length of the shell. Spiral
sculpture of very weak, smooth narrow
threads. Growth lines crude on the last
whorl. Outer lip not flaring, but smooth
and thin. Columella thin and narrow.
Exterior colour light brown. Range is
from the Aleutians to Kodiak Island,
Alaska.

Finely-striate Buccinum
3.5 in (9 cm)

Finely-striate Buccinum,
Buccinum striatissimum Sowerby, 1899.
Shell fairly large, relatively thin-shelled, whitish, with a high acute spire and an aperture one-third the length of the shell. Whorls very well rounded, the suture well indented. Surface covered with very fine spiral threads. Growth lines weak, but made more evident when the thin, grey periostracum is worn away. Aperture round, white, with the outer lip uniformly reflected. Siphonal notch short, narrow but distinct. Interior of aperture white. Occurs in deep water from Japan to Alaska; uncommon.

Norwegian Volute Whelk,
Volutopsius norvegicus (Gmelin, 1791).
Shell large, copious, with a tall spire and a large aperture about half the length of the shell. Whorls well rounded, smoothish except for very fine growth lines. Suture finely indented and sometimes with small wrinkles below it. Outer lip smooth, enamel white and reflected in the upper half. The lower edge is confluent with the hardly evident siphonal region. Columella slightly glazed and strongly arched. The animal is creamy yellow with purplish-brown specklings. It lives on soft, muddy bottoms and feeds on chinoderms. The single eggs hatch out as crawling young snails. It is moderately common in cold water south to the Gulf of St. Lawrence, Newfoundland, Scotland and Scandinavia.

Norwegian Volute Whelk
5 in (13 cm)

Chestnut Buccinum
3 in (7.5 cm)

Chestnut Buccinum,
Volutopsius castaneus (Mörch, 1858).
Shell fusiform, rather solid, with four whorls, the early one being bulbous and smooth. Aperture large, slightly larger than half the length of the shell and slightly flaring above. Siphonal canal weakly defined. Exterior surface brownish and smoothish, except for coarse axial wrinkles appearing more as deformities. Common on rocks offshore from the Aleutians to Kodiak Islands, Alaska.

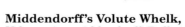

Melon Volute Whelk
5 in (13 cm)

Melon Volute Whelk
Volutopsius melonis (Dall, 1891).
Shell large, spire short, aperture two-thirds the length of the shell. Two nuclear whorls, smooth, white. Remainder of whorls have crowded, well-rounded, straight axial ribs crossed by very numerous, crowded, rounded, rough spiral threads. Colour ashen purplish-grey with a white, narrow columella. Aperture large, purple-brown within, and with as very thin, smooth outer lip. Operculum one-quarter the area of the aperture, chitinous, brown with the nucleus at one end. An uncommon deep-water species from northern Japan and the Bering Sea.

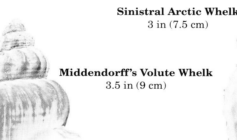

Middendorff's Volute Whelk
3.5 in (9 cm)

Middendorff's Volute Whelk,
Volutopsius middendorffi Dall, 1891.
Shell large and copious, resembling the Norwegian Volute Whelk, but with a less flaring lip, a more pronounced siphonal canal and with fewer and larger whorls in the spire. This is a common offshore species in the Bering Sea area and northern Alaska.

Sinistral Arctic Whelk
3 in (7.5 cm)

Sinistral Arctic Whelk,
Pyrolofusus deformis (Reeve, 1847)
One of the few normally 'left-handed' or sinistrally coiling whelks in the northern hemisphere. Shell solid, sinistral, whitish grey, with many low, irregular spiral cords. Nuclear whorls bulbous. Aperture has a thin slightly waved outer lip and is enamel white with brown staining within.
Uncommon offshore in the Arctic Seas; Alaska, Greenland and north-western Europe.

Behring's Neptune,
Beringion behringi (Middendorff, 1844).
Shell large, fusiform, dextral, with four or five well-rounded whorls, the first two smooth and bulbous, but usually badly eroded. Suture coarsely indented. Aperture slightly more than half the length of the entire shell. Siphonal canal well developed but short. Outer lip not flaring, but thin, smooth and strong. Exterior has five or six weak spiral cords and weak, coarse low ribs. There is a generally eroded look to this purplish-brown shell. Formerly called *Beringius beringi*. Uncommon offshore in the Bering Sea.

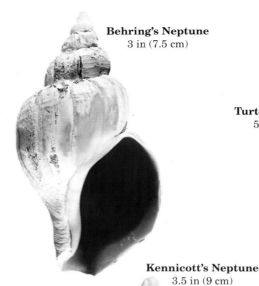

Behring's Neptune
3 in (7.5 cm)

Turton's Neptune
5 in (13 cm)

Kennicott's Neptune
3.5 in (9 cm)

Kennicott's Neptune,
Beringion kennicottii (Dall, 1907).
Shell large, not very heavy. Characterized by about nine strong, arched, somewhat rounded axial ribs extending from suture to suture and, on the body whorl, extending three-quarters the way down. Spiral sculpture of microscopic scratches, except on the base where there are a dozen or so weak threads. Periostracum light brown, thin and usually flakes off from dried specimens. Shell chalky grey. Moderately common offshore from 10–164 ft (3–50 m) from the Aleutians to Cook's Inlet, Alaska. Many of these Arctic whelks serve as the food for marine mammals.

Turton's Neptune,
Neoberingius turtoni (Bean, 1834).
Shell large, broadly fusiform, thin-shelled but strong; two nuclear whorls bulbous, white and smooth. Spire acute, tall with well-rounded whorls bearing numerous weakly beaded spiral threads. Aperture less than half the length of the entire shell. Outer lip thin, sharp but strong. Siphonal canal produced below and open. Colour whitish grey, with an overlying thin periostracum which is yellowish in colour. Moderately common offshore in the Arctic Seas, Scandinavia south to the North Sea; Labrador to Newfoundland and the Gulf of St. Lawrence.

Pygmy Colus
0.8 in (2 cm)

Hairy Colus
2.5 in (6.5 cm)

Marshall's Neptune
5.5 in (14 cm)

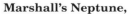

Pygmy Colus,
Colus pygmaeus (Gould, 1841).
Shell small, fusiform, fairly fragile, with a straight-sided, pointed apex and rounded whorls. Exterior chalk white, with numerous fine spiral threads covered with a light olive-grey, thin smoothish periostracum. Aperture about half the length of the shell. This is one of several boreal species of *Colus* found in the northern hemisphere. This small one extends offshore from the Gulf of St. Lawrence to off North Carolina.

Hairy Colus,
Colus pubescens (Verrill, 1882).
Shell of moderate size, fusiform, solid with a straight-sided spire. It is similar to the Pygmy Colus, but is larger, with a longer aperture and the sutures are not as deeply impressed nor as wide. Spiral sculpture of numerous crowded incised lines. Periostracum dark brown, thin, velvety when wet but flakes off when dry. Outer lip thin and sharp. Siphonal canal moderately long. Very commonly dredged from 96–3937 ft (30–1200 m) from Arctic Canada to off South Carolina.

Marshall's Neptune,
Beringion marshalli (Dall, 1919)
Shell large, fusiform, spire elongate with well-rounded whorls and a neatly impressed suture. Colour of shell whitish flesh, covered with a thin, pale brownish periostracum. At the shoulder on the last whorl are low, oblique irregular ridges. Siphonal canal moderately long, open and white within. Operculum black, horny and large. Uncommon offshore in the Bering Sea and Alaska.

Double-sculptered Neptune
4 in (10 cm)

Double-sculptured Neptune,
Neptunea intersculpta (Sowerby, 1899).
Shell large, broadly fusiform. Whorls
well rounded. Sculpture of numerous
fine, raised spiral cords, alternating
between large and small. Siphonal
canal fairly long and bent to the left.
Aperture glossy tan and smooth within.
Uncommon offshore in the northern
Pacific from Japan to Alaska.

Upright Neptune
4 in (10 cm)

Upright Neptune,
Neptunea ithia (Dall, 1891).
Shell large, elongate, fusiform and
rather narrow. Aperture less than half
the length of the entire shell. Surface
smoothish, colour ashen white.
Uncommon offshore from British
Columbia to northern California.

Simple Colus
2.5 in (6.5 cm)

Simple Colus,
Colus gracilis (da Costa, 1778).
Shell fusiform, elongate, with a tall,
straight-sided spire. Protoconch
smooth, slightly swollen. Whorls
moderately convex with about 60 low,
spiral threads, crossed occasionally by
axial growth lines. Aperture oval,
cream-white. Columella enamel white,
arched. Siphonal canal fairly long and
twisted slightly to the left. Colour of
shell white, with a yellowish-brown,
soft periostracum. Lives on sandy mud
bottoms from 96–1968 ft (30–600 m)
deep from Norway to off Portugal.
C. alaber (Kobelt) is a synonym.

Spitzbergen Colus
3 in (7.5 cm)

Jeffrey's Colus
2 in (5 cm)

Twisted Colus
2.5 in (6.5 cm)

Spitzbergen Colus,
Colus spitzbergeni (Reeve, 1855).
Spindle-shaped, rather light-shelled.
Spire elongate. Whorls well rounded
with 12 to 14 small, low, flat-topped,
equally sized, spiral cords.
Periostracum thin, reddish brown.
Arctic Seas to Maine and Scandinavia;
Bering Sea to Washington State.
Common offshore from 3–465 ft
(1–142 m) .

Jeffreys' Colus,
Colus jeffreysianus (Fischer, 1868).
Shell fusiform, similar to the Simple
Colus, but fatter and with a
proportionately longer aperture. The
siphonal canal is shorter. Spiral
sculpture coarser, with about 30 spiral
threads on the last whorl. Shell white,
rarely with a pinkish-brown tint.
Periostracum pale yellow. This
carnivorous snail lives on sandy mud
bottoms from 196–2296 ft (60–700 m).
Ranges from Norway to off Spain. A
synonym appears to be *turgidulus*
(Friele).

Twisted Colus,
Colus tortuosus (Reeve, 1855).
Shell elongate, fusiform, whitish with a
yellowish periostracum. Sutures well
indented. Outer lip thin and sharp.
Siphonal canal long, slim and twisted
to the left. Uncommon offshore in
88–3894 ft (27–1187 m). Ranges along
the north coast of Scandinavia. This
species is considered by some workers
to be a mere variant of Jeffreys' Colus.

Iceland Colus,

Colus islandicus (Gmelin, 1791).
Shell broadly fusiform. Three nuclear
whorls, bulbous and set obliquely to the
rest of the shell. Whorls slightly
convex. Siphonal canal long and almost
straight. Outer lip thin and strong.
Surface whitish, with numerous fine,
subdued spiral ridges and covered by a
pale brownish, smooth periostracum.
Aperture about half the length of the
shell. Outer lip thin, smooth and
strong. These carnivorous snails live on
sandy mud bottoms from 32–9842 ft
(10–3000 m) deep. They lay a leathery,
dome-shaped capsule on rocks and each
may contain several thousand minute
eggs. Ranges in the Arctic Seas from
Canada to Scandinavia.

Ovum Arctic Whelk
1.5 in (4 cm)

Iceland Colus
5 in (13 cm)

Herendeen's Colus,

Colus herendeenii (Dall, 1902).
Shell elongate-fusiform with about
seven whorls that are slightly convex.
Aperture ovate and less than half the
length of the entire shell. Sutures
narrow and very deep. Whorls with
numerous deep, incised lines between
which are formed flat-topped, narrow
spiral cords. Colour white and overlaid
by a thin, yellowish periostracum.
Uncommon off the Aleutian Islands
and to the Shumagin Islands, Alaska,
in fairly deep water.

Herendeen's Colus
2.5 in (6.5 cm)

Ovum Arctic Whelk,

Liomesus ovum (Turton, 1825).
Shell fairly small, ovate-fusiform,
smooth, creamy white, with convex
whorls. Nuclear whorls very small.
Growth lines not apparent unless the
outer lip had been previously broken.
Columella short, with an abrupt twist
at the end. Outer lip slightly flaring
and round at the base. Parietal wall
has a large, glazed white area.
Periostracum very thin and
translucent. Common in the northern
waters of north-western Europe.
Synonym: *L. dalei* (Sowerby, 1825).

Common Northwest Neptune
5 in (13 cm)

Fat Colus
2 in (5 cm)

Stimpson's Colus
4 in (10 cm)

Fat Colus,

Colus ventricosus (Gmelin, 1791).
Shell fusiform but very fat, with well-
rounded whorls and an aperture that is
slightly longer than half the entire
shell. Spiral sculpture of very faint,
raised lines. Siphonal canal open along
its length and slightly twisted. Outer
lip thin, sharp and strong. Colour of
shell whitish grey. Periostracum
brownish and fairly thick. Uncommon
offshore from Nova Scotia to
Massachusetts.

Stimpson's Colus,

Colus stimpsoni (Mörch, 1867).
Fusiform, very similar to the Iceland
Colus, but is fatter and has a less
produced nuclear whorl. Shell chalky
white, but covered with a semi-glossy,
light- to dark-brown, moderately thin
periostracum. Sculpture of numerous
incised spiral lines. Fairly common
from 10–3280 ft (3–1000 m). Found off
Labrador and Newfoundland south to
off North Carolina.

Common Northwest Neptune,

Neptunea lyrata (Gmelin, 1791).
Shell large, broadly fusiform, solid,
fairly heavy. Has five or six strongly
convex whorls bearing about eight
strongly to poorly developed, raised
spiral cords, two of which are usually
seen in each whorl in the spire. Faint
spiral threads are also present.
Exterior dull whitish brown. Fairly
common in Alaska from shore to 328 ft
(100 m); off Oregon and northern
California it occurs in deeper water.

New England Neptune,
Neptunea lyrata subspecies *decemcostata* (Say, 1826).
Broadly fusiform, solid. Characterized by its greyish-white, rather smooth shell which bears seven to ten very strong, squarish, reddish-brown spiral cords. The upper whorls show two or three cords. There is an additional band of brown just below the suture. This is a common soft-bottom carnivore found offshore and distributed from off Nova Scotia to off North Carolina. It is often brought into lobster traps by hermit crabs. A form or possibly subspecies, *N. lyrata turnerae* A. H. Clarke, 1956, has a shorter spire and broader shell. It ranges from Grand Manan Island, New Brunswick, to Mount Desert Island, Maine.

Phoenician Neptune,
Neptunea lyrata subspecies *phoenicea* (Dall, 1891).
Elongate-fusiform, with five or six well-rounded whorls bearing numerous small, raised, smooth, rounded spiral cords, seven on the upper whorls, 20 weaker ones on the body whorl. Colour of shell a uniform taffy brown with lighter cords and threads. Aperture ovate, a little greater than half the length of the shell, slightly flaring, and blending in below with the short broad siphonal canal. Columella and inside of aperture white. Commonly dredged off the northern coast of British Columbia.

New England Neptune
4 in (10 cm)

Disreputable Neptune
3 in (7.5 cm)

Phoenician Neptune
4 in (10 cm)

Disreputable Neptune,
Neptunea despecta (Linnaeus, 1758).
Fusiform, usually appearing worn and unattractive. Colour dingy white or brownish tan. Eight whorls very convex, the last being ventricose. Sometimes spirally banded with light chestnut. Spiral sculpture of fine, crowded threads. Upper whorls usually have two large, crude spiral cords which gradually disappear on the body whorl. Aperture just less than half the length of the shell and somewhat flaring. This species is quite variable and has had many subspecies described. It is found offshore in deep water from Arctic Canada to Maine and in Scandinavia and the Shetland Islands.

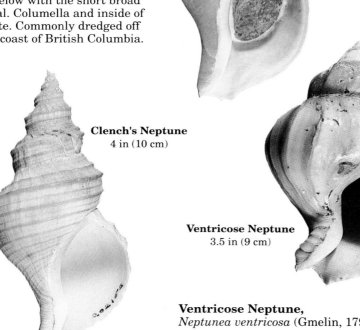

Clench's Neptune
4 in (10 cm)

Ventricose Neptune
3.5 in (9 cm)

Ancient Neptune
4 in (10 cm)

Clench's Neptune,
Neptunea despecta subspecies *clenchi* A. H. Clarke, 1956.
Similar to the Disreputable Neptune, but more elongate, with a higher spire and with much stronger spiral cords. The siphonal canal is not as twisted and is longer. It occurs along the northern Arctic areas of Canada in several feet of water.

Ventricose Neptune,
Neptunea ventricosa (Gmelin, 1791).
Shell fat, heavy and solid. The swollen last whorl may bear weak or strong, rounded slanting axial ribs. Columella strongly twisted to the right. The siphonal fasciole often with scale-like fimbriations. Colour of shell a dirty brownish-white. Aperture white or flushed with brownish purple. Moderately common offshore. Ranges across the Arctic Ocean, especially in northern Alaska; also Scandinavia, northern Scotland and Iceland.

Ancient Neptune,
Neptunea antiqua (Linnaeus, 1758).
Large, strong shell, yellowish to grey, with weak, fine spiral threads. Whorls rounded, swollen. Outer lip strong and smooth. Siphonal canal short, slightly twisted. A rare all-white form occurs in the North Sea. Sometimes specimens have a deep-orange mouth. Freaks may be sinistral (left-handed). An edible species, common around the British Isles; Scandinavia and France; offshore to 3280 ft (1,000 m).

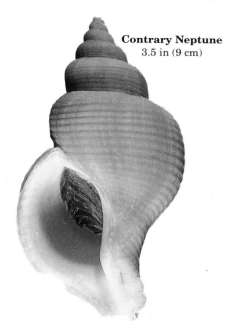

Contrary Neptune
3.5 in (9 cm)

Smirnia Neptune,
Neptunea smirnia (Dall, 1919).
Fusiform, fairly large, with a large,
slightly flaring aperture which is
greater than half the entire length of
the shell. Surface smoothish, except for
four or five very weak, low, flat spiral
cords on the early whorls. Last two
whorls smooth-shouldered with fine,
faint, silky growth lines. Colour tan
with a brown-stained aperture. A
common soft bottom species in
328–984 ft (100–300 m) of water.
Occurs from northern Japan to Alaska
and south off Washington State.

Smirnia Neptune
3.5 in (9 cm)

Heros Neptune
4 in (10 cm)

Contrary Neptune,
Neptunea contraria (Linnaeus, 1771).
Shell fusiform, sinistrally coiled (left-
handed), with a pointed spire, well-
rounded whorls and a well-indented
suture. Sculpture of numerous
crowded, squarish, raised weakly
beaded cords. Colour of shell a rich
light brown with a white aperture and
siphonal canal. Outer lip slightly
flaring and slightly crenulated.
Operculum half the size of the
aperture, brown, chitinous and with a
terminal nucleus. A moderately
common offshore species found from
Portugal south into the Mediterranean.

Heros Neptune,
Neptunea heros (Gray, 1850).
Shell large, heavy, fusiform with the
shoulders angled by an irregular spiral
cord. Axial ribs subdued and irregular.
One spiral cord is usually prominent on
the middle of the upper whorls. Scales
on siphonal fasciole. Colour tawny
brown. Aperture whitish. Operculum
chitinous, brown, almost as large as the
aperture and its nucleus at the
terminal end. Lives offshore in Arctic
Seas from Japan to Alaska; uncommon.

Tabled Neptune
3 in (7.5 cm)

Stiles Neptune
4 in (10 cm)

Tabled Neptune,
Neptunea tabulata (Baird, 1863).
Shell fusiform, solid, with eight white
whorls covered with a thin, brown
periostracum. Characterized by the
wide, flat channel next to the suture. It
is bounded by a raised, scaly or
fimbriated spiral cord. Remainder of
whorl with numerous sandpapery
spiral threads. Aperture white and one
third the length of the entire shell.
Siphonal canal moderately long, and
sometimes with a very small, narrow
chink-like umbilicus. Moderately
common offshore from 196–1312 ft
(60–400 m), extending from British
Columbia to San Diego, California.

Stiles Neptune,
Neptunea stilesi A. G. Smith, 1968.
Shell very broadly fusiform with a
short spire and large last whorl. Outer
lip not flaring. Siphonal canal
relatively short. Columellar edge raised
and glossy white. Colour of shell dingy
white to tan or yellowish and
occasionally reddish brown. Major
sculpturing of widely spaced, distinct,
rounded, low spiral cords which are
darker brown. Uncommon from
223–820 ft (68–250 m). Range is from
off Vancouver Island, British Columbia,
to Washington.

Kroyer's Colus,
Plicifusus kroyeri (Moller, 1842).
Shell fusiform, with about seven
rounded whorls bearing numerous,
distinct, rounded axial ribs. Suture
narrowly and deeply indented. Exterior
covered with a shiny, olive-brown
periostracum. Aperture round, slightly
less than half the length of the shell.
Outer lip thin, slightly flaring.
Columella has a built-up, narrow
callus, and is quite twisted at the lower
end. An offshore circumpolar species
from the Bering Sea and Greenland to
Norway.

Kroyer's Colus
3 in (7.5 cm)

Ivory Colus
3 in (7.5 cm)

Fenestrate Colus
1.5 in (4 cm)

Ivory Colus,
Siphonorbis ebur (Mörch, 1869).
Similar to the Fenestrate Colus, but
the spire is shorter, whorls more
rounded, aperture about half the length
of the shell, and lacking the axial ribs.
Sculpture of numerous, irregularly
placed fine spiral threads crossed by
even finer lines of growth. Siphonal
canal short and slightly leaning to the
left. Shell alabaster white. Arctic
waters of north-west Scandinavia and
Iceland.

Fenestrate Colus,
Siphonorbis fenestratus (Turton, 1834).
Somewhat fusiform, with a high spire
of about seven slightly convex whorls.
White, ovate aperture about one third
the length of the shell. Siphonal canal
short, slightly twisted. Suture strongly
indented. Sculpture in upper whorls of
numerous, rounded axial plicae crossed
by several, smaller spiral threads.
Nuclear whorls large and smooth.
Colour of shell white. Animal white,
siphon has many dark streaks.
Uncommon on gravel and sand
bottoms. Ranges from Newfoundland
to Scandinavia and rarely in the
northern British Isles. Alias *Turrisipho
fusiformis* (Broderip, 1830), not Borson,
1820.

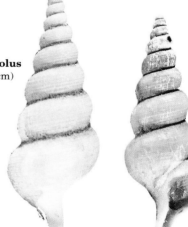

Destiny Colus
1.5 in (4 cm)

Howse's Colus
1.5 in (4 cm)

Howse's Colus,
Siphonorbis howsei (Marshall, 1911).
Shell fusiform, solid, white, smoothish
except for weak irregular spiral
threads. Aperture about half the length
of the entire shell. Suture finely
indented. Outer lip thin, strong and
smooth. Columella arched, the siphonal
canal usually twisted to the left.
Periostracum thin, translucent
yellowish. Occurs offshore from 114–
557 ft (35–170 m) in north-west
Europe.

Destiny Colus,
Turrisipho lachesis (Mörch, 1869).
Shell elongate-fusiform, with about
eight very rounded whorls. Spire high;
aperture small, about one quarter the
length of the entire shell. Siphonal
canal relatively short and narrow.
Suture well impressed. Axial sculpture
absent. Whorls covered by numerous,
crowded, small flattish spiral cords.
Colour of shell dirty-white; small
aperture white with a large brown
chitinous operculum. Periostracum,
when present, is soft and grey. This
uncommon carnivore lives on soft mud
bottoms offshore in the area of Norway.

Ample Fragile Buccinum
1.5 in (4 cm)

Dire Whelk
1 in (2.5 cm)

Livid Macron
1 in (2.5 cm)

Ample Fragile Buccinum,
Volutharpa ampullacea (Middendorff, 1848).
Shell small, fragile, ovate with a low spire. Aperture more than half the length of the shell; outer lip thin and flaring below. Siphonal canal short, its notch U-shaped. Nuclear whorl small and white. Four remaining whorls convex, smoothish. Colour of shell cream with broad axial streaks of yellow brown or purplish. Suture slightly channeled. Periostracum thin, fuzzy and greyish green. This is a moderately common cold-water species living on gravel bottoms. It ranges from the Bering Sea to off British Columbia.

Livid Macron,
Macron lividus (A. Adams. 1855).
Strong, solid shell, with five whorls which are covered with a thick, felt-like, dark-brown periostracum. Shell yellowish. Outer lip sharp, strong and near its base bearing a small, spiral thread. Columella strongly concave and white. Upper end of aperture narrow, with a small, short channel and with a white tooth-like callus on the parietal wall. Siphonal canal short and slightly twisted. Base of shell with a half dozen incised spiral lines. Operculum chitinous, oval and brown. Very common under stones at low tide. Ranges from California to Mexico.

Dire Whelk,
Searlesia dira (Reeve, 1846).
Shell small, solid, fusiform with an acute spire, bearing nine to 11 low rounded axial ribs. Spiral sculpture of numerous unequal-sized spiral threads. Siphonal canal short and slightly twisted to the left. Aperture slightly more than half the length of the shell and coloured tan. Outer lip not flaring and made crenulate by the numerous short, whitish spiral teeth just inside the aperture. Columella concave, thickened by an orange-brown, glossy callus. This is a common shallow-water species ranging from Alaska to Monterey, California.

Perry's Fragile Buccinum
2.5 in (6.5 cm)

Kellet's Whelk
4 in (10 cm)

Perry's Fragile Buccinum,
Volutharpa ampullacea subspecies *perryi* (Jay, 1855).
Very similar to typical *ampullacea* from Alaska, but usually larger, more rotund and with a smaller, finer apex. The outer lip is usually wider and more flaring. Common offshore in northern Honshu Island, Japan.

Kellet's Whelk,
Kelletia kelleti (Forbes, 1850).
Shell very heavy and solid, broadly fusiform with a fine, wavy suture and a sharp, crimped outer lip. Whorls slightly concave between the suture and the shouldered periphery. The latter bears ten strong, rounded, elevated knobs per whorl. Base with about six to ten incised spiral lines. Aperture glossy and white. Very common from northern California to Mexico in subtidal rocky areas, as well as in Japan. This is the only member of the genus.

Busycon Whelks
(Family Melongenidae)

These large, carnivorous snails are mainly tropical in distribution, but in eastern United States the *Busycon* whelks extend up into the cooler waters of New England. The siphonal canal is narrow and fairly open, and the columella is without strong folds. This group is an ancient American subfamily, Busyconinae, with less than a dozen living, shallow-water species. The abundant Knobbed Whelk and Channeled Whelk of eastern United States are sometimes used as food. Eggs are laid in long strings of wafer-shaped, horny capsules, each containing several dozen individuals that hatch as live crawling young in about five weeks. Adults feed on the hardshell clam, prying open the valves with the edge of their shelly outer lip.

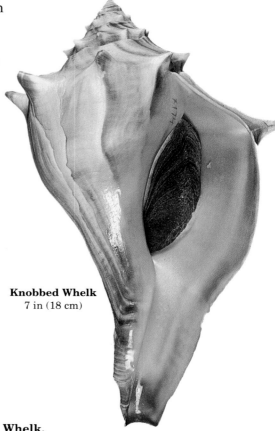

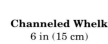

Channeled Whelk
6 in (15 cm)

Knobbed Whelk
7 in (18 cm)

Channeled Whelk,
Busycotypus canaliculatus (Linnaeus, 1758).
Shell fairly large, lightweight, fusiform with a relatively low spire and a large aperture that is three-quarters the length of the shell. Characterized by a deep, squarish, rather wide channel running along the suture. Periostracum heavy, felt-like and grey. The squarish shoulder is weakly beaded in the earlier whorls. This is the most northern of the genus *Busycon* endemic to eastern United States and belongs to the family Melongenidae. It feeds on clams and lays strings of disk-shaped capsules containing young shells. Fairly common in shallow water from Cape Cod to north-eastern Florida. Introduced to California prior to 1948.

Knobbed Whelk,
Busycon carica (Gmelin, 1791).
Shell large, dextral or 'right-handed', with low tubercles on the shoulder of the last whorl. Aperture light orange-yellow, but sometimes brick-red. The young show axial streaks of brownish purple. Common in shallow water where it feeds on clams. Ranges from the south shore of Cape Cod to the Carolinas. It is gradually replaced from North Carolina south to north-eastern Florida with the sturdier subspecies, *eliceans* (Montfort, 1810), which has larger spines and a swollen mid-section.

Spindles
(Family Fasciolariidae)

The graceful elongate spindle shells, belonging to the subfamily Fusininae, are mainly deep-water in distribution and confined to equatorial areas. Only two species are likely to be encountered in the northern hemisphere, namely Harford's Spindle off British Columbia to California, and the Syracuse Spindle of the Mediterranean, Portugal and the Azores. The shells are usually well ribbed, with a long siphonal canal and a chitinous operculum. Other member of the family include the tulip shells, *Fasciolaria,* of the West Indies.

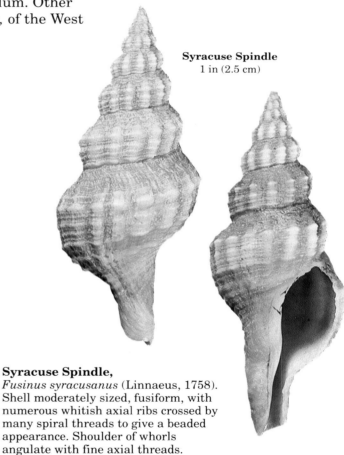

Syracuse Spindle
1 in (2.5 cm)

Harford's Spindle
2 in (5 cm)

Harford's Spindle,
Fusinus harfordi (Stearns, 1871).
Shell of moderate size, fusiform, solid with a white aperture half the length of the shell. Exterior dark, orange-brown, with 11 or 12 wide, rounded ribs crossed by small, sharply raised, fine scaled spiral cords. Inside the aperture there are numerous weak, white spiral lirae. Siphonal canal moderately long. Columella straight and glossy white. The soft parts of living specimens give off a luminescent pinkish glow. This genus belongs in the family Fasciolariidae. The species is uncommon off British Columbia to northern California.

Syracuse Spindle,
Fusinus syracusanus (Linnaeus, 1758).
Shell moderately sized, fusiform, with numerous whitish axial ribs crossed by many spiral threads to give a beaded appearance. Shoulder of whorls angulate with fine axial threads. Suture minutely indented. Colour tan with spiral bands of brown on the base of the last whorl. Siphonal canal long and open. Brown bands on the base of the last whorl. Fairly common offshore from 13–131 ft (4–40 m) in the Mediterranean, Portugal and the Azores.

Nassa Mud Snails
(Family Nassariidae)

Giant Western Nassa
1.5 in (2 cm)

These small sand- and mud-dwelling snails are common scavengers in most parts of the world, particularly in warm seas where there are large stretches of flats left exposed at low tide. The operculum is chitinous, oval and usually has a serrated edge.

Eastern Mud Snail
0.8 in (2 cm)

Giant Western Nassa,
Nassarius fossatus (Gould, 1849).
One of the largest known nassas.
Orange-brown to grey in colour. Early whorls coarsely beaded; last whorl with about a dozen coarse, variously sized, flat-topped spiral threads and short axial riblets. A common intertidal species from Vancouver Island to Mexico.

Eastern Mud Snail,
Ilyanassa obsoleta (Say, 1822).
A gregarious, abundant species on intertidal mud flats. Shell ovate, solid, smoothish with a high slightly convex spire. Aperture one-third the length of the shell. Colour dark brown with a narrow, tan colour band on the middle of the last whorl. Aperture chocolate brown. Columella with a strong spiral tooth at the base. Ranges from Quebec to north-east Florida; introduced to British Columbia and California.

Western Lean Nassa,
Nassarius mendicus (Gould, 1849).
Spire high. Outer lip not thickened.
Sculpture of numerous small beads.
Colour yellowish grey. Common in shallow water from Alaska to California. The subspecies *cooperi* (Forbes, 1850) has weaker spiral threads and about seven to nine strong, whitish, smoother axial ribs which persist to the last of the body whorl. Colour greyish yellow, often with fine, spiral brown or mauve lines. Very common in more southern waters.

Western Lean Nassa
0.8 in (2 cm)

Western Fat Nassa,
Nassarius perpinguis (Hinds, 1844).
Fairly thin-shelled but strong, with a
straight, acute spire and an aperture
less than half the length of the shell.
Outer lip fragile. Characterized by a
neat beaded sculpture. Parietal wall
glazed over with tan while the
remainder of the shell is yellowish
brown. There is a small white tooth on
the upper part of the inner wall.
Columella arched and ending below
with a single spiral lira. Inside of outer
lip has fine lirae. This is very abundant
on intertidal flats to a depth off 328 ft
(100 m) from Vancouver Island to Baja
California.

Western Fat Nassa
1 in (2.5 cm)

Common Eastern Nassa
0.5 in (1 cm)

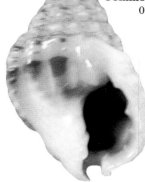

Pygmy Nassa
0.5 in (1 cm)

Pygmy Nassa,
Nassarius pygmaeus (Lamarck, 1822).
Shell small, with an acute spire,
swollen last whorl, strongly sculptured
with axial ribs bearing round beads.
Aperture small, ovate and encircled
with a thick beaded outer lip and
arched glossy columella. Base of
columella has two whitish swellings.
Nine or ten small teeth within the
outer lip. Siphonal canal wide and with
a gutter above it on the last whorl.
Colour brownish grey, sometimes with
three subdued spiral bands. Uncommon
just offshore to 656 ft (200 m) on sandy
bottoms. Ranges from southern
Norway, the Shetlands to the British
Isles. Some workers place it in the
genus, or subgenus, *Hinia*.

Common Eastern Nassa,
Nassarius vibex (Say, 1822).
Shell small, nut solid, with a well-
developed parietal shield. Last whorl
has about a dozen, poorly developed
axial ribs which are coarsely beaded.
Colour grey brown to whitish with a
few blotches or broken bands of darker
brown. Inside the outer lip has four or
five enamel teeth, the largest at the
top. Siphonal canal recurved; columella
has two small spiral lirae at the base.
Parietal shield sometimes yellowish. A
common intertidal mudflat species
ranging from southern Cape Cod to
Florida, Texas and to Brazil.

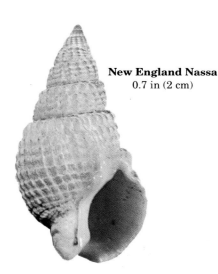

New England Nassa
0.7 in (2 cm)

New England Nassa,
Nassarius trivittatus (Say, 1822).
Rather light shelled, with eight or nine
whorls which are slightly channeled
below the suture. Apex acute. Spiral
sculpture of four or five rows of strong
distinct beads. Parietal wall glazed
with white enamel. Outer lip sharp and
thin. Colour yellowish grey. Lives in
shallow water down to 228 ft (70 m) on
sand. Common from Newfoundland to
off north-east Florida.

Thickened Nassa,
Nassarius incrassatus (Ström, 1768).
A small thick shell with an acute spire
and small aperture surrounded by a
thickened lip. Five whorls with ten to
12 rounded axial ribs crossed by
numerous spiral ridges. Suture wavy.
Parietal shield and outer lip enamel
white. Behind the lip is a swollen varix.
Inside of outer lip with five or six small
lirae. Colour reddish buff to yellow
grey, sometimes with a subsutural
darker band. Common in large colonies
in muddy areas. Its range extends from
most of western Europe into the
Mediterranean. Belongs to the
subgenus *Tritonella*.

Thickened Nassa
0.5 in (1 cm)

Calthrate Nassa
0.8 in (2 cm)

Western Mud Nassa
0.7 in (2 cm)

Reticulated Nassa
1 in (2.5 cm)

Clathrate Nassa,
Nassarius clathratus (Born, 1778).
Shell solid, ovate. Whorls slightly
rounded, each bearing about 16 low,
rounded, slanting ribs which are
crossed by numerous crowded spiral
cords. Fasciole sulcus deep. Suture
indented and wavy. Outer lip thick,
sharp and finely crenulated. Spiral
lirae within the outer lip. Parietal wall
has a raised left edge. Colour of shell
tan cream. Uncommon in shallow water
in the Mediterranean, Iberian
Peninsula and the Azores.

Western Mud Nassa,
Nassarius tegula (Reeve, 1853).
Shell moderately heavy, with a heavy,
whitish or brown-stained parietal
callus. Body whorl smoothish around
the middle, but with a spiral row of
fairly large nodes below the suture. In
the spire, the nodes are usually divided
in two. Base of body whorl with a few
weak spiral threads. Outer lip thick.
Colour olive grey with a narrow whitish
spiral band. A common mud-flat species
from California south to Panama.

Reticulated Nassa,
Nassarius reticulatus (Linnaeus, 1758).
Solid, heavy, coarse shell, quite
variable in its sculpturing which may
be coarsely beaded or with widely
spaced, coarsely knobbed axial ribs.
Suture well indented, usually with a
row of separate beads below it. Parietal
wall well callused. Colour glossy white
with fine brown spiral lines and
occasional dark blotches. These
scavengers live in pockets of soft sand
among rocky intertidal areas and range
from the Black Sea north to the British
Isles and Norway.

Little Horn Nassa,
Nassarius corniculum (Olivi, 1792).
Shell elongate-oval, the aperture about
half the length of the entire shell.
Surface glossy smooth. Parietal wall
raised, narrow and glossy. Inside of
outer lip has about eight small strong
teeth. Colour of shell rosy tan with
small cream flames below the well-
impressed suture and with small dots
on the broad spiral bands of light
brown. Common on muddy flats in the
Mediterranean and Iberian Peninsula.

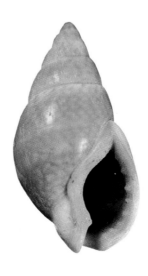

Little Horn Nassa
0.5 in (1 cm)

Olive Shells
(Family Olividae)

Although the glossy and attractive olive shells are associated with tropical waters, there are two species that have invaded the cooler waters of the Eastern Pacific. There is no operculum in the true *Oliva*, but some smaller *Olivella* have a chitinous one. All species are carnivorous scavengers. There are no olive shells in western Europe.

Beatic Dwarf Olive
0.5 in (1 cm)

Purple Dwarf Olive,
Olivella biplicata (Sowerby, 1825). Quite solid, globular-elongate. Upper columella wall with a heavy white callus. Lower end of columella with a raised spiral fold which is cut by two or three spiral incised lines. Colour bluish grey with violet stains around the fasciole and lower part of the aperture. Abundant in summer months in sandy bays and beaches. Ranges from Vancouver Island to Baja California.

Purple Dwarf Olive
1 in (2.5 cm)

Beatic Dwarf Olive,
Olivella baetica Carpenter, 1864. Small, light-shelled, glossy and coloured a drab tan with weak purplish-brown maculations arranged in axial flames. Fasciole white, often stained with brown. A moderately common shallow-water sand species living from Kodiak Island, Alaska to Baja California.

San Pedro Dwarf Olive
0.5 in (1 cm)

San Pedro Dwarf Olive,
Olivella pedroana (Conrad, 1856). Resembles the Beatic Dwarf Olive, but much heavier and stouter. Parietal callus heavy. Exterior coloured light brown to grey with long distinct axial zigzag stripes of dark brown. Fasciole and callus always white. Moderately common from northern California to Mexico; uncommon in Oregon.

Mitres and False Mitres

(Families Mitridae and Volutomitridae)

**Alaskan
False Mitre**
1.5 in (4 cm)

Both families are related, but their internal anatomy is different. The Volutomitridae are mainly cold-water dwellers, there being two from the Atlantic and one in the north-west Pacific. The Mitridae are mainly tropical. Both have two to four strong, oblique spiral folds, or teeth, on the columella.

Ebony Mitre
1.2 in (3 cm)

Little Trumpet Mitre
0.7 in (2 cm)

False Greenland Mitre
1 in (2.5 cm)

Alaskan False Mitre,
Volutomitra alaskana Dall, 1902.
Fusiform, solid, resembling the Greenland False Mitre, but having a longer aperture and a thicker, smooth greenish-brown periostracum. In both species the early whorls are badly eroded. This is a carnivorous species living in deep water from the Pribilof Islands, Alaska to off San Diego, California.

Ebony Mitre,
Mitra ebenus (Lamarck, 1811).
Fusiform, solid, smooth, with slightly convex whorls and an indented suture. Aperture slightly more than half the length of the shell. Surface smooth, with about ten low, rounded ribs. Colour blackish brown. Upper third of the last whorl with a narrow spiral band of tan. Columella with two large and two small slanting folds. Outer lip thickened, with tiny teeth on the inner edge. Moderately common in rock pools in Mediterranean and Portugal.

False Greenland Mitre,
Volutomitra groenlandica (Moller, 1842).
Fusiform, solid, white with a dark-brown periostracum. Smoothish, the nuclear whorls smooth, the others with fine spiral scratches. Minute axial riblets on the early whorls. Columella with four folds. Operculum chitinous. Uncommon. Canada to Maine; Greenland to Norway.

Little Trumpet Mitre,
Mitra cornicula (Linnaeus, 1758).
Similar to the Ebony Mitre, but with smaller, weaker columella folds, a smooth outer lip, and about seven or eight spiral threads on the base of the shell. Lacks ribs. Colour glossy brown. A common littoral species of the Mediterranean extending to the Azores and to Portugal.

Nutmegs
(Family Cancellariidae)

This curious family of small, carnivorous snails is widespread throughout the tropics, but the colder waters at both poles support a genus of ribbed, broadly fusiform snails belonging to the subfamily Admetinae. There is no operculum in this family. The shells of the Admete snails have very weak folds on the columella, while those of the true *Cancellaria* nutmegs bear two or three strong columella folds. They all feed on marine worms.

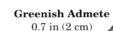

Greenish Admete
0.7 in (2 cm)

Northern Admete
0.7 in (2 cm)

Greenish Admete,
Admete viridula (Fabricius, 1780).
Shell thin, broadly fusiform, the spire slightly more than half the length of the entire shell. Whorls rounded and bearing numerous low, rounded axial ribs on the upper half. Squarish spiral cords form beads on the axial ribs. Suture well indented and bounded above by one or two spiral threads. Aperture and columella white, the latter has three very weak folds. Emits a greenish liquid when disturbed. Common offshore in north-west Europe.

Northern Admete,
Admete couthouyi (Jay, 1839).
Shell lightweight but strong, obese, with six shouldered whorls. Suture wavy. Sculpture of coarsely beaded riblets crossed by numerous spiral wavy threads. Columella strongly arched and bearing two to five very weak spiral folds near the middle. Colour dull white, covered with a brownish periostracum. Commonly dredged offshore from the Arctic Seas to California and to off Massachusetts.

Margin Shells
(Family Marginellidae)

Nearly all members of this family of colourful glossy shells are found in tropical waters, especially in West Africa and the Indo-Pacific region. The operculum is absent. Only one species, the Boreal Marginella, has ventured into the cooler waters of New England.

The world's largest species, *Afrivoluta pringlei* Tomlin, from South Africa reaches 3 inches (7.5 cm) in length, but members of the genus *Granulina* rarely exceed quarter-inch (2 or 3 mm).

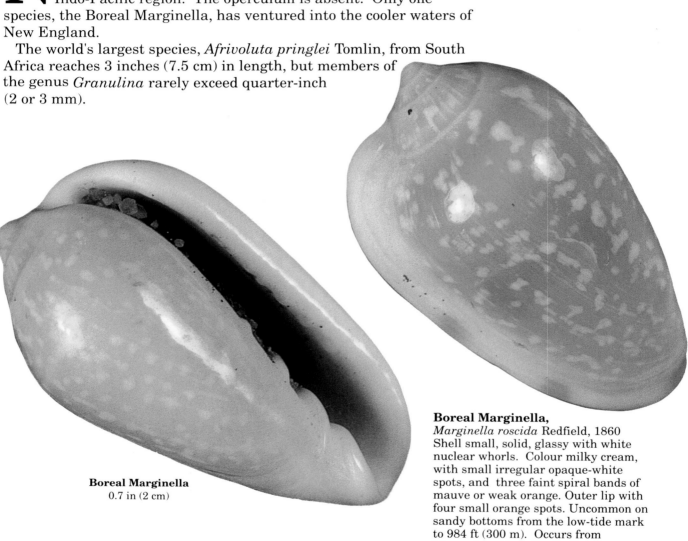

Boreal Marginella
0.7 in (2 cm)

Boreal Marginella,
Marginella roscida Redfield, 1860
Shell small, solid, glassy with white nuclear whorls. Colour milky cream, with small irregular opaque-white spots, and three faint spiral bands of mauve or weak orange. Outer lip with four small orange spots. Uncommon on sandy bottoms from the low-tide mark to 984 ft (300 m). Occurs from Massachusetts to South Carolina.

Volutes
(Family Volutidae)

This is a major family of large carnivorous snails that are popular with shell collectors. Most have several strong spiral plicae or folds on the columella. They are mainly tropical in distribution, with many colourful species living in West Africa and Australia. The Music Volute of the West Indies bears a claw-like, horny operculum, but most volutes lack this feature. Only one volute exists in the cold waters of the North Pacific, and the only volute in western Europe is the Spotted Flask.

Spotted Flask
2.5 in (6.5 cm)

Stearns' Volute
4 in (10 cm)

Spotted Flask,
Ampulla priamus (Gmelin, 1791). Shell oval, thin-shelled but strong, with only three or four convex whorls. Smooth, shiny, light brown with six distantly placed rows of small round dots of reddish brown on the last whorl. Outer lip thin and sharp. No operculum. Frequently dredged in fairly deep water off Spain and Portugal. *Halia* is a synonym. This species is a desirable collectors' item.

Stearns' Volute,
Arctomelon stearnsi (Dall, 1872). Shell large, fusiform, strong; the exterior is chalky grey with mauve-brown undertones. Aperture semi-glossy and light brown. Nuclear whorls bulbous, smooth, but often eroded away. Columella brownish with two large folds and a third weaker one below. Locally common offshore in Alaska.

Cones
(Family Conidae)

The well-known, colourful cones are represented in warm waters by several hundred species, but only the Mediterranean Cone comes as far north as Portugal. Cones have their radular teeth modified into hollow harpoon-shaped teeth that permit the injection of a strong neurotoxin into their prey. Most venomous cones feed on small live fish, worms or other marine snails, but several human deaths have been recorded from stings inflicted by tropical south-west Pacific cones.

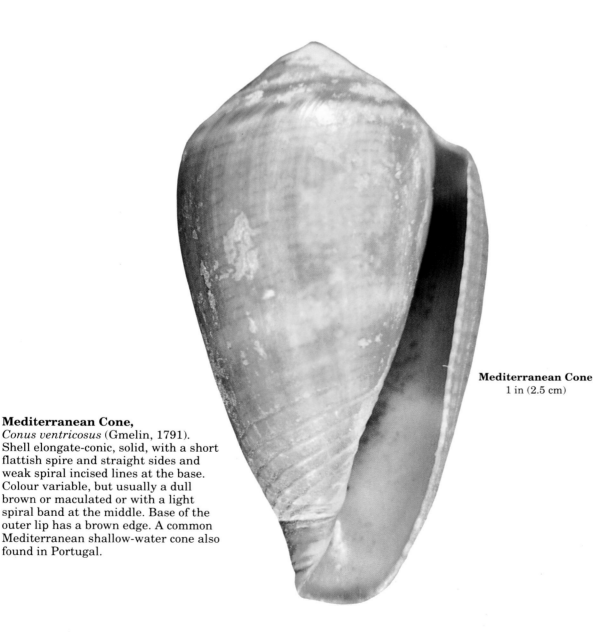

Mediterranean Cone
1 in (2.5 cm)

Mediterranean Cone,
Conus ventricosus (Gmelin, 1791).
Shell elongate-conic, solid, with a short flattish spire and straight sides and weak spiral incised lines at the base. Colour variable, but usually a dull brown or maculated or with a light spiral band at the middle. Base of the outer lip has a brown edge. A common Mediterranean shallow-water cone also found in Portugal.

Turrids
(Family Turridae)

This is a very large, worldwide family with hundreds of genera and thousands of species, thus making it a difficult group to identify without extensive, well-illustrated monographs. Most are fusiform and rather small, with a slit notch or U-shaped canal at the top of the outer lip, known as the 'turrid' notch. Operculum is chitinous.

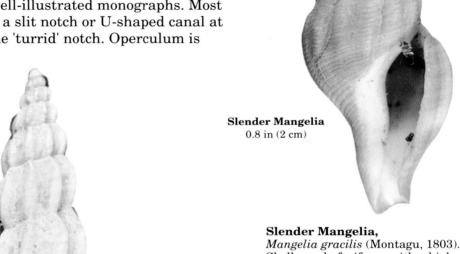

Slender Mangelia
0.8 in (2 cm)

Attenuated Mangelia
0.5 in (1 cm)

Slender Mangelia,
Mangelia gracilis (Montagu, 1803). Shell evenly fusiform, with a high, acute spire. Nine whorls, bearing ten to 14 rounded axial ribs which are on the upper third of the last whorl. Spiral sculpture of minute threads over-riding the ribs. Outer lip sharp, thickened behind by a swollen varix, and with a small, but deep 'turrid' notch. Colour cream with yellow banding. Occurs on gravel bottoms from 23–492 ft (7–150 m) from the Mediterranean to the southern British Isles.

Attenuated Mangelia,
Mangelia attenuata (Montagu, 1803). Shell slender, smooth, with about eight prominent slanting ribs running from suture to suture. Varix thick. Lives on sandy clay from 16–492 ft (5–150 m) from Norway to the Mediterranean.

Elegant Lora,
Oenopota elegans (Moller, 1842). Shell small, elongate, with the acute spire two-thirds the length of the entire shell. Whorls slightly shouldered and bearing about 18 low, rounded, slightly slanting axial ribs which are crossed by numerous incised lines, thus forming small rounded beads. Found offshore in the Bering Sea and Canada; south to New England.

Elegant Lora
0.7 in (2 cm)

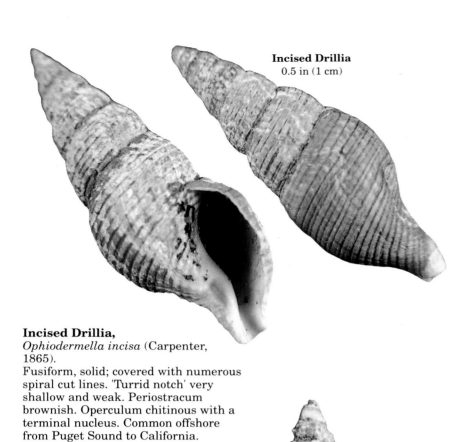

Incised Drillia
0.5 in (1 cm)

Goode's Aforia
3.5 in (9 cm)

Incised Drillia,
Ophiodermella incisa (Carpenter, 1865).
Fusiform, solid; covered with numerous spiral cut lines. 'Turrid notch' very shallow and weak. Periostracum brownish. Operculum chitinous with a terminal nucleus. Common offshore from Puget Sound to California.

Goode's Aforia,
Aforia goodei (Dall, 1890).
Shell fairly large, lightweight, fusiform and chalky white. There is a strong spiral cord on the shoulder of the whorls. Above it are axial growth scars showing the former 'turrid notches'. Common from off British Columbia to southern Chile.

Perverse Turrid,
Antiplanes voyi (Gabb, 1866).
Shell elongate, fusiform, coiled counter-clockwise (sinistrally), with a high straight-sided spire. Colour chalky white, with a greenish brown periostracum, usually worn away for the most part. Sinus on outer lip shallowly V-shaped. Early protoconch whorls smooth, globular. A cold-water offshore species ranging from northern Japan to Alaska and south to California.

Perverse Turrid
2 in (5 cm)

Bubble Shells
(Families Acteonidae, Scaphandridae and Haminoeidae)

Open Paper-bubble
1.5 in (4 cm)

The great snail subclass Opisthobranchia contains a vast number of diverse hermaphrodites that includes the naked seaslugs, or nudibranchs, as well as the seahares with their reduced internal shells, and the bubble shells with their very delicate coiled shells. Some are vegetarians, others carnivorous. Most lay jelly-like egg masses from which free-swimming veliger larval stages emerge. Most lack an operculum, with the exception of *Acteon*.

Open Paper-bubble,
Philine aperta (Linnaeus, 1767).
Shell fragile, translucent, oval with a very large, wide aperture. Outer lip projects above the apex. Pale-yellow animal covers the shell. The skin is capable of secreting a protective layer of sulphuric acid. Within the stomach of all *Philine* are three solid, flat gizzard plates. It lives on sandy bottoms and preys upon small molluscs and polychaete worms. This is a common offshore species ranging from Norway to the Mediterranean, as well as South Africa and the Indian Ocean.

Lathe Acteon
0.5 in (1 cm)

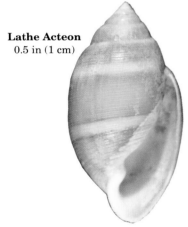

Wooden Canoe-bubble
1 in (2.5 cm)

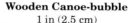

Lathe Acteon
Acteon tornatilis (Linnaeus, 1758).
Shell broadly fusiform, solid, with a convex spire and long aperture three-quarters the length of the entire shell. Base of columella with a strong, enamel-white spiral fold. Outer lip smooth, sharp and strong. Sculpture of numerous very fine, spiral incised lines becoming stronger towards the base of the shell. Colour pinkish yellow with three lighter spiral bands, the upper one being just under the impressed suture, the other two being bordered by a dark-brown line. Operculum chitinous. Occurs offshore from Iceland to Spain.

Wooden Canoe-bubble,
Scaphander lignarius (Linnaeus, 1758).
Shell solid, opaque, ovate-oblong, with the upper half constricted. Apex slightly sunken. Columella arched and with a thickened callus. Exterior cream, with numerous fine spiral scratches and brown lines. Colour variable from yellow to brownish green. Animal white or orange, with large fleshy lobes of the foot. A common sublittoral sand-dwelling species which feeds on small worms and bivalves. It ranges from the British Isles to the Mediterranean and the Canary Islands.

Giant Canoe-bubble
1.5 in (4 cm)

Giant Canoe-bubble,
Scaphander punctostriatus Mighels, 1841.
Shell lightweight, ovate-oblong. Apex with a slightly sunken area. Aperture constricted above the outer lip, projecting above the apex. Shell smoothish except for numerous spiral rows of microscopic elongate punctations. Colour chalk white, with a straw periostracum. Moderately common offshore on sand. Ranges from the Arctic Seas to Florida; Greenland and Iceland, uncommon.

Gould's Paper-bubble
0.7 in (2 cm)

Sowerby's Paper-bubble
0.5 in (1 cm)

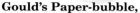

Gould's Paper-bubble,
Haminoea vesicula Gould, 1855.
Shell very fragile, globular, translucent-yellow with a thin rusty-brown or yellowish-orange periostracum. There is a very small perforation at the concealed apex. Similar to *H. virescens*, but the body whorl is larger, the aperture smaller and the columella thickened at the base and forming an indented umbilicus. Belongs in the family Haminoeidae. A common, littoral bay species ranging from southern Alaska to the Gulf of California.

Sowerby's Paper-bubble,
Haminoea virescens (Sowerby, 1833).
Shell, fragile, globular and translucent greenish yellow in colour. Aperture very large and open. Upper part of the outer lip high and narrowly winged. No apical hole. The animal is dark green with yellowish markings: dots on the head shield, mottlings on the parapodia. A common, shallow-water species of the open coast. It prefers sandy areas where there are beds of seagrass where it lays small gelatinous egg masses on the stems of weeds. Found from Puget Sound, Washington to the Gulf of California.

Solitary Paper-bubble
0.5 in (1 cm)

Bubble Akera
0.7 in (2 cm)

Watery Paper-bubble
0.5 in (1 cm)

Solitary Paper-bubble,
Haminoea solitaria (Say, 1822).
Shell fragile, oblong, with the aperture as long as the entire shell. Apertural lip arising on the right side of the apical perforation. Spiral sculpture of numerous, very fine scratches. Colour translucent amber to whitish. Prefers a shallow sandy area where there is protective grasses. It lays its gelatinous egg masses on the stems of weeds. This is a common carnivorous species distributed from Cape Cod to off North Carolina.

Watery Paper-bubble,
Haminoea hydatis (Linnaeus, 1758).
Shell fragile, globular, inflated, translucent white or yellowish, with the aperture slightly longer than the spire. Columella thickened with a white glaze. Exterior surface smooth except for fine irregular growth lines. Soft parts are light brown and cover most of the shell. The anterior cephalic disc bears two small black eyes on the dorsal surface. This species feeds on small bivalves. It occurs in muddy sand in subtidal areas from the British Isles to the Mediterranean.

Bubble Akera,
Akera bullata Müller, 1776.
Shell fragile, globular and the whorls enrolled at the apex. The shell is carried externally at the hind end of an elongate animal which has two elongate parapodia extending over the back of the animal and part of the shell. Lacks tentacles. Soft parts pale grey to orange with many small white and black spots and streaks. A purple fluid may be secreted if the animal is disturbed. It ranges from Norway, throughout the British Isles, south into the Mediterranean.

Sea Butterflies
(Order Pteropoda)

The world's oceans are heavily populated with these small, abundant snails that live near the surface and form a large part of the planktonic hordes upon which most life in the seas depends, particularly some species of whales and oceanic fishes. The shells are delicate, glassy and translucent. The hermaphroditic animals have two large wing-like extensions of the foot that enable them to swim and dart about quite rapidly. There is no operculum, but they have a set of radular teeth. There are 15 genera and about 100 species, most with a worldwide distribution in both cold and warm seas.

Dead shells of the pteropods are continually raining down on the bottom of the ocean. In some areas the deposits are several feet (metres) thick and are referred to as 'pteropod ooze'.

There are two major orders of Pteropoda, one being the naked or shell-less Gymnosomata which includes the common, inch-long (3 cm), cigar-shaped **Common Clione**, *Clione limacina* (Phipps, 1774). The other order, Thecosomata, develop protective, glassy shells. Some are quite small, less than one-eighth inch (2 mm), and bear a sinistral snail shell.

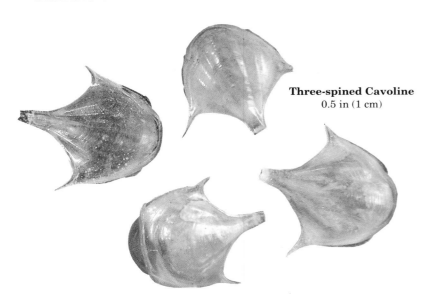

Three-spined Cavoline
0.5 in (1 cm)

Pyramid Clio
0.7 in (2 cm)

Three-spined Cavoline,
Diacria trispinosa (Blainville, 1821). Shell small, glassy, with a long lateral spine on each side and a very long terminal one which falls off in later life. Dorsal lip thickened. Aperture scarcely discernible. Ventral side of shell very slightly convex. A worldwide pelagic species extending from the tropics into cool waters.

Pyramid Clio,
Clio pyramidata Linnaeus, 1767. Shell of an angular form, compressed, colourless and with lateral keels. A cross-section of the front end is always angular at the sides. There is usually a ridge extending longitudinally along the back. Surface has wavy ribs. A worldwide pelagic species and popular food of whales.

Uncinate Cavoline,
Cavolinia uncinata (Rang, 1829).
Shell small, glassy, translucent and
brownish. Dorsal lip with a thin
margin. Ventral lip not more developed
than the dorsal one. Shell with distinct
lateral points. Upper lip flattened
posteriorly. This is usually a warm-
water, pelagic species found in the
Atlantic as far north as Newfoundland
and Alaska. There are five common
species in this genus.

Uncinate Cavoline
0.5 in (1 cm)

Cigar Pteropod,
Cuvierina columnella (Rang, 1827).
Shell small, cylindrical, shaped
somewhat like a fat cigar. Surface
smooth. A cross-section is almost
circular. Behind the aperture there is a
slight constriction. This is the only
species in the genus and it is worldwide
in distribution.

Cigar Pteropod
0.4 in (1 cm)

Terrestrial Snails
(SUBCLASS PULMONATA ORDER BASOMMATOPHORA)

There are over 25,000 kinds of air-breathing snails throughout the world with most of them found in wooded areas, gardens or in tropical trees. They include the freshwater lymnaeid and physid pond snails, as well as the small brown seaside snails of the family Melampidae.

Mouse Melampus
0.3 in (7 mm)

Marsh Snails
(Family Melampidae)

Usually associated with the damp, grass-covered marshes of estuaries are the numerous melampus snails characterized by their small, barrel-shaped shells with small, shelly teeth within the aperture. Some tropical members of the family may reach a length of 3 inches (7.5 cm), but those in the temperate regions are much smaller. They are usually very abundant wherever they become established.

These airbreathers belong to the subclass Pulmonata, Order Basommatophora. They are hermaphrodites and have only one pair of tentacles, with the eys mounted at the tip ends.

Mouse Melampus,
Ovatella myosotis (Draparnaud, 1801). Shell small, ovate-fusiform, dark brown and semi-glossy. Spire elevated, with seven or eight slightly convex whorls with a distinct suture and below which is a spiral marginal line. Inner lip of adults have three white folds. Umbilicus minute. Two or three teeth within the outer lip. Locally common in temperate marshes in north-west Europe; from Nova Scotia to the West Indies; and from Washington to California.

Eastern Melampus,
Melampus bidentatus Say, 1822. Shell thin but strong with five or six whorls, the last one being three-quarters the length of the entire shell. Spire short and blunt. Colour of fresh specimens brownish horn, smooth and shining, with three or four darker narrow bands. Commonly eroded and grey. Inner lip with two strong folds; inside of outer lip with several raised threads. Abundant in salt marshes on stems of grasses. These vegetarians lay their jelly-like egg masses on the marsh grasses. Occurs from eastern Quebec to Texas and the West Indies.

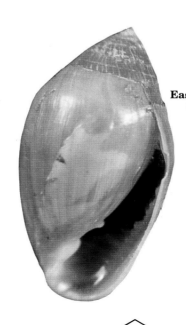

Eastern Melampus
0.6 in (1.5 cm)

TUSK
SHELLS

Tusk Shells
(CLASS SCAPHOPODA)

This group of sand-dwelling molluscs are worldwide in distribution, but has fewer than a thousand species. The shell is open at both ends. The narrow end protrudes above the sandy bottom where water in drawn in and expelled at alternating intervals. At the large end, the conic-shaped foot and dozens of ciliated, prehensile threads project through the sand. Tusk shells feed upon single-celled foraminifera. They have a radula but no operculum. Identification depends upon the nature of the slits at the small end of the shell and in the nature of the ribbing.

Western Straight Tusk
1.2 in (3 cm)

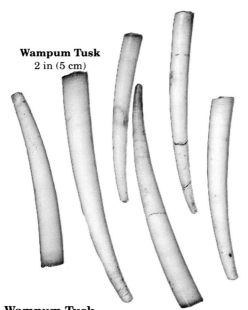

Wampum Tusk
2 in (5 cm)

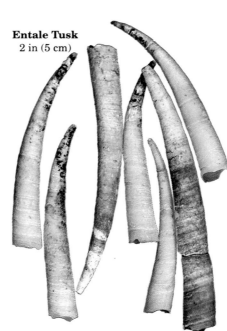

Entale Tusk
2 in (5 cm)

Western Straight Tusk,
*Laevidentalium rectius*s (Carpenter, 1864).
Almost straight, slender and long and attenuated towards the apex. Thin-shelled and fragile. Surface glossy and smoothish. Colour bluish white, somewhat translucent, with some opaque-white flecks and rings. Apical opening without a notch. Moderately common offshore from Alaska to Panama.

Wampum Tusk,
Antalis pretiosum (Sowerby, 1860).
Moderately curved and solid; opaque-white, ivory-like, commonly with faint dirty-yellow rings of growth. Apex has a short notch on the convex side. A common offshore species living in sandy mud. It was used extensively as money by the north-west Indian tribes. It ranges from Alaska to Baja California.

Entale Tusk,
Antalis entalis (Linnaeus, 1758).
Moderately curved, solid, round in cross-section and finely striate longitudinally. Colour ivory white, sometimes with a rusty stain on the narrow end, caused by a mixture of mud and sand in which it burrows. Margin of larger end often jagged. Small end has a very short, oblique pipe or tubular appendage having a pear-shaped opening. This is a common sand-dwelling offshore species found in Arctic waters from Iceland and Norway south to off Portugal.

Western Atlantic Tusk
1.2 in (3 cm)

Western Atlantic Tusk,
Antalis occidentale (Stimpson, 1851).
Sixteen to 18 primary ribs, fairly distinct in the young stages. Sculptureless in the senile stage. Round in cross-section. Common offshore from Newfoundland to off North Carolina.

Stimpson's Tusk
2 in (5 cm)

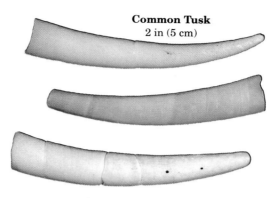

Common Tusk
2 in (5 cm)

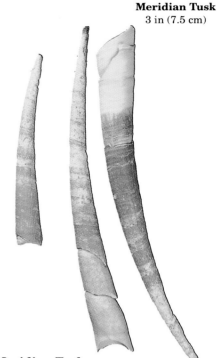

Meridian Tusk
3 in (7.5 cm)

Stimpson's Tusk,
Antalis entalis stimpsoni (Henderson, 1920).
This North American subspecies is hardly distinguishable from its European counterpart. Shell round in cross-section and dull ivory-white in colour. Region of the apex always very eroded and chalky. Surface uneven, with some longitudinal wrinkles in better preserved specimens. Common from 32–6560 ft (10–2000 m). Ranges from off Nova Scotia to Massachusetts.

Common Tusk,
Antalis vulgaris (da Costa, 1778).
Moderately curved, solid and wide. Circular in cross-section. Opaque-white, sometimes tinted with yellowish brown or rose towards the narrow, apical end. Sculpture of about 30 fine, crowded longitudinal striae at the apex. Aperture oblique, thin and jagged. Anal opening small, round or ovate and occupying a very short tube. No notch or slit present. Common offshore in muddy and sandy areas from southern England and Ireland southwards into the Mediterranean.

Meridian Tusk,
Fissidentalium meridionale (Pilsbry and Sharp, 1897).
Fairly large, mouse grey, oval in cross-section. Tip has 16 riblets; large end has up to 90 riblets. Periostracum glossy grey. Apical notch deep on the convex side. It lives in deep water offshore from Massachusetts to Brazil.

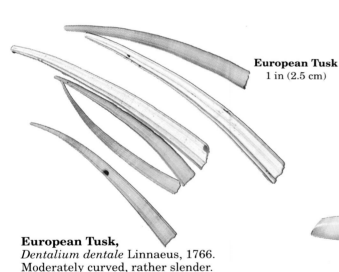

European Tusk
1 in (2.5 cm)

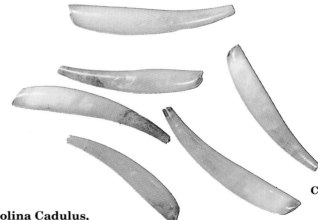
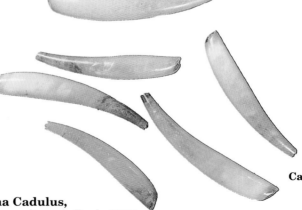

Carolina Cadulus
0.3 in (7 mm)

European Tusk,
Dentalium dentale Linnaeus, 1766.
Moderately curved, rather slender. Opaque white, sometimes suffused with rose at the smaller end. Sculpture of about ten strong, rounded longitudinal ribs near the apex, becoming 18 to 20 near the aperture. Aperture rounded, polygonal, slightly oblique. Anal orifice small, circular and with very thick walls. No notch or slit present. This is a southern species living offshore from Portugal south into the Mediterranean and the Adriatic.

Carolina Cadulus,
Cadulus carolinensis Bush, 1885.
Shell small, white, without sculpture, elongate and slightly swollen at the lower end. Apex has four shallow slits. In cross-section the shell is oval round. Commonly dredged in shallow water from off North Carolina to Texas.

THE
CHITONS

Chitons
(CLASS POLYPLACOPHORA)

These rock-dwelling elongate molluscs have eight shelly plates bound together at the sides by a leathery girdle which may be smooth, hairy or covered with small shelly scales. The flat foot occupies most of the underside, and the small head possesses a mouth with radular teeth, but without tentacles or eyes. The anus is posterior and the gills are strung along the sides of the foot. All species are marine and most are vegetarians. Many are rocky shore dwellers and a few exist in deep waters. There are about 600 species throughout the world.

Northern Red Chiton
1 in (2.5 cm)

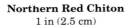

Northern Red Chiton,
Tonicella rubra (Linnaeus, 1767). Oblong, moderately elevated and with the valves rather rounded. Upper surfaces smooth except for fine growth wrinkles. Coloured light tan over which are orange-red marblings. Interior of valves bright pink. Girdle reddish brown, covered with minute, elongate, separate scales. Common on hard surfaces from 10–656 ft (3–200 m). Arctic Seas to Connecticut; also Bering Strait to northern California; Norway to Portugal.

Mottled Red Chiton,
Tonicella marmorea (Fabricius, 1780). Oblong to oval, elevated and rather sharply angular. Upper surface smoothish with microscopic granulations. Interior of valves tinted with rose. Girdle leathery and without scales or bristles. Common from 10–328 ft (3–100 m). Greenland to Massachusetts; Japan and Alaska to Washington State; Norway to the British Isles.

Mottled Red Chiton
1 in (2.5 cm)

Lined Red Chiton
1.2 in (3 cm)

Lined Red Chiton,
Tonicella lineata (Wood, 1815).
Valves shiny smooth, orange to deep
red with oblique black lines bordered
with white. Interior of valves white.
Girdle naked. Common in shallow
water from Japan to Alaska to
northern California.

Mertens' Chiton
1.5 in (4 cm)

Mertens' Chiton
Lepidozona mertensii (Middendorff,
1847).
Oval in shape; colour variable:
commonly yellowish with dark reddish-
brown streaks and maculations.
Central areas of the valves have strong
longitudinal ribs and smaller cross
ridges which give a netted appearance.
Anterior valve has 30 or more radial
rows of tiny warts. Interior of valves
whitish. Girdle has alternating yellow
and reddish bands and is covered with
tiny, low, smooth split-pea scales.
Abundant in shallow water on hard
surfaces. Ranges from the Aleutian
Islands to Baja California, Mexico.

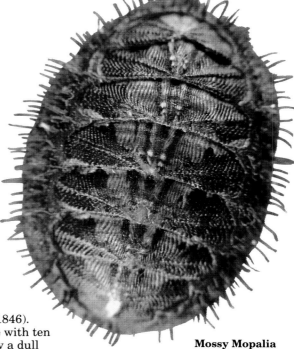

Mossy Mopalia,
Mopalia muscosa (Gould, 1846).
Oblong to oval. Head valve with ten
beaded ribs. Colour usually a dull
brown, blackish olive or grey. Interior
of valves blue green, rarely stained
with pink. Girdle with stiff hairs
resembling a fringe of moss. Many
varieties were described. This is a
common intertidal species ranging
along the entire coast from Alaska to
Baja California, Mexico.

Mossy Mopalia
1.5 in (4 cm)

Hinds' Mopalia,
Mopalia hindsii (Reeve, 1847).
Very similar to the Mossy Mopalia, but
generally smoother. Girdle brown,
rather thin and fairly wide, and almost
naked except for a few short hairs.
Interior of valves white with short
crimson rays under the beaks. This is a
moderately common species found on
the underside of intertidal rocks.
Alaska to Mexico.

Hinds' Chiton
1 in (2.5 cm)

Eastern American Chiton
0.8 in (2 cm)

Eastern American Chiton,
Chaetopleura apiculata (Say, 1830).
Small, oblong to oval. Valves slightly
carinate. Central area of valves with 15
to 20 longitudinal rows of raised neat
beads. Lateral areas distinctly defined,
raised, and bearing numerous larger
beads. Interior of valves white or
greyish. Girdle narrow, mottled cream
and brown, and microscopically
granulose and sparsely scattered with
short transparent hairs. A common
species attached to small rocks and to
dead shells in shallow water. It ranges
from Cape Cod to both sides of Florida.

Magdalena Chiton,
Stenoplax magdalenensis (Hinds,
1844).
Shell fairly large, elongate. Colour
brown or grey green. Sides of the valves
with fine wavy ribs. The front slope of
the anterior valve is very concave.
Scales on the girdle are round and
finely striate. Interior of valves pinkish
with a blue spot at the anterior end of
each valve. Moderately common on
intertidal rocks. A southern species
from California to Mexico.

Magdelena Chiton
3 in (7.5 cm)

Smooth European Chiton,
Callochiton septemvalvis (Montagu, 1803).
Shell small, oval, girdle rather wide and spiculose. Valves moderately elevated with straight sides. Colour varying from brick-red to brown, sometimes mottled with white, yellow or orange. Exterior of valves microscopically granulose and bearing tiny black 'eyes'. Girdle covered with microscopic short and long needles. Moderately common in shallow water to 1640 ft (500 m), sometimes on red algae. Ranges from Norway to the Mediterranean. Formerly called *Chiton laevis* Montagu.

Smooth European Chiton
1 in (2.5 cm)

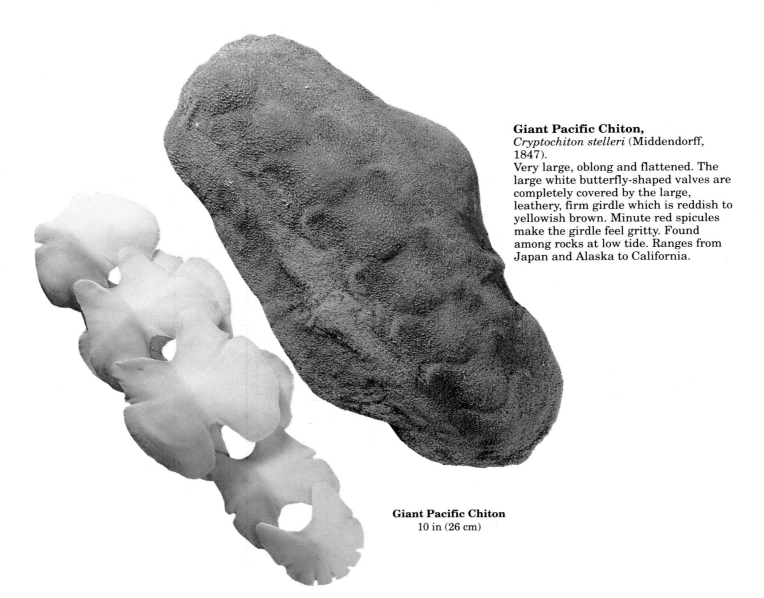

Giant Pacific Chiton,
Cryptochiton stelleri (Middendorff, 1847).
Very large, oblong and flattened. The large white butterfly-shaped valves are completely covered by the large, leathery, firm girdle which is reddish to yellowish brown. Minute red spicules make the girdle feel gritty. Found among rocks at low tide. Ranges from Japan and Alaska to California.

Giant Pacific Chiton
10 in (26 cm)

THE
BIVALVES

The Bivalves
(CLASS BIVALVIA)

The class Bivalvia or Pelecypoda includes such molluscs as the clams, oysters and scallops. There are about 10,000 living species, most living in the world's seas, but many found only in freshwater rivers and lakes.

The soft parts lack a true head and radular teeth, and are protected by two shelly valves, hence the name 'bivalves'. Locomotion is accomplished by a tongue-like foot that protrudes from the front end. Some species, like the oysters, become permanently attached to the substrate. At the rear are two fleshy tube-like siphons, sometimes fused into one, through which water is inhaled or exhaled. Microscopic forms of vegetable matter are drawn in over the mucus-covered gills and passed into a small mouth. In most clams the sexes are in separate individuals, but a few are hermaphroditic or can change sex periodically. Eggs are sometimes brooded within the gills or may be shed into the open sea where released sperm can fertilize them. The larval or veliger forms of bivalves float and swim freely, sometimes for many miles before they settle down on the bottom and change into shelly bivalves. Bivalves may have a life span of two to one hundred years.

The valves of bivalves are held together by one or two adductor muscles, and are kept ajar by a chitinous, elastic ligament which may sometimes be located internally between the teeth of the hinge. The shape and number of hinge teeth, the outline of the muscle scars on the inside of the valves, and the exterior sculpturing are used in identifying the various species.

Awning Clams
(Family Solemyacidae)

This is a relatively obscure and primitive-looking group of bivalves living in mud in U-shaped burrows that are open at each end. The oblong, cigar-shaped shells lack hinge teeth and are covered with a thin, glossy, brown periostracum which extends well beyond the margins of the shell. The foot is large and sucker-like at the broadened flat end. The short siphonal opening is bordered by fleshy tentacle-like appendages. The ligament is internal and near the posterior beak end. These clams harbour symbiotic bacteria to reduce sulphur oxides. The family appears to be absent in north-western Europe.

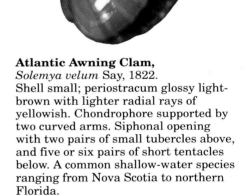

Atlantic Awning Clam
1 in (2.5 cm)

Boreal Awning Clam,
Solemya borealis Totten, 1834.
Shell fragile, oblong, somewhat compressed laterally and with a glossy, rayed, chestnut-brown periostracum. Interior of valves greyish blue. Siphonal opening with three pairs of long tentacles on the upper part, and 15 smaller ones bordering the lower half. Moderately common offshore from Nova Scotia to Connecticut.

Boreal Awning Clam
2.5 in (6.5 cm)

Atlantic Awning Clam,
Solemya velum Say, 1822.
Shell small; periostracum glossy light-brown with lighter radial rays of yellowish. Chondrophore supported by two curved arms. Siphonal opening with two pairs of small tubercles above, and five or six pairs of short tentacles below. A common shallow-water species ranging from Nova Scotia to northern Florida.

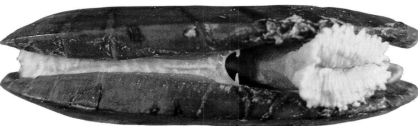

Toga Awning Clam
2 in (5 cm)

Toga Awning Clam,
Solemya togata (Poli, 1795).
Shell fragile; periostracum reddish brown with lighter rays. Offshore in mud from Portugal to West Africa and the Mediterranean.

Nut Clams
(Family Nuculidae)

These small, hard-shelled clams have been abundant since the earliest development of bivalves during the Ordovician, 500 million years ago. They are characterized by their pearly interior and numerous 'taxodont' teeth in the hinge. Below the beak is a chitinous resilium set in a cup, or chondrophore. There is no pallial sinus scar. The edge of the shell is crenulated in some species. Nut clams are worldwide in distribution and are well-represented in cold waters where they serve as food for bottom fish.

Atlantic Nut Clam
0.3 in (7 mm)

Atlantic Nut Clam,
Nucula proxima Say, 1822.
Very small, solid, obliquely ovate, smooth. Colour greenish grey with microscopic, embedded, axial grey lines and prominent, irregular, brownish concentric rings. Outer shell overcast with an oily iridescence. Ventral edge minutely crenulated. A common shallow-water species found in sand and mud. Ranges from Nova Scotia to Florida and to Texas.

Smooth Nut Clam
0.2 in (5 mm)

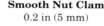

Smooth Nut Clam,
Nucula tenuis (Montagu, 1808).
Shell very small, ovate, smooth, except for irregular growth lines. Colour a shiny olive-green, sometimes with darker lines of growth. No radial lines present. Ventral edge smooth. Moderately common offshore in Arctic Seas south to Florida; south to Spain; Japan to Alaska and south to California.

Sulcate Nut Clam,
Nucula sulcata Bronn, 1831.
Shell solid, equivalve; beaks behind the
mid-line; triangular in outline. Lunule
with irregular, broad transverse
corrugations. Periostracum not shiny,
but olive-yellow with red patches.
Sculpture of fine radiating riblets and
concentric lines, making the surface
finely decussate. Margin crenulate.
Some 22 to 29 anterior teeth; 12 to 14
posterior teeth. Lives on mud bottoms
offshore. Ranges from Norway to the
Mediterranean and north-west Africa.

Sulcate Nut Clam
0.6 in (1.5 cm)

Turgid Nut Clam
0.5 in (1.2 cm)

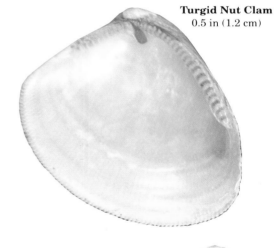

Nuclear Nut Clam
0.4 in (1 cm)

Nuclear Nut Clam,
Nucula nucleus (Linnaeus, 1758).
Shell small, ovate; beaks behind the
mid-line; triangular in outline. Never
with radiating lines. Ventral edge
crenulate. Common offshore on sandy,
coarse bottoms from Norway to Africa;
Labrador to Florida; Alaska to Mexico.

Turgid Nut Clam,
Nucula turgida Leckenby and
Marshall, 1875.
Shell small, solid, equivalve, triangular
in shape. Beaks slightly behind the
mid-line. Sculpture of very fine
microscopically beaded concentric lines.
Colour greyish white, with a glossy,
olive-yellow periostracum. Rarely with
purple rays on the beaks. Anterior
hinge line with 20 to 30 teeth; posterior
section with ten to 14 teeth. Margin of
valves crenulate. Common on sandy
mud bottoms down to 295 ft (90 m).
Ranges from Norway to the
Mediterranean and West Africa.
Formerly called *N. nitida* Sowerby,
1833, not Brown, 1827.

Pointed Nut Clams
(Family Nuculanidae)

These nut clams have a porcelaneous, rather than pearly, shell, and are usually rather drawn out or pointed at the posterior end. The chondrophore cup between the rows of taxodont teeth is rather large.

Fossa Nut Clam
1 in (2.5 cm)

Fossa Nut Clam,
Nuculana fossa (Baird, 1863).
Shell elongate, moderately fat and smoothish, except for small, pronounced concentric ribs at the anterior end and on the beaks. Dorsal area of rostrum is smoothish, depressed and bounded by two weak radial ribs. Found in sand offshore from Alaska to Puget Sound, Washington.

Pointed Nut Clam,
Nuculana acuta (Conrad, 1831).
Shell very small, solid, rounded at the front end, pointed at the rear. Apex of the pallial sinus is broadly U-shaped. Concentric ribs evenly sized and evenly spaced extend over the rib which borders the dorsal surface of the pointed end. Colour white with a thin yellowish periostracum. This is a common shallow-water species ranging from Cape Cod to Brazil.

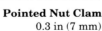

Pointed Nut Clam
0.3 in (7 mm)

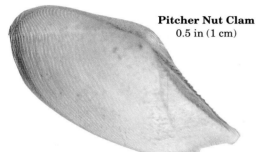

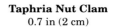

Taphria Nut Clam
0.7 in (2 cm)

Pitcher Nut Clam
0.5 in (1 cm)

Pitcher Nut Clam,
Nuculana pella (Linnaeus, 1758).
Shell small, elongate, with a pointed,
somewhat upturned posterior end.
Escutcheon bordered on either side by a
fine serrated ridge. Sculpture of
numerous fine wavy, slightly oblique
concentric lines. Colour greyish white.
Common offshore in white sand.
Ranges from Portugal to the
Mediterranean Sea.

Taphria Nut Clam,
Nuculana taphria (Dall, 1897).
Shell small, shiny greenish brown,
with prominent concentric sculpture
and with the beaks near the centre.
Rostrum bluntly pointed and slightly
upturned at the end. Commonly
dredged offshore from California to
Mexico.

Almond Yoldia,
Yoldia amygdalea Valenciennes, 1846.
Shell thin, compressed laterally,
elongate and narrowing at the
posterior end. The anterior ventral
margin has a small concave depression.
Moderately common in Arctic Seas to
California, the Gulf of Maine, and to
Norway.

Almond Yoldia
2 in (5 cm)

File Yoldia
2 in (5 cm)

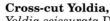

File Yoldia,
Yoldia limatula (Say, 1831).
Thin-shelled, elongate, narrowing at
the posterior end. Umbones very small,
halfway between the ends of the shell.
Exterior glistening greenish tan to
chestnut. Interior glossy white. A
common species in subtidal muddy
sand areas.

Cross-cut Yoldia
1.2 in (3 cm)

Cross-cut Yoldia,
Yoldia scissurata Dall, 1897
Shell elongate-oval, compressed, with
the beaks central, and the keel on the
dorsal margin of the rostrum well
produced and gently curved. Sculpture
of numerous oblique concentric cut
lines. Shell whitish with a glossy, olive-
brown periostracum. About two dozen
fine teeth in the hinge on either side of
the spoon-shaped chondrophore.
Ranges offshore from Alaska to Orgeon.

Cooper's Yoldia
3 in (7.5 cm)

Broad Yoldia
2 in (5 cm)

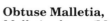

Obtuse Malletia
0.6 in (1.5 cm)

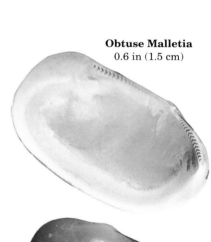

Cooper's Yoldia,
Yoldia cooperi Gabb, 1865.
Shell large, laterally compressed, with
its anterior two-thirds broadly oval,
and the posterior third narrowly
produced into a short rostrum with a
slightly concave dorsal edge. Sculpture
of numerous concentric incised lines.
Pallial sinus deep and U-shaped.
Colour light yellow with a thin glossy
periostracum. Uncommon offshore in
California.

Broad Yoldia,
Yoldia thraciaeformis Storer, 1838.
Fairly large; characterized by its broad,
squarish upturned posterior end and
coarse flaky periostracum.
Chondrophore large. Exterior with an
oblique ridge running from the beak to
the posterior ventral margin.
Moderately common in shallow water.
Found from Greenland to off North
Carolina and from Alaska to Puget
Sound, Washington.

Obtuse Malletia,
Malletia obtusa (M. Sars, 1872).
Shell small, roundly oblong, slightly
swollen. Beaks one third back from the
rounded anterior end. Lunule and
escutcheon absent. Ligament external,
elongate and prominent. Colour chalky
white, covered externally by a
chestnut-brown, glossy periostracum.
Found off Massachusetts to North
Carolina and from Norway to off West
Africa. Uncommon and deep-water
dweller.

Ark Clams
(Families Arcidae and Limopsidae)

Ark shells are distributed in most warm-water seas around the world, with only a few extending into cooler waters. The oblong, sturdy shells are characterized by a straight hinge bearing many, small interlocking 'taxodont' teeth. In the true arks, there is a natural gape in the ventral edge of the shell through which passes the foot that spins a strong cluster of byssal threads.

Transverse Ark
1 in (2.5 cm)

Four-sided Ark
1.3 in (3 cm)

Four-sided Ark,
Arca tetragona Poli, 1795.
Shell solid, box-shaped, with the widely separated beaks in the front half of the shell. There is a wide ventral gape where the massive green byssus protrudes. Exterior finely reticulated and dirty white to yellowish with a brown periostracum. Ligament in a number of grooves radiating from the beaks across the cardinal area. Hinge plate straight, with 40 to 50 small teeth. Common in shallow water from Norway to the Mediterranean.

Transverse Ark,
Anadara transversa (Say, 1822).
Shell solid, quadrate-oval; left valve overlaps the right valve. Thirty to 35 ribs per valve, those on the left valve usually beaded. Ligament long, narrow and pustulose. Fairly common in mud below low-tide mark. Ranges from Cape Cod to Florida and to Texas.

Blood Ark
2 in (5 cm)

Blood Ark,
Anadara ovalis (Bruguière, 1789).
Shell fat and oval, white, with 26 to 35 smooth ribs. Ligament very narrow and depressed; beaks close together. Periostracum blackish brown, hairy and fairly thick. Flesh and blood are red. A common shallow-water ark found from Cape Cod to Texas.

Ponderous Ark,
Noetia ponderosa (Say, 1822).
Shell solid and heavy. Beaks point
posteriorly; valves of the same size.
Posterior muscle scar raised to form a
weak flange. Ribs raised, square in
cross-section, and split down the centre
by a fine incised line. Periostracum
thick, black, but wears off at the beaks.
A common shallow-water species
normally found in warm waters from
Virginia to Texas. Fossils occur in Cape
Cod.

Ponderous Ark
2 in (5 cm)

Milky Ark
0.5 in (1 cm)

Sulcate Limopsis
0.5 in (1 cm)

Nodulose Ark
0.5 (1 cm)

Milky Ark,
Arcopsis lactea (Linnaeus, 1767).
Shell small, solid, rhomboidal in
outline; somewhat compressed. Beaks
just in front of the mid-line and far
apart. Hinge plate has 40 to 50 small
teeth. Exterior yellowish white, with a
light-brown periostracum, sometimes
overhanging the margins. Sculpture of
fine radiating ribs crossed by
concentric ridges. Interior whitish;
muscle scars raised. A common
intertidal species attached to rocks in
sandy areas. Ranges from the southern
coast of Britain to the Mediterranean
and to South Africa.

Nodulose Ark,
Acar nodulosa (Müller, 1776).
Shell small, solid, elongate-rhomboidal,
with a narrower front end and a
broader, spathate hind end. Beaks
nearer the smaller front end and set
slightly apart. Ligament long, narrow
and arrow-shaped. Hinge has about
seven teeth in front, and about 12
slanting ones at the posterior end.
Sculpture of worn reticulation and
beads. Periostracum thin and light
brown. Interior of valves white. Byssal
gape very small. A common offshore
and deep-water species ranging from
Norway to Portugal.

Sulcate Limopsis,
Limopsis sulcata Verrill and Bush,
1898.
Shell small, obliquely oval, with
prominent rounded ribs which are
finely cut on the upper edge by short
radial grooves. Inner margin of the
valves smooth. Colour dull white.
Periostracum thick, tufted, extending
beyond the ventral edge of the shell.
Hinge arched, with about six small
teeth on either side of the centre.
Ligament external, small, central and
triangular. Moderately common in sand
offshore to about 2296 ft (700 m).
Ranges from Cape Cod to Texas and the
West Indies. Belongs to the family
Limopsidae.

Bittersweet Clams
(Family Glycymerididae)

The sturdy, oval bittersweet clams of the family Glycymerididae have an arched hinge with a few taxodont teeth. The exterior is either smooth or strongly ribbed. Most species are tropical- or temperate-dwelling in sandy areas. There is no gape or byssus produced by the adults.

West Coast Bittersweet
1 in (2.5 cm)

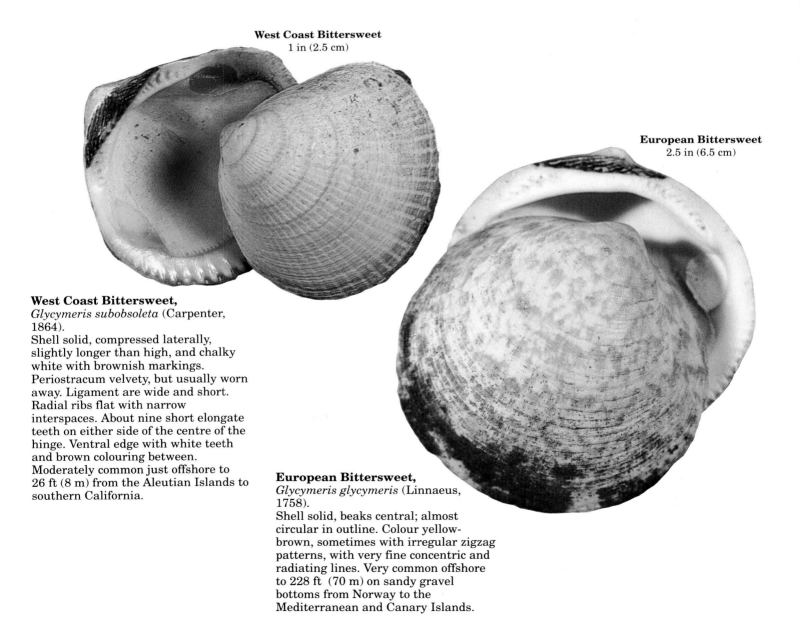

European Bittersweet
2.5 in (6.5 cm)

West Coast Bittersweet,
Glycymeris subobsoleta (Carpenter, 1864).
Shell solid, compressed laterally, slightly longer than high, and chalky white with brownish markings. Periostracum velvety, but usually worn away. Ligament are wide and short. Radial ribs flat with narrow interspaces. About nine short elongate teeth on either side of the centre of the hinge. Ventral edge with white teeth and brown colouring between. Moderately common just offshore to 26 ft (8 m) from the Aleutian Islands to southern California.

European Bittersweet,
Glycymeris glycymeris (Linnaeus, 1758).
Shell solid, beaks central; almost circular in outline. Colour yellow-brown, sometimes with irregular zigzag patterns, with very fine concentric and radiating lines. Very common offshore to 228 ft (70 m) on sandy gravel bottoms from Norway to the Mediterranean and Canary Islands.

Mussels
(Family Mytilidae)

European Date Mussel
2.7 in (7 cm)

The mussel family is quite diverse, with many genera and species, some of which have been accidentally introduced around the world on ships' bottoms and floating logs. Mussels become attached to hard substrates by means of a multi-threaded byssus spun by a short foot. A few species burrow into peat, rocks and coral. Many are an important food for man, especially in France and Japan where they are farmed in large intertidal areas.

Among the mussels of the family Mytilidae are several elongate species of date mussels that are adapted for boring by means of carbonic acid and shell rotation into rocks, shells and coral.

Blue Mussel
2.5 in (6.5 cm)

European Date Mussel,
Lithophaga lithophaga (Linnaeus, 1758).
Elongate, cigar-shaped. Umbo at the narrow anterior end. Exterior light brown with fine growth lines. Interior bluish white. No hinge teeth. Bores in shallow-water rocks. Portugal to the Mediterranean and Adriatic Seas.

Blue Mussel,
Mytilus edulis Linnaeus, 1758.
Shell spathate, with the umbones at the narrow end. Ventral margin often curved. Colour blue black with eroded areas of chalky purple. Periostracum varnish-like. Interior pearly white with a deep blue border. Occasionally specimens have rays of brownish yellow. Occurs in large numbers attached to intertidal rocks in the lower Arctic Ocean south to South Carolina; south to California; and in western Europe south to the Black Sea.

Californian Mussel
5 in (13 cm)

Mediterranean Blue Mussel
4 in (10 cm)

Mediterranean Blue Mussel,
Mytilus galloprovincialis Lamarck, 1822.
Similar to the Blue Mussel, but is usually larger, broader, and more angular. The mantle edge of the animal is blue black, whereas in *edulis* it is straw coloured. Periostracum dark and shiny. A common intertidal species farmed in western Europe.

Californian Mussel,
Mytilus californianus Conrad, 1837.
Shell large, thick, inflated. Ventral margin straight. With a dozen weak radial ribs and coarse growth lines. Abundant intertidally from the Aleutians to north-west Mexico.

Falcate Date Mussel
3 in (7.5 cm)

California Date Mussel
1 in (2.5 cm)

Falcate Date Mussel,
Adula falcata (Gould, 1851).
Very elongate, cylindrical, slightly
curved. Beaks rounded and about one-
eighth the length from the swollen
anterior end. A strong angular rib runs
from the beaks to the base of the
posterior end. Sculpture of numerous
vertical, wavy and slightly beaded ribs
are over the entire shell. Colour shiny
chestnut-brown. A fairly common rock-
borer in shallow water from Coos Bay,
Oregon, to Mexico

Californian Date Mussel,
Adula californiensis (Philippi, 1847).
Similar to the Falcate Date Mussel, but
chubbier, not as elongate and has a
smooth surface. A velvety, hair-like
periostracum covers the compressed
posterior end. Colour a shiny chocolate-
brown. It makes burrows in hard rocks
in shallow water. Moderately common
from British Columbia to southern
California.

Non-boring Date Mussel
1 in (2.5 cm)

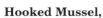
Hooked Mussel
1.5 in (4 cm)

Non-boring Date Mussel,
Adula diegoensis (Dall, 1911).
Mytiloid in shape, with rather large, fat,
inrolled umbones near the anterior end.
Chestnut brown in colour. Abundant in
colonies attached to wharf pilings and
breakwaters. Ranges from Oregon south
to Sonora, Mexico.

Hooked Mussel,
Ischadium recurvum (Rafinesque,
1820).
Flattish, rather wide, with numerous
wavy axial ribs. Colour of exterior dark
greyish brown; inside purplish to rosy
brown with a narrow blue-grey border.
Three or four small teeth at the edge of
the posterior end. A common brackish
water rock-dweller living from Cape Cod
to the West Indies.

Senhouse's Mussel
1 in (2.5 cm)

Senhouse's Mussel,
Muscilista senhousei (Benson, 1842).
Shell small, rather fragile, thin-shelled
and coloured green to bluish green with
delicate, zigzag brownish flames. Ends
with fine radiating striae. Lunule with a
crenulated margin. Common; makes
nests on mud flats and attaches to
wooden pilings. Introduced from Asia to
Washington to central California.

Atlantic Ribbed Mussel,
Geukensia demissa (Dillwyn, 1817).
Lightweight, but strong, elongate,
blackish brown in colour, often shiny,
and with strong, rough, radial,
bifurcating ribs. Interior bluish white
with the posterior end flushed with
purple. Interior margins crenulated. No
tiny teeth at the umbones, as in the
Hooked Mussel. An abundant intertidal
species nestled in peat and grass
marshes. Ranges from the Gulf of
St Lawrence to north-east Florida.
Introduced to northern California.

Atlantic Ribbed Mussel
3 in (7.5 cm)

False Tulip Mussel,
Modiolus modiolus subspecies
squamosus Beauperthuy, 1967.
Almost identical to half-grown
Northern Horse Mussels, but rarely
over 2 in (5 cm). Exterior brownish
purple, with an oblique whitish ray.
Umbones small, not swollen, and
always white. A common southern
subspecies found in shallow water in
south-eastern United States.

False Tulip Mussel
2 in (5 cm)

Northern Horse Mussel
4 in (10 cm)

Northern Horse Mussel,
Modiolus modiolus (Linnaeus, 1758).
Shell strong, oblong, swollen, with a
coarse, rather thick blackish brown
periostracum with long smooth hairs.
Beaks always white and not swollen.
Adult shells chalky mauve-white. No
hinge teeth. A common circumpolar,
subtidal mussel found as far south as
New Jersey, central California and
south to France.

Tulip Mussel,
Modiolus americanus (Leach, 1815).
A common southern species which is
fatter than the Horse Mussel. Umbones
swollen and coloured rose or purplish.
Exterior blushed with rose. Interior
pearly white. Ranges from South
Carolina to Brazil and Bermuda.

Tulip Mussel
3 in (7.5 cm)

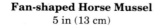
Fan-shaped Horse Mussel
5 in (13 cm)

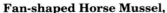

Fan-shaped Horse Mussel,
Modiolus rectus (Conrad, 1837).
Oblong, rectangular, well-inflated and
thin-shelled. Colour bluish white with
a yellowish-brown periostracum.
Exterior with fine growth lines.
Interior pearly white, tinged with pink.
Lives burrowed in mud with the broad
margin exposed. In 3–147 ft (1–45 m) of
water from British Columbia to Mexico.

Bearded Horse Mussel,
Modiolus barbatus (Linnaeus, 1758).
Shell broad at one end, somewhat
compressed, and coloured yellow and
reddish. Covered with a thick, yellow-
brown, hairy periostracum. Interior
lustrous, very pale blue, tinted with
pink. Margins smooth. Lives among
rocks from low tide mark to 328 ft
(100 m). Common from southern
British Isles to the Mediterranean.

Bearded Horse Mussel
1 in (2.5 cm)

Black Musculus
2 in (5 cm)

Discord Musculus
1.5 in (4 cm)

Black Musculus,
Musculus niger (Gray, 1824).
Small black mussels with the
sculpturing divided into three oblique
areas. The centre section has
microscopic, concentric, wavy threads
and pimples; the two end sections with
strong, axial, decussated riblets.
Exterior black; interior pinkish. A
common shallow-water species,
sometimes encased in a 'cocoon' of its
own byssal threads. Ranges from the
Arctic Seas to Washington and to off
North Carolina, as well as to the
British Isles.

Discord Musculus,
Musculus discors (Linnaeus, 1767).
Oblong, fairly fragile. Periostracum
brown to black. Centre section smooth,
except for weak growth lines. Interior
bluish white with a slight iridescence.
Common intertidal in algae and
offshore from the Arctic Seas to New
York, Puget Sound in the west, and to
the Mediterranean.

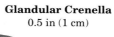

Glandular Crenella
0.5 in (1 cm)

Glandular Crenella,
Crenella glandula (Totten, 1834).
Shell small, ovate, thin, brownish
periostracum with fine decussate
riblets. Margin crenulated. Hinge finely
dentate. Foot worm-shaped with a disc-
shaped end. A very common offshore
species ranging from Labrador to off
North Carolina.

Adriatic Horse Mussel
1.5 in (4 cm)

Adriatic Horse Mussel,
Modiolus adriaticus Lamarck, 1822.
Shell small, brittle, swollen, with the
beaks a short distance from the
anterior end. Colour yellow with
reddish rays or irregular zigzag
streaks. Interior pearly white, with the
external rays showing through. Found
offshore to 262 ft (80 m) from the
British Isles to the Mediterranean.

Pen Shells
(Family Pinnidae)

Although mostly tropical and temperate in distribution, one species reaches into cooler European waters. They are quite fragile and live buried in soft mud or sand. A large clump of byssal threads attached to a firm object keeps them from being uprooted. The largest known living species, *Pinna nobilis* Linnaeus, 1758, comes from the Mediterranean where its golden byssal threads were used to make gloves and socks. Commensal crustacea quite commonly are found within the mantle cavity of this clam. Octopus are known to attack pen shells by inserting a stone between the gaping valves and then devouring the contents.

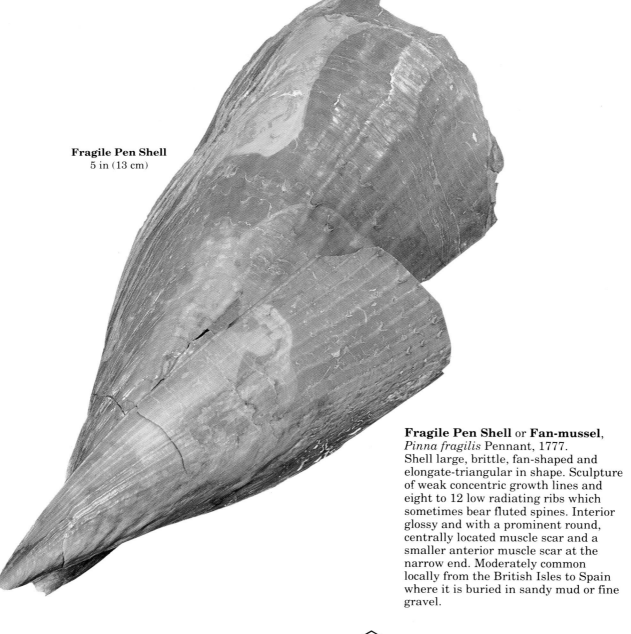

Fragile Pen Shell
5 in (13 cm)

Fragile Pen Shell or **Fan-mussel**, *Pinna fragilis* Pennant, 1777. Shell large, brittle, fan-shaped and elongate-triangular in shape. Sculpture of weak concentric growth lines and eight to 12 low radiating ribs which sometimes bear fluted spines. Interior glossy and with a prominent round, centrally located muscle scar and a smaller anterior muscle scar at the narrow end. Moderately common locally from the British Isles to Spain where it is buried in sandy mud or fine gravel.

Scallops
(Family Pectinidae)

Atlantic Deepsea Scallop
7 in (18 cm)

The well-known, edible scallops are worldwide in distribution and contain hundreds of species divided into about 50 genera. Scallops are capable of swimming in short zigzag spurts by snapping together their two shelly valves. The hinge has no teeth but there is a central black resilium. There are numerous small eyes set along the margins of the fleshy mantle. In some countries only the circular adductor muscle is eaten. St. James' Scallop has long been a religious symbol and extensively used in heraldry and art design.

Atlantic Deepsea Scallop,
Placopecten magellanicus (Gmelin, 1791).
Shell large, almost circular. Lightweight but strong. Both valves flattish to slightly convex. Exterior rough with numerous, very small, raised threads. Colour variable from grey to dirty white and sometimes rayed with purplish red. Ears unequal. Common offshore. A commercial species ranging from the Maritime Provinces of Canada to off North Carolina.

Great Scallop
4 in (10 cm)

Great Scallop,
Pecten maximus (Linnaeus, 1758).
Shell solid and circular in outline; ears equal; the right (lower) valve is quite convex and slightly overlaps the flat left (upper) valve. Upper valve has 15 to 17 broad radiating ribs and is coloured red brown. Bottom valve white to cream with tints of yellow and pink. Young specimens are attached by a small byssus. Common in sandy areas offshore from 3–393 ft (1–120 m). Distributed from Norway south to Portugal.

St James' Scallop
Pecten jacobaeus (Linnaeus, 1758).
The Great Scallop is replaced in Spain and throughout the Mediterranean by this species or subspecies. The shell has more pronounced, squarish ribs. It is a common, shallow water seafood.

St. James' Scallop
5 in (13 cm)

Giant Pacific Scallop,
Pecten caurinus Gould, 1850.
Shell large, circular in outline. The upper (left) valve is almost flat, reddish grey with about 17 low, rounded ribs; lower valve moderately deep, whitish with a few more, stronger, rather flat-topped ribs. This is a popular commercial species found offshore from the Aleutians to northern California.

Giant Pacific Scallop
7 in (18 cm)

Seven-rayed Scallop
1.5 in (4 cm)

Bald Scallop   2 in (5 cm)

Seven-rayed Scallop,
Pseudamussium septemradiatum (Müller, 1776).
Shell brittle, almost circular in outline; ears about the same size and with four to six riblets. Valves with five to eight low, rounded ribs which increase in width towards the margins. Surface with numerous radiating scratches, crossed by concentric lines. Colour of left valve brick red or purplish brown; right valve whitish with some brick red near the umbones. Rarely all-white. A common offshore scallop in 40–656 ft (12–200 m) around the British Isles. Extends from Norway to north-west Africa.

Bald Scallop,
Proteopecten glaber (Linnaeus, 1758).
Shell solid, both valves about the same thickness and with the ears about the same size. Right (lower) valve with ten or 11 raised riblets; left valve with six or seven weaker low ribs. Ears with fine riblets. Colour variable and usually bright. Moderately common offshore from Portugal to the Mediterranean.

Iceland Scallop,
Chlamys islandica (Müller, 1776).
Solid, both valves about the same convexity, oval-oblong, one ear twice as long as the other. Has about 50 coarse, irregular ribs which split in two near the margin of the valve. Rarely the ribs are grouped in twos, threes or fours. Colour usually dirty grey or cream, but some may be tinged with peach, yellow or purplish both inside and out. A very common offshore species of Arctic Seas from Japan to Alaska to Puget Sound; Greenland to Massachusetts; and Iceland and Norway to the Shetland Islands.

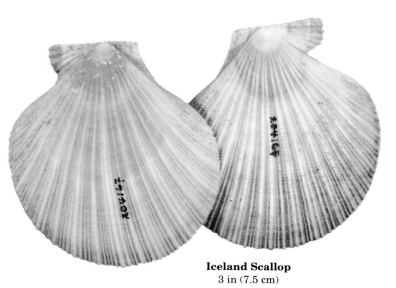

Iceland Scallop
3 in (7.5 cm)

Variable Scallop,
Chlamys varia (Linnaeus, 1758).
Fan-shaped; anterior ears long. Colours variable. Sculpture of 25 to 35 prominent spined ribs. Margins strongly crenulate. A common shallow-water species found under stones. Ranges from Denmark and the British Isles to the Mediterranean.

Kitten Scallop,
Camptonectes tigerinus (Müller, 1776).
Shell small, fan-shaped, almost equivalve, with the anterior ears about three times as long as the posterior ones. Colours and patterns variable: white, cream, grey, brown and purple, with spots, streaks and maculations. Ribs variable in number up to 30. Growth stages are sometimes prominent. Ears with three to five small riblets. Lower margin of the byssal notch with minute teeth. Margin usually crenulate. Found commonly from the low-tide mark to a depth of 328 ft (100 m) on sand and gravel bottoms. Ranges from Iceland and Norway to Spain.

Kitten Scallop
1 in (2.5 cm)

Variable Scallop
2.5 in (6.5 cm)

Sulcate Scallop,
Chlamys sulcata (Müller, 1776).
Shell small, solid, brittle; anterior ears about three times as long as the posterior ones. Colour dirty white, yellowish or red brown. Sculpture of 20 to 40 radiating ribs with narrower riblets in between, usually clumped in threes or fours to give a sulcate surface. Ears with small riblets and with strong folds between the prominent byssal notch and the beaks. An uncommon small scallop off the coasts north-west Europe.

Snow Scallop
2.5 in (6.5 cm)

Snow Scallop,
Chlamys nivea (Macgillivray, 1825).
Very similar to the Variable Scallop, but it has many more ribs, generally up to 45. It may be pure white or yellow or orange in colour. Locally common on the west coast of Scotland.

Sulcate Scallop
1.7 in (4 cm)

Pacific Spear Scallop,
Chlamys hastata hastata (Sowerby, 1843).
Shell solid, somewhat fan-shaped. Right valve (with byssal notch) has about 18 to 20 strongly spined, primary ribs which have five to seven much smaller, weakly spined secondary riblets in between; left valve has ten or 11 distantly spaced, scaled primary ribs, with 12 to 16 weak, beaded secondary ribs in between. Colours are bright orange, red or lemon. A southern form found offshore along the Californian coast. The subspecies *hericia* (Gould, 1850) or Pacific Pink Scallop has stronger ribs, is more spinose and occurs from Alaska to Oregon.

Pacific Spear Scallop
2 in (5 cm)

Hinds' Scallop
2.5 in (6.5 cm)

Atlantic Bay Scallop
2.5 in (6.5 cm)

Hinds' Scallop,
Chlamys rubida (Hinds, 1845).
With microscopic reticulations between
the ribs near either the beaks or the
margins of the valves. Left valve has
three rows of spines on the primary
ribs. Right valve lighter in colour with
smoothish ribs. Common just offshore
from Alaska to California.

Atlantic Bay Scallop,
Argopecten irradians (Lamarck, 1819).
Shell solid, almost circular, moderately
inflated, with almost equal-sized ears.
Each valve is about the same thickness,
and the lower one is slightly lighter in
colour. With 17 or 18 low, roundish ribs.
Colour usually drab grey-brown with
indistinct dark-brown mottlings. Rarely
yellowish or greyish orange. This is a
common, edible scallop found at depths
of 3–64 ft (1–20 m). Ranges from the
north shore of Cape Cod to New Jersey.

Queen Scallop
3 in (7.5 cm)

Giant Rock Scallop
7 in (18 cm)

Hunchback Scallop
1.5 in (4 cm)

Queen Scallop,
Aequipecten opercularis (Linnaeus,
1758)
Shell fairly large, evenly fan-shaped
with almost equal-sized ears. Upper
(left) valve more convex than the lower
(right) valve. Circular in outline.
Sculpture of about 19 to 22 rounded
radial ribs crossed by fine concentric
corrugations. Byssal notch with small
teeth. Margin strongly crenulate.
Colour variable, with mottlings of red,
pink, brown or purple on a yellow or
whitish background. When young, it
lives attached by its byssus to the
bottom, but in its adult stage it is a
frequent swimmer, usually to avoid the
predatory starfish, *Asteria*. Found
offshore on sandy gravel or shelly
bottoms. A common edible species
ranging from Norway to Portugal and
into the Mediterranean.

Hunchback Scallop,
Hinnites distortus (da Costa, 1778).
A small, permanently attached scallop,
growing in its early life in the shape of
a *Chlamys*, but then becoming
irregular in various shapes as it grows
older. Upper valve has about 60 prickly
ribs. Colour white, yellow, reddish or
brownish and often mottled. Lives in
rock crevices or in kelp holdfasts.
Ranges from Norway to the Azores.

Giant Rock Scallop,
Hinnites giganteus (Gray, 1825).
A heavy, massive shell characterized by
the early '*Chlamys*-like' shell at the
beaks. The young shells have a mauve
spot on the inside of the hinge line and
measure half-inch (1.5 cm) long .
Adults are large, heavy with coarse,
irregular radial riblets. Interior white
with a purple hinge area. Attaches to
rocks by the right valve. Moderately
common offshore from British
Columbia to southern California.

Jingle Shells
(Family Anomiidae)

Saddle Jingle Shell
2 in (5 cm)

The thin, semi-translucent jingle shells have a remarkably strong shell and are frequently cast up on beaches. The lower valve has a round notch through which passes the strong attachment byssus. The top (or left) valve is usually convex. The flesh of the mollusc, although edible, has a very strong taste of alum. There are less than a dozen species in the family and many have been spread by boats and floating logs.

Common Jingle Shell,
Anomia simplex Orbigny, 1842.
Shell strong, irregularly oval, smoothish and thin-shelled. Upper free valve quite convex; lower valve flat and with a large hole near the apex. Colour either translucent yellow or orange with a silvery sheen. Specimens buried in mud become blackened. Byssus forms a round calcified base where it is attached. Common on logs and dead shells from Cape Cod to Texas and to Brazil.

Common Jingle Shell
1.5 in (4 cm)

Saddle Jingle Shell,
Anomia ephippium Linnaeus, 1758.
Right (lower) valve thin, fragile, smaller and flatter than the more solid left (upper) valve. Colour white with occasional mottling of pink or purple. The left valve has three muscle scars. Interior of shell pearly white, purplish or brown. The surface of the shell usually takes on the shape of the shell or object to which the jingle shell is attached. This species has a very wide distribution from Scandinavia to the Mediterranean and West Africa.

Prickly Jingle Shell
0.7 in (2 cm)

False Pacific Jingle
3 in (7.5 cm)

Prickly Jingle Shell,
Anomia squamula (Linnaeus, 1758).
Shell small, irregularly rounded, moderately fragile. Upper valve convex, rough, often with small prickles. Sometimes has rather long spines. Lower valve flat, with a small hole near the hinge end. Left valve muscle scars small. Colour drab, opaque whitish tan. A common cold-water species attaching itself to rocks and broken shells from the low tide mark to 1968 ft (600 m). Ranges from Labrador to off North Carolina; and from Iceland to France.

False Pacific Jingle
Pododesmus macroschisma (Deshayes, 1839).
Shell resembling a jingle shell, with very coarse, irregular radiating ribs. Upper valve has only two muscle scars. Lower valve with a hole. Colour greenish white and somewhat pearly. Common on stones, wharf pilings and other shells from 3–228 ft (1–70 m). It is very often found attached to the backs of the *Haliotis* abalone shells. Ranges from Japan to Alaska to Mexico.

File Clams
(Family Limidae)

These remarkable clams have many long tentacles extending from the margin of the mantle. By snapping their valves together, the lima clams are able to swim clumsily through the water. They also produce a small byssal anchor and sometimes will build a protective nest of byssal threads. Many colourful species are tropical and hide under corals, while others are deep-sea and grow to over 5 inches (13 cm) in length.

Hians File Clam
1.5 in (4 cm)

Inflated File Clam
1.5 in (4 cm)

Inflated File Clam,
Limaria inflata (Gmelin, 1791).
Shell thin but strong, white, obliquely elongate. One ear is twice as long as the other. The black resilium is small, triangular and located in the centre of the hinge. Valves rather well-inflated. Sculpture of about 25 small, thread-like riblets which bear small beads where concentric growth lines cross. The margin of the valve bears a small prickle wherever a rib ends. A southern Mediterranean species extending north to France.

Hians File Clam,
Limaria hians (Gmelin, 1791).
Shell thin, but strong, brown and very obliquely elongate. Byssal notch in the right anterior ear is very small. Wide dorsal gape. Beaks far apart, with 50 radiating riblets crossed by concentric lines. Tentacles red and orange. Common from Norway to the Azores.

Loscomb's File Clam
0.8 in (2 cm)

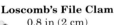

Loscomb's File Clam,
Limaria loscombi (Sowerby, 1820).
With a broad black cardinal area. Ears equal. Fifty distinct, beaded riblets. Margin with minute prickles. Offshore from Norway to the Mediterranean and Azores.

Giant European File Clam
Acesta excavata (Fabricius, 1779).
Shell large, strong, swollen and greyish white. Hinge short, thick, without teeth and externally having an oblique ligamental pit. Sculpture of numerous fine radial incised lines. Margins smoothish. In life, the soft parts bear long whitish tentacles. Uncommon offshore from Norway to the Iberian Peninsula.

Giant European File Clam
5 in (13 cm)

Oysters
(Family Ostreidae)

Crested Oyster
2.5 in (6.5 cm)

T he abundant and well-known oysters have served mankind as a seafood for many centuries. Of the three common species now living in western Europe, only one is native, the other two were probably introduced many years ago.

Crested Oyster,
Ostrea equestris Say, 1834.
Usually oval, with raised margins which are crenulated. The attached valve has a flat interior with a rather high vertical margin on each side. Muscle scar almost central. Interior greenish pearly. Edge of upper valve has a row of fine denticles. Uncommon from Virginia south to Texas and to Brazil.

Giant Pacific Oyster
8 in (20 cm)

Giant Pacific Oyster,
Crassostrea gigas (Thunberg, 1793). Shell large, of various shapes, but generally characterized by its elongate shape, its coarse, widely spaced concentric lamellae or very coarse longitudinal fluting or ridges. Interior enamel white, often with a faint purplish stain on the muscle scar. A common shallow-water species of Japan now established from British Columbia to California. In Europe, where it was introduced many years ago it is called the Portuguese Oyster, *Crassostrea angulata* (Lamarck, 1818).

Eastern American Oyster
5 in (13 cm)

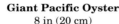

Common European Oyster
4 in (10 cm)

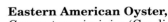

Common European Oyster,
Ostrea edulis Linnaeus, 1758. Shell roughly circular in outline. Exterior rough, with deep radiating ribs and concentric ridges. Upper or right valve flat and brownish. Interior whitish with green or red-brown blotches. Common offshore from Norway to the Black Sea.

Eastern American Oyster,
Crassostrea virginica (Gmelin, 1791). The valve margins are only slightly wavy or are straight. Lower valve cupped. The muscle scar is usually coloured a deep purple. Harvested commercially along the east coast of North America.

Lucine Clams
(Family Lucinidae)

These circular, laterally compressed clams are recognized by the very long, narrow anterior muscle scar. The clams have very short siphons and hence there is no pallial sinus. The long foot creates a tunnel in the sandy mud for drawing in water to the gills.

Boreal Lucina
1.2 in (3 cm)

Northeast Lucina
2.5 in (6.5 cm)

Northeast Lucina,
Lucinoma filosa (Stimpson, 1851).
Almost circular, compressed, white,
with a thin yellowish periostracum.
Beaks small, close together and
centrally located. No anterior lateral
teeth present. Sculpture of sharp,
concentric ridges. Common offshore
from Newfoundland to north Florida
and to Texas.

Boreal Lucina,
Lucinoma borealis (Linnaeus, 1758).
Almost circular, solid, white with a thin
brown periostracum. Strong concentric
ridges are sometimes eroded away. Two
small cardinal teeth in each valve. One
of them is bifid. Margin of valves
smooth. Lives in shallow water to
328 ft (100 m) in sandy mud. Ranges
from Norway to the Baltic and south to
the Mediterranean.

Western Ringed Lucina,
Lucinoma annulata (Reeve, 1850).
Oval to circular and slightly inflated.
With strong raised, concentric threads.
Colour chalky grey to white, overlaid
by a thin, greenish-brown
periostracum. Fairly common from
19–492 ft (16–150 m) from Alaska to
southern California.

Western Ringed Lucina
2 in (5 cm)

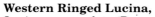

Cleft Clams
(Family Thyasiridae)

These small, white clams are usually somewhat trigonal in shape and have a chalky texture. The beaks are hooked forward and the hinge bears no prominent teeth. The posterior dorsal margin of the valve is usually deeply furrowed. Pallial line without a sinus. Ligament is in a dorsal groove and partly external. The family is worldwide in distribution with the majority found in cool waters.

Atlantic Cleft Clam
0.5 in (1 cm)

Atlantic Cleft Clam,
Thyasira trisinuata Orbigny, 1842. Shell small, oblong, fragile and translucent white. Hinge weak and only a very long, weak posterior lateral tooth. Posterior slope of shell has two strong radial grooves. Common offshore from Nova Scotia to the West Indies; Alaska to California.

Pacific Cleft Clam
2 in (5 cm)

Pacific Cleft Clam,
Thyasira bisecta Conrad, 1849. Shell almost square in side view and moderately obese. Characterized by the almost vertical, straight anterior end. Ligament long and flush with the dorsal margin of the shell. Shell chalky white and covered with a thin yellowish periostracum. Uncommon from 26–984 ft (8–300 m). Occurs in Japan and Alaska and south to Oregon.

Diplodont Clams
(Family Ungulinidae)

These small, round, white clams are capable of building complicated, compact nests of periostracal material and detritus. There are two small, but distinct, cardinal teeth in each valve. The left anterior and right posterior ones are split or bifid. Lateral teeth absent in some species. No pallial sinus present.

Rotund Diplodont
1 in (2.5 cm)

Rotund Diplodont,
Diplodonta rotundata (Montagu, 1803). Shell small, solid, equivalve. Beaks almost central. Colour dull white; periostracum light yellow. Sculpture of fine concentric lines and a few microscopic radiating lines. Single anterior and posterior lateral teeth present. Burrows into muddy sand. Common from the British Isles to the Mediterranean.

Pacific Orb Diplodont
1 in (2.5 cm)

Pacific Orb Diplodont,
Diplodonta orbellus Gould, 1852. Shell oval to almost circular in outline, quite inflated and smoothish, except for moderately coarse growth lines. Beaks small and pointing slightly forward. Ligament posterior to the beaks is long, raised and conspicuous. Builds small nests of periostracal material. Common in shallow water to offshore from Alaska to Panama.

Jewel Boxes
(Family Chamidae)

These are sturdy, usually spiny, bivalves attached to rock surfaces or to buoys. They resemble the Spiny Oysters, *Spondylus*, but lack the ball-and-socket type of hinge and have instead large amorphous teeth in the hinge. Most species live in temperate or tropical waters.

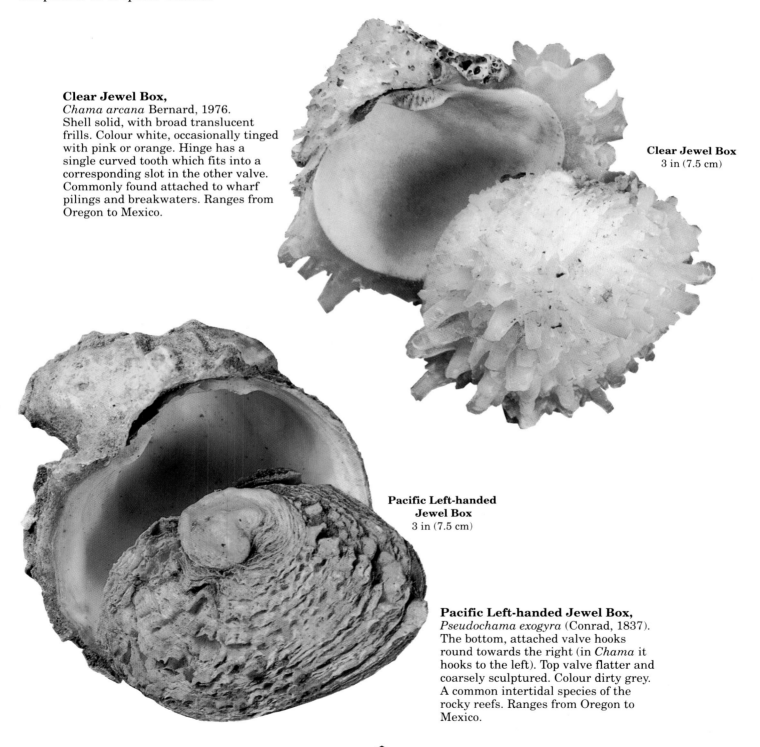

Clear Jewel Box,
Chama arcana Bernard, 1976. Shell solid, with broad translucent frills. Colour white, occasionally tinged with pink or orange. Hinge has a single curved tooth which fits into a corresponding slot in the other valve. Commonly found attached to wharf pilings and breakwaters. Ranges from Oregon to Mexico.

Clear Jewel Box
3 in (7.5 cm)

Pacific Left-handed Jewel Box
3 in (7.5 cm)

Pacific Left-handed Jewel Box,
Pseudochama exogyra (Conrad, 1837). The bottom, attached valve hooks round towards the right (in *Chama* it hooks to the left). Top valve flatter and coarsely sculptured. Colour dirty grey. A common intertidal species of the rocky reefs. Ranges from Oregon to Mexico.

Cardita Clams
(Family Carditidae)

This ancient group of stout, ribbed clams with heavy, irregular hinges bearing strong teeth is widely distributed from the tropics to the polar seas. In the genus *Cyclocardia*, the shell is roundly trigonal, white, with a rough blackish periostracum. The internal margins of the valves are crenulate. Lateral teeth are absent. Some tropical Cardita are quite colourful.

Northern Cardita
1 in (2.5 cm)

Fine-ribbed Cardita
1 in (2.5 cm)

Northern Cardita,
Cyclocardia borealis (Conrad, 1831). Shell strong and obliquely heart-shaped. Beaks elevated and turned forward. Has about 20 rounded, moderately rough or beaded radial ribs. Colour white, but usually covered with a thick, velvety brown periostracum. Lunule small but very deeply sunk. A common offshore species ranging from Labrador to off North Carolina.

Fine-ribbed Cardita,
Cyclocardia crebricostata
  (Krause, 1885).
Shell strong, elongate-oval, with about 24 strong, slightly curved radial ribs which are squarish in cross-section and smoothish. Inner margin crenulate. Periostracum fuzzy, smoothish, light brown and generally worn off at the beaks. Moderately common on gravel bottoms offshore from Point Barrow, Alaska, to Oregon.

Stout Cardita,
Cyclocardia ventricosa (Gould, 1850). Rounded-trigonal; velvety periostracum. With 18 to 20 wide, beaded radial ribs. Common offshore from Alaska to California.

Stout Cardita
0.8 in (2 cm)

Astarte Clams
(Family Astartidae)

Most members of this family are inhabitants of cold waters, usually at moderate depths where the bottom is silty or muddy. The shells of the astarte clams are solid, thick, oval to triangular in shape, chalky white in colour, and usually covered with a thick dark periostracum. The external ligament and the resilium are behind the beaks. There is no pallial sinus. Usually there are three cardinal teeth in the left valve and two in the right.

Sulcate Astarte
1 in (2.5 cm)

Smooth Astarte
1 in (2.5 cm)

Smooth Astarte,
Astarte castanea (Say, 1822).
Shell solid, fairly small, trigonal in outline and quite compressed. Beaks pointed and hooked forward. Lunule large and shallow. Exterior smoothish. Colour a glossy light-brown. Inner margins finely crenulate. This is a common offshore species ranging from Nova Scotia to off New Jersey.

Sulcate Astarte,
Astarte sulcata (da Costa, 1778).
Shell oval, slightly compressed. With 25 to 55 prominent, broad radial ribs. Lunule and eschutcheon prominent. Inner margin finely crenulate. Periostracum light brown. Colour of shell white to salmon-pink. Common offshore from Greenland and Iceland to the Mediterranean.

Montagu's Astarte,
Astarte montagui (Dillwyn, 1817).
Somewhat elongate; variable in sculpture and colour but generally with fine concentric, evenly spaced riblets in the region of the beaks, with less prominent, irregularly spaced ones throughout the lower two-thirds of the shell. Periostracum dark brown. This is a widespread, abundant species in Arctic Seas, south to Maine and to British Columbia, usually in 32–984 ft (10–300 m).

Montagu's Astarte
1 in (2.5 cm)

Crenate Astarte
1 in (2.5 cm)

Crenate Astarte,
Astarte crebricostata Forbes, 1847.
Shell solid, ovate, moderately
compressed. Numerous concentric
ridges are strong, rounded and evenly
spaced. Internal margin of valves finely
crenulate. Colour of periostracum dark
brown. Found in shallow water in
Arctic Seas and in deep water off
eastern United States; Greenland.

Waved Astarte
(1.5 in (3 cm)

Waved Astarte,
Astarte undata Gould, 1841.
Similar to the Crenate Astarte but less
elongate, with its beaks near the centre
and with fewer and stronger concentric
ridges. Very common offshore in New
England waters. Ranges from Labrador
to off New Jersey.

Cockles
(Family Cardiidae)

The well-known cockle family is worldwide in distribution and contains several dozen genera and several hundred living species. The shells vary from the large and copious *Cardium* of West Africa to the flat, heart-shaped *Corculum* of the East Indies. The foot of the cockles is large and muscular and the siphons are quite short. The ligament is external.

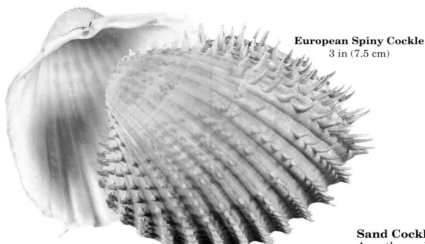

European Spiny Cockle
3 in (7.5 cm)

Sand Cockle
2.5 in (6.5 cm)

European Spiny Cockle,
Acanthocardia aculeata (Linnaeus, 1767).
Thin-shelled but strong, broadly oval in outline and with 20 to 22 strong radial ribs, each bearing a row of spines down the middle. Right valve with two anterior laterals and one posterior lateral. Interior of valves radially furrowed. Colour yellowish brown, with darker blotches. Subtidal to 98 ft (30 m). Rare in Britain; commoner southwards into the Mediterranean.

Sand Cockle,
Acanthocardia spinosa (Lightfoot, 1786).
Broadly oval, with about 35 small squarish radial ribs, those at the anterior end bearing smooth rounded scales, and those at the posterior end having numerous short spines. Colour yellow brown. A Mediterranean species ranging north to Portugal.

Tuberculate Cockle,
Acanthocardia tuberculata (Linnaeus, 1758).
Elongate-oval, with the beaks near the anterior end. With 21 to 23 weakly beaded radial ribs. Colour light brown. A common shallow-water cockle from the British Isles to the Mediterranean.

Tuberculate Cockle
2.5 in (6.5 cm)

Hians Cockle
3 in (7.5 cm)

Morton's Egg Cockle
1 in (2.5 cm)

Hians Cockle,
Ringicardium hians (Brocchi, 1814).
Shell similar to the European Spiny
Cockle, but larger, with a wide gape at
the larger posterior end, and with
stronger, narrower, more distantly
spaced radial ribs. The spines on the
posterior and anterior ribs are longer
and sharper. A fairly common, more
southerly species living from low-tide
mark to 98 ft (30 m), from the Iberian
Peninsula into the Mediterranean.

Morton's Egg Cockle,
Laevicardium mortoni (Conrad, 1830).
Thin-shelled, small, swollen and oval.
Surface smooth, glossy, yellowish
brown with darker zigzag markings
and with fine concentric ridges which
may be minutely pimpled. This
common food for ducks lives in sand
from 3–20 ft (1–6 m) of water. It ranges
from Cape Cod to Texas.

Heavy Egg Cockle
3 in (7.5 cm)

Greenland Cockle
4 in (10 cm)

Heavy Egg Cockle,
Laevicardium crassum (Gmelin, 1791).
Shell solid, obliquely oval, with the
beaks well in front of the mid-line.
Colour dirty yellow, sometimes with red
and brown blotches and zigzag
markings, especially near the beaks.
Periostracum thin, greenish yellow.
Sculpture of 40 to 50 very faint, smooth
radial riblets. No spines or scales.
Interior cream tan. Margins crenulate.
This common species lives among
broken shell and gravel from Norway to
the Mediterranean and the Cape Verde
Islands.

Greenland Cockle,
Serripes groenlandicus (Bruguière,
1789).
Shell fairly large, solid, inflated, with a
slight gape at the pointed posterior
end. Exterior smoothish, brownish
grey. Interior dull white. Beaks
inflated. Ligament large and strong.
No lunule or pallial sinus. Foot of
animal mottled red. Common offshore
from 20–393 ft (6–120 m) in Arctic
Seas to Massachusetts and to Puget
Sound, Washington State.

Nuttall's Cockle,
Clinocardium nuttallii (Conrad, 1837).
Shell fairly large, roundly oval,
moderately compressed and usually
with 33 to 37 coarse, radial ribs with
half-moon beads. Older specimens are
worn smooth. Beaks nearer the
anterior end and considerably rolled in.
Interior whitish, with the margins
showing distinct ribbing. Colour drab
grey, with a thin, brownish-yellow
periostracum. A common offshore
sand-loving cockle ranging from the
Bering Sea and Alaska to off southern
California.

Nuttall's Cockle
4 in (10 cm)

Iceland Cockle
3 in (7.5 cm)

Common European Cockle
1.5 in (4 cm)

Iceland Cockle,
Clinocardium ciliatum (Fabricius,
1780).
Fairly large, roundly oval, moderately
compressed, with 32 to 38 ridged radial
ribs which are crossed by coarse
concentric lines of growth. Exterior
drab greyish yellow with weak, narrow,
concentric bands of darker colour.
Interior ivory. Periostracum grey.
Common from Alaska to Puget Sound,
and from Greenland to Massachusetts.

Common European Cockle,
Cerastoderma edule (Linnaeus, 1758).
Shell solid, broadly oval, with in-rolled
beaks almost touching each other. With
22 to 28 squarish radial ribs, each
with numerous weak scales. Right
valve with two anterior and two
posterior lateral teeth. Interior of
valves white and stained brown around
the muscle scars. Margins crenulate
inside. Abundant near estuaries from
Norway to Portugal and West Africa.

Northern Dwarf Cockle,
Cerastoderma pinnulatum (Conrad,
1831).
Shell small, thin-shelled, somewhat
compressed, obliquely oval in outline,
with 22 to 28 wide, flat ribs which have
numerous arched scales on the anterior
and posterior ribs. Ligament
inconspicuous, but strong. Lunule and
escutcheon poorly defined. Margins
strongly crenulate. Colour cream or
rarely orange brown. Periostracum thin
and yellowish. Very common offshore
from Labrador to North Carolina.

Northern Dwarf Cockle
0.5 in (1 cm)

Trough Clams
(Family Mactridae)

C alled trough shells in England and surf clams in New England, these large smooth clams are recognized by the small spoon-shaped compartment, or chondrophore, in the centre of the hinge. Into this fits the pad-like, black resilium which keeps the valves ajar. Most of these species are fished commercially in cooler American waters.

Catilliform Surf Clam
4.5 in (11.5 cm)

California Mactra
2 in (5 cm)

California Mactra,
Mactra californica Conrad, 1837.
Shell elongate-oval, moderately fragile, smooth, and with peculiar concentric undulations on the beaks. The velvety yellowish-brown periostracum forms an angular ridge along the top posterior edge of each valve. This small species is fairly common in lagoons of California, but rarer in Puget Sound.

Catilliform Surf Clam,
Spisula catilliformis (Conrad, 1867).
Shell solid, oval, with the beaks slightly nearer the anterior end. Moderately obese. Dull ivory, commonly stained reddish brown, with numerous irregular growth lines. Periostracum glossy, thin and usually worn off. Pallial sinus deep. Sometimes washed ashore. Ranges from Washington to central California.

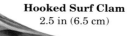

Hooked Surf Clam
2.5 in (6.5 cm)

Stimpson's Surf Clam,
Spisula polynyma (Stimpson, 1860).
Large, solid. Colour dirty white with a coarse varnish-like periostracum. Pallial sinus large. Common offshore from the Arctic Seas to Rhode Island; Japan to Puget Sound.

Stimpson's Surf Clam
4 in (10 cm)

Hooked Surf Clam,
Spisula falcata (Gould, 1850).
Elongate at the narrower anterior end. Low beaks nearer the rounded posterior end. Anterior upper margin slightly concave. Exterior chalky, with a brown shiny periostracum. Common from Washington to California.

Alaskan Gaper
8 in (20 cm)

Atlantic Surf Clam
5 in (13 cm)

Atlantic Surf Clam,
Spisula solidissima (Dillwyn, 1817).
Shell large, strong, elongate-oval and
smoothish, except for small, irregular
growth lines. Lateral teeth bear very
tiny saw-tooth ridges. Colour yellowish
white with a thin, yellowish-brown
periostracum. In the hinge, the small
oval, black-brown ligament, which is
close to the dorsal margin, does not
have a shelly ridge between it and the
larger chondrophore cup, as is the case
in *Mactra*. An abundant, shallow-
water, edible species commercially
dredged offshore. Occurs from Nova
Scotia to off South Carolina.

Alaskan Gaper,
Tresus capax (Gould, 1850).
Shell large, oval-elongate, with a dip or
bulge in the ventral margin. Gapes at
the posterior end. Cardinal teeth small,
and lateral teeth very small. Ligament
external and separated from the
cartilage pit by a shelly plate. Common
in shallow water in sandy mud from
Alaska to northern California.

Subtruncate Trough Clam
1 in (2.5 cm)

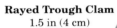

Rayed Trough Clam
1.5 in (4 cm)

Rayed Trough Clam,
Mactra corallina (Linnaeus, 1758).
Shell brittle, ovate; beaks in the mid-
line and curled inward and slightly
forward. Colour creamy white with
purplish around the beaks, and usually
with brown rays. Periostracum light
brown. Interior purplish white. Pallial
sinus deep. Widely distributed from
Norway to the Black Sea and to
Senegal.

Subtruncate Trough Clam,
Spisula subtruncata (da Costa, 1778).
Fairly small, ovate-triangular and
solid; beaks nearer the front end.
Colour greyish white to brownish.
External ligament is short and narrow
just behind the beaks. Sculpture of
coarse, concentric lines. Lunule and
eschutcheon with fine ridges. Laterals
finely serrated. Pallial sinus shallow.
An abundant offshore sand-lover
occurring from Norway to the Black
Sea and the Canary Islands.

Solid Trough Clam,
Spisula solida (Linnaeus, 1758).
Shell of medium size, solid, ovate,
beaks central and the exterior
smoothish, except for irregular growth
stoppages. Shell whitish grey;
periostracum light brown but usually
worn away. Pallial sinus short and
rounded at the end. Adductor muscle
scars recessed. Hinge teeth strong;
with a fairly large chondrophore. Shape
of this clam may vary from truncate to
oval. Found from 3–492 ft (1–150 m)
from Finland to Spain and Morocco.

Solid Trough Clam
1.5 in (4 cm)

Elliptical Trough Clam
1 in (2.5 cm)

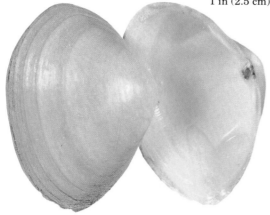

European Otter Clam
5 in (13 cm)

Elliptical Trough Clam,
Spisula elliptica (Brown, 1827).
Shell small, solid, oval-elongate with
the beaks slightly nearer the well-
rounded anterior end. Posterior end
slightly more pointed. Ventral margin
slightly swollen. Right valve with two
separate cardinal teeth and two
anterior and two posterior laterals.
Laterals in left valve are serrated.
Pallial sinus small, U-shaped. Exterior
smoothish. Interior glossy white.
Exterior tan with a smooth, shiny
brownish periostracum. Common in
muddy sand and fine gravel from the
Arctic to the English Channel,
sometimes as deep as 295 ft (90 m).

European Otter Clam,
Lutraria lutraria (Linnaeus, 1758).
Shell fairly large, solid, oval-elongate
in outline and gaping at both ends;
beaks nearer the front end and directed
inward. Colour yellowish brown with
an olive-brown, thin periostracum.
Internal ligament, black, triangular
and set in a large chondrophore. Pallial
sinus large and oval at the closed end.
Lower margin of the pallial sinus scar
is separated from the pallial line below
it. Common from 3–295 ft (1–90 m)
from Norway to the Baltic,
Mediterranean and West Africa.

Oblong Otter Clam,
Lutraria magna (da Costa, 1778).
Shell similar to the European Otter
Clam, but more elongate, with the
dorsal margin behind the beak concave,
and with the beaks closer to the front
end. The lower section of the pallial
sinus is confluent with the main pallial
scar. This member of the subfamily
Lutrariinae is a common shallow-water
clam living from the British Isles to the
Mediterranean.

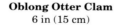

Oblong Otter Clam
6 in (15 cm)

Gould's Pacific Mactra,
Mactra nasuta Gould, 1851.
Similar to the California Mactra, but
more oval at the ventral margin,
without concentric undulations on the
beaks, and with a very distinct raised
radial ridge on the posterior dorsal
margin. Colour glossy white with a
thin, shiny yellowish-tan periostracum.
This is a more southerly, less common
clam ranging from California to
Colombia.

Gould's Pacific Mactra
3.5 in (9 cm)

Giant Wedge Clams
(Family Mesodesmatidae)

Shallow-water clams with heavy shells that are wedge-shaped. Hinge teeth strong, the resilium and ligament internal.

Arctic Wedge Clam
1.5 in (4 cm)

Arctic Wedge Clam,
Mesodesma arctatum (Conrad, 1830). Heavy for its size, elongate-oval. The posterior end is truncate and has a very short pallial sinus. Anterior end narrower and compressed. Chondrophore oblique. The lateral teeth have fine comb-like teeth on each side. Common offshore from Greenland and Labrador to Maryland.

Razor Clams
(Family Pharellidae)

This widespread family of razorfish or razor clams is predominantly a cold-water group characterized by their elongate and compressed shape, reduced hinge teeth and smooth, glossy periostracum.

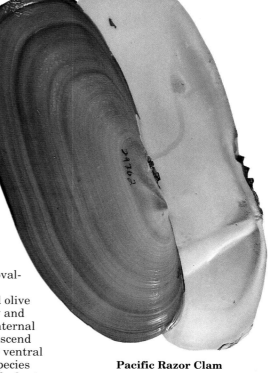

Squamate Razor Clam
3 in (7.5 cm)

Pacific Razor Clam,
Siliqua patula (Dixon, 1788).
Shell lightweight but strong, oval-oblong, laterally compressed. Periostracum varnish-like and olive green in colour. Interior glossy and whitish with a purple flush. Internal rib below the tiny cardinals descend obliquely towards the anterior ventral margin. An abundant edible species found in shallow water from Alaska to central California.

Pacific Razor Clam
5 in (13 cm)

Atlantic Jackknife Clam
9 in (22 cm)

Squamate Razor Clam,
Siliqua squamata Blainville, 1827.
With a prominent internal rib descending straight down towards the ventral margin. Dull white with a glossy periostracum with chestnut-brown concentric bands. Uncommon offshore from Newfoundland to Cape Cod.

Atlantic Jackknife Clam,
Ensis directus (Conrad, 1843).
Shell long, cylindrical, smooth, moderately curved and with sharp edges. Gapes widely at each end. Shell white, covered with a thin, varnish-like, brownish-green periostracum. Left valve has two very small vertical cardinals near the beak end, and each valve has a long, low, inconspicuous posterior lateral tooth. A common edible species living in sand burrows from southern Labrador to South Carolina.

Atlantic Razor Clam,
Siliqua costata Say, 1822.
Shell delicate, compressed, thin-shelled. Exterior with a shiny, greenish periostracum. Interior glossy, purplish white, with a strong white rib. Very common in shallow water in firm sand from the Gulf of St Lawrence to off North Carolina.

Atlantic Razor Clam
2 in (5 cm)

Narrow Jackknife Clam
4 in (10 cm)

Narrow Jackknife Clam,
Ensis ensis (Linnaeus, 1758).
Slightly bowed. Colour tan white with
reddish-brown blotches. Anterior end
rounded. Periostracum greenish brown
to yellowish green and glossy. Right
valve with one cardinal and two lateral
teeth; left valve with two cardinals and
two laterals. Fairly common in silty
sand from the intertidal zone down to
64 ft (20 m). Ranges from Norway to
the Mediterranean.

Blunt Jackknife Clam,
Solen sicarius Gould, 1850.
Shell elongate-rectangular, with very
slightly curved dorsal and ventral
margins. The anterior beak end is
obliquely truncate, and the posterior
end is rounded and slightly
compressed. *Solen* differs from *Ensis* in
having only a single tooth usually
located at the very anterior end of the
valve. Periostracum varnish-like and
olive greenish. Common on sandy mud
flats from British Columbia to
California.

Giant Razor Clam,
Ensis siliqua (Linnaeus, 1758).
Elongate-rectangular with rounded,
gaping ends and almost straight
margins. Beaks inconspicuous at the
anterior end. Colour white with reddish
streaks and blotches. Periostracum
dark green. Interior white with
purplish tints. This common species is
larger and stouter than the Narrow
Jackknife Clam. Occurs from Norway
to the Baltic and into the
Mediterranean.

Giant Razor Clam
8 in (20 cm)

Blunt Jackknife Clam
3.5 in (9 cm)

European Razor Clam
5 in (13 cm)

Pellucid Razor Clam,
Cultellus pellucidus (Pennant, 1777).
Shell brittle, beaks very small;
rectangular in outline with rounded
corners. Both ends gaping. Colour dull
white with a yellowish-green
periostracum. Right valve with one
cardinal; left valve with two cardinals.
Anterior muscle scar as long as the
ligament. Lives in muddy sand
between 13–393 ft (4–120 m). Common
from Norway to Portugal.

Pellucid Razor Clam
1 in (2.5 cm)

European Razor Clam,
Solen vagina Linnaeus, 1758.
With parallel margins; obliquely
truncate at the anterior end and
squarely rounded at the other end.
Colour yellowish with brownish growth
lines. Each valve has one cardinal but
no laterals. Synonym is *S. marginatus*
Montagu (and Pulteney). This species
is found just offshore where it burrows
into sandy bottoms. Ranges from
Norway into the Baltic and down into
the Mediterranean.

Tellins
(Family Tellinidae)

This worldwide family of bivalves is known for its very colourful shells with a simple architecture. Most are smooth, laterally compressed and rather thin-shelled. There is a slight twist at the posterior end. There are two small cardinal teeth, one of which is bifid.

Great Alaskan Tellin
3.5 in (9 cm)

Bodegas Tellin,
Tellina bodegensis Hinds, 1845. Narrowly elongate, laterally compressed, with the posterior end narrow and drawn out. Dorsal and ventral margins almost parallel. Pallial line long and narrow. Exterior with concentric threads. Fairly common from 3–98 ft (1–30 m) in sand from Canada to Mexico.

Great Alaskan Tellin,
Tellina lutea Wood, 1828. Shell strong, elongate-oval, quite compressed laterally and with a posterior twist to the right. Chalky white, commonly with a pink flush. Periostracum greenish brown. External ligament prominent. Pallial sinus three-quarters the length of the interior. Commonly found from 3–118 ft (1–36m) from Japan to Alaska and northern British Columbia.

Bodegas Tellin
2 in (5 cm)

Modest Tellin
0.8 in (2 cm)

Modest Tellin,
Tellina modesta Carpenter, 1864. Small and thin-shelled; compressed laterally, elongate and moderately pointed at the posterior lower corner. Surface white with an iridescent sheen and with fine concentric grooves. There is a well-formed radial rib inside just behind the anterior muscle scar. Common in sandy areas from shore to about 164 ft (50 m). Ranges from Alaska to Mexico.

Salmon Tellin,
Tellina nuculoides (Reeve, 1845). Small, oval, white with widely spaced growth lines. Interior with a rose tint. Ligament behind the beaks is prominent. Characterized by about four to seven prominent, concentric, former growth-stop lines which are usually stained dark brown. Common from low tide to offshore from the Aleutians to central California. Formerly called *Tellina salmonea* Carpenter, 1864.

Salmon Tellin
0.5 in (1 cm)

Story Tellin
0.7 in (2 cm)

Donax Tellin
1 in (2.5 cm)

Story Tellin,
Tellina fabula (Gmelin, 1791).
Shell small, elongate-oval, with the
posterior end pointed. Right valve
slightly more convex than the left.
Posterior end twisted towards the
right. Colour white or tinged with
yellow or orange. Periostracum
yellowish. Sculpture of concentric lines.
In the left valve diagonal lines cross
them. Pallial sinus deep, broad,
quadrate. Common in sand 3–164 ft
(1–50 m). Occurs from Norway to the
Black Sea and north-west Africa.

Donax Tellin,
Tellina donacina Linnaeus, 1758.
Shell small, thin-shelled but strong;
right valve slightly more convex than
the left one. External ligament large.
Colour grey to yellowish with pink
rays; sometimes all white. Sculpture of
many evenly spaced concentric ridges.
Interior pearly white with yellow or
pink blush. Pallial sinus scar almost
touches the anterior adductor muscle.
A common shallow-water species in
coarse sand from Orkney, south to the
Black Sea and Azores.

Fleshy Tellin
1 in (2.5 cm)

Balthica Macoma,
Macoma balthica (Linnaeus, 1758).
Shell fairly small, oval, moderately
compressed. Colour dull whitish,
sometimes flushed with pink.
Periostracum thin, grey and flakes off
when dry. Pallial sinus reaches half
way to anterior muscle scar in left
valve. An abundant intertidal and
offshore species in Arctic waters south
to estuaries in Norway to Portugal;
Greenland to off Georgia.

Fleshy Tellin,
Angulus incarnatus (Linnaeus, 1758).
Shell laterally compressed, oval-
elongate, with a rounded ventral
margin. Colour a uniform pink with a
narrow white radial ray at the
posterior, slightly pointed end. A
shallow-water sand-lover, mainly in the
Mediterranean but sometimes found
north to Portugal.

Balthica Macoma
1 in (2.5 cm)

Chalky Macoma,
Macoma calcarea (Gmelin, 1791).
Oval-elongate, moderately compressed,
but somewhat inflated at the larger
anterior end. Beaks three-fifths the
way towards the narrow, slightly
twisted posterior end. *Macoma* do not
have lateral teeth. Grey periostracum
usually worn away except at margins.
Pallial sinus in left valve does not
reach the anterior muscle scar. Much
shorter in right valve. A common cold-
water species found offshore in Arctic
waters from Greenland to New York,
and from the Bering Sea to Washington
State.

Chalky Macoma
2 in (5 cm)

Doleful Macoma
1.5 in (4 cm)

Thick Tellin
2.5 in (6.5 cm)

Thick Tellin,
Arcopagia crassa (Pennant, 1777).
Circular in outline; beaks almost in the
centre; somewhat compressed. Colour
dirty tan with the beaks tinged with
orange or pink radial rays. Exterior
with concentric ridges with fine
radiating lines showing between.
Common offshore from Norway to
Senegal.

Bent-nose Macoma,
Macoma nasuta (Conrad, 1837).
Rather compressed and strongly
twisted to the right at the posterior
end. Pallial sinus scar in the left valve
reaches the anterior muscle scar.
External ligament large and black. A
very common Pacific coast species
living in mud in quiet waters from
shore to 164 ft (50 m); southern Alaska
to Mexico.

Queen Charlotte Macoma
1 in (2.5 cm)

Bent-nose Macoma
3 in (7.5 cm)

Queen Charlotte Macoma,
Macoma carlottensis Whiteaves, 1880.
Shell extremely fragile, inflated and
with a very short, external,
inconspicuous ligament. Pallial sinus
large, rounded at its extremity, and
reaching beyond the centre of the
valve. Colour translucent white with a
thin, glossy periostracum. Common
offshore. Ranges from Alaska to
Mexico.

Doleful Macoma,
Macoma moesta (Deshayes, 1855).
Shell ovate, inflated, with the beaks
two-thirds the way back from the
larger rounded end. Periostracum
yellowish olive. Posterior end short,
slightly angular, and finely wrinkled at
the angle. Pallial sinus rounded,
smaller in right valve. Common
offshore in muddy areas. Arctic Seas;
Greenland and Alaska.

Tenta Macoma
0.8 in (2 cm)

Tenta Macoma,
Macoma tenta (Say, 1837).
Shell oval-elongate, somewhat
compressed, rather fragile. Colour
white with a delicate iridescence on the
smooth exterior. Posterior end slightly
twisted to the left. Interior glossy
white, tinted with yellow and with fine
radiating lines, which produce a finely
serrated margin. Two diverging
cardinals in the right valve, a single
one in the left. A common shallow-
water species from Cape Cod to Florida
and to Brazil.

Fouled Macoma,
Macoma inquinata (Deshayes, 1855).
Shell oval-elongate, moderately
inflated, very slightly twisted at the
posterior end. Pallial sinus in left valve
almost reaches the bottom of the
anterior muscle scar. Colour chalky
white. Periostracum grey with fine
concentric growth lines. Posterior
ventral margin has a weak
embayment. A moderately common
offshore clam ranging from Japan and
the Bering Sea to off southern
California.

Fouled Macoma
2 in (5 cm)

Brota Macoma,
Macoma brota Dall, 1916.
Shell moderately elongate, moderately
inflated and rather thick-shelled.
Beaks two-thirds towards the posterior
end. This is fairly common in shallow
water and is one of the largest of the
Pacific Coast macomas. Ranges from
the Arctic Ocean to Puget Sound,
Washington.

Brota Macoma
3 in (7.5 cm)

Flat Tellin
2.5 in (6.5 cm)

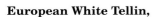

European White Tellin
1.5 in (4 cm)

European White Tellin,
Angulus albicans (Gmelin, 1791).
Shell solid, brittle, elongate-oval.
Beaks small and central. Posterior end
pointed with a straight dorsal margin.
Anterior end wider and more rounded.
Pallial sinus very large and long.
Concentric sculpture of microscopically
incised lines, more prominent at the
larger anterior end. Growth lines of
different shades of cream or grey are
prominent. A shallow-water, fairly
common species ranging from the
Iberian Peninsula into the
Mediterranean.

Flat Tellin,
Angulus planatus (Linnaeus, 1758).
Shell fairly large, compressed, oval in
outline. Beaks slightly nearer the
larger evenly rounded anterior end.
Exterior white, smoothish, with weak
concentric scratches and colour growth
lines. Hinge without lateral teeth.
Pallial sinus large. Narrower posterior
end with two weak, rounded radial
ridges. Periostracum thin and
brownish. Found on sand bars at low
tide from Portugal to West Africa and
the Mediterranean.

White Sand Macoma
3.5 in (9 cm)

White Sand Macoma,
Macoma secta (Conrad, 1837).
Shell large, with an almost flat left
valve, a rather inflated right valve and
a wide and short ligament which is
sunk partially into the shell. There is a
large, oblique rib-like extension just
behind the hinge inside each valve.
Common in sand in bays and intertidal
flats from British Columbia to Mexico.

Yoldia-shaped Macoma,
Macoma yoldiformis Carpenter, 1864.
Shell fairly small, oval-elongate,
compressed laterally, moderately
rounded at each end with a small but
distinct twist to the right at the
posterior end. Colour a uniform glossy
porcelaneous white. Rarely translucent
with an opalescent sheen. Common on
sandy intertidal flats down to 164 ft
(50 m). Ranges from Alaska to southern
California.

Yoldia-shaped Macoma
0.6 in (1.3 cm)

Wedge Clams
(Family Donacidae)

Members of this worldwide family are small wedge clams or coquina clams, unique in their preference for a habitat along wave-dashed, sandy beaches. Water intake through their two long siphons is possible only during the interval when waves are dashing up or down the slope of the beach. Uprooted wedge clams quickly burrow back below the sand surface as the water recedes. They usually occur in large colonies and are fed upon by sandpipers and other shorebirds. In the cooler, more northerly parts of their distribution adults are killed off by severe winters. Floating larvae from the south replenish the colonies in the spring. The shells are wedge-shaped. The hinge has two cardinals and an anterior and a posterior lateral tooth in each valve.

Coquina 0.5 in (1 cm)

Banded Wedge-clam
1.2 in (3 cm)

Banded Wedge-clam,
Donax vittatus (da Costa, 1778). Shell wedge-shaped, elongate-triangular. Anterior end triangular; posterior end rounded, its dorsal margin straight. Exterior smoothish, except for fine, evenly spaced, incised radiating lines. Interior white and stained with purple, rarely orange. Pallial sinus deep. Margins coarsely crenulate. Found in sand on beaches down to 64 ft (20 m). Rare in Norway; more common south to the Mediterranean.

Coquina,
Donax variablis Say, 1822. Shell small, wedge-shaped. Ventral margin of the valves straight and almost parallel with the dorsal margin. The more compressed anterior end is commonly smoother. Internal margin of the valves minutely denticulate. Colour very variable and usually bright. In warm waters shells may be bright orange, reddish or purplish, but from Maryland north the colour is dull white with purplish rays. Ranges from New York to southern Florida and to Texas.

Truncate Wedge-clam,
Donax trunculus Linnaeus, 1758. Shell wedge-shaped, similar to the Banded Wedge-clam, but with a shorter, more rounded anterior end. Right valve without lateral teeth. Posterior margin smooth within, but serrated at the anterior end. Colour tan with radial rays of purplish. Periostracum glossy, translucent tan. Interior white with purple-brown stains. Occurs on sand flats and down to 228 ft (70 m) from Portugal to the Black Sea.

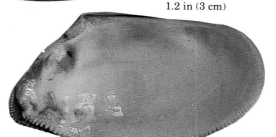

Truncate Wedge-clam
1.2 in (3 cm)

Sunset Clams
(Family Psammobiidae)

These fairly large clams resemble the tellin clams but are generally larger, with purple and reddish colours, and with a large, external ligament that is attached to a prominent shelly ridge. No lateral teeth. Pallial sinus is large.

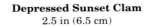

Depressed Sunset Clam
2.5 in (6.5 cm)

Depressed Sunset Clam,
Gari depressa (Pennant, 1777). Shell solid, evenly elongate, with the beaks almost at the centre. Right valve a little more convex. Colour cream with purplish rays. Periostracum thick and greenish brown. Lives in coarse sand in 3–164 ft (1–50 m). Ranges from the North Sea to West Africa.

Californian Sunset Clam,
Gari californica (Conrad, 1849). Elongate-oval, fairly strong; the low beaks are nearer the anterior end. Sculpture of strong, irregular concentric growth lines. Colour dirty white with faint, narrow radial rays of purple. Periostracum brownish. Common from 3–164 ft (1–50 m), and often washed ashore after storms. Ranges from the Aleutians to California.

Faroes Sunset Clam
2 in (5 cm)

Faroes Sunset Clam,
Gari fervensis (Gmelin, 1791). Elongate, with the posterior and narrower end bearing a rounded keel. Surface has crowded concentric threads. Colour of variable purples and brownish pinks with a few rays. Common offshore from Norway to West Africa.

Tellin-like Sunset Clam,
Gari tellinella (Lamarck, 1818). Shell small, solid, oval-elongate in outline. Colour whitish cream with tints of orange, red or purplish. Periostracum very thin. Ligament brown. Sculpture of fine concentric and radiating lines. Growth stoppages evident. Right valve with two bifid cardinals. No lateral teeth. A common shallow-water clam found from Iceland and Norway to the Mediterranean.

Tellin-like Sunset Clam
1 in (2.5 cm)

Tagelus Razor Clams
(Family Solecurtidae)

These shallow water-, sometimes brackish water-dwelling clams in the genera *Pharus, Solecurtus* and *Tagelus* usually live in mud and communicate with the water above by means of two separate siphons. Most have conspicuous periostracum. The shells are elongate-quadrate and widely gaping at both ends. The hinge plate is weak and narrow, with one or two small cardinal teeth under the beaks. Pallial sinus well developed. Many species are tropical but a few live in temperate waters.

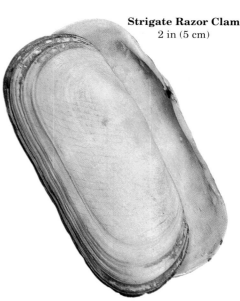

Strigate Razor Clam
2 in (5 cm)

Bean Razor Clam
5 in (13 cm)

Strigate Razor Clam,
Solecurtus strigillatus (Linnaeus, 1758).
Quadrate in shape; gaping at both ends; hinge plate weak and narrow. The right valve has two strong, horizontally jutting cardinal teeth just under the centrally located beaks. Left valve with one cardinal. Exterior with numerous obliquely set incised lines. A shallow-water, sand-living clam from the Mediterranean and north to southern France.

Bean Razor Clam,
Pharus legumen (Linnaeus, 1758).
Shell elongate-cylindrical, brittle, with the inconspicuous beaks almost centrally located. Both ends gaping and rounded. Colour yellowish white with a yellowish-green periostracum. Ligament prominent, external and dark brown. Right valve with a tiny vertical cardinal and one long ridge-like anterior lateral and a short projecting posterior lateral. White rib inside. Pallial sinus short. Common from Norway to the Mediterranean.

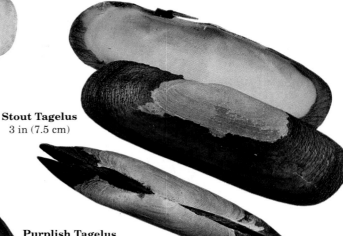

Stout Tagelus
3 in (7.5 cm)

Purplish Tagelus
1.5 in (4 cm)

Purplish Tagelus,
Tagelus divisus (Spengler, 1794).
Elongate, sub-cylindrical, fragile and smooth. The valves are reinforced internally by a very weak radial rib. Colour of shell whitish purple, covered externally with a very thin, brown, glossy periostracum. A common shallow-water species on sand flats from Massachusetts to Brazil.

Stout Tagelus,
Tagelus plebeius (Lightfoot, 1786).
Oblong, sub-cylindrical, rather inflated, rounded posteriorly, obliquely truncate anteriorly. Hinge with two small projecting cardinal teeth, with a large bulbous callus just behind them. Exterior smoothish, with tiny irregular scratches. Periostracum brownish yellow. Moderately common below the surface of sand flats. Ranges from Cape Cod to Texas and to Brazil.

Furrow Clams
(Family Scrobiculariidae)

Shells of medium size, usually white, resembling the Semele Clams in having an oblique resilium buried within the hinge, but they lack lateral teeth. The posterior end is usually not bent to one side. The *Abra* clams were previously placed in the family Semelidae.

White Abra Clam
0.8 in (2 cm)

Flat Furrow Clam
2.5 in (6.5 cm)

White Abra Clam,
Abra alba (Wood, 1815).
Shell small, white, brittle, broadly oval; posterior with a slight twist to the right. Hinge weak and narrow, with the narrow, brown internal ligament in a grooved, triangular chondrophore. Pallial sinus large. Common in mud or muddy gravel from low-tide mark to 216 ft (66 m). Ranges from Norway to the Black Sea and to Senegal.

Flat Furrow Clam
Scrobicularia plana (da Costa, 1778).
Shell almost round in outline; compressed; with the beaks almost at the centre. Colour greyish brown or light yellow. Internal ligament large, obliquely slanting and set in the chondrophore. This intertidal clam lives from Norway south to Senegal.

Semele Clams
(Family Semelidae)

Most semele clams are sturdy and oval in shape, with a slight posterior bend. The resilium is elongate and set inside the hinge at an oblique angle in a small chondrophore. Hinge with two cardinal and one or two lateral teeth. The pallial sinus is large and rounded. The family is worldwide in distribution with the most colourful species living in tropical waters.

Californian Cumingia
1.2 in (3 cm)

Rose Petal Semele,
Semele rubropicta Dall, 1871.
The black resilium is in an oblique gutter which is buried in the hinge. Shell oval-elongate, with the beaks nearer the front end. Has irregular growth lines and many radial incised lines. Colour chalky grey to tan with faint rays of light mauve. Interior glossy white, with mauve at both ends of the hinge. Uncommon offshore. Ranges from Alaska to Mexico.

Rose Petal Semele
1.5 in (4 cm)

Californian Cumingia,
Cumingia californica Conrad, 1837.
Shell strong, elongate-oval, moderately compressed. Resilium internal and supported by a spoon-shaped chondrophore. One cardinal and two elongate lateral teeth in each valve. Pallial sinus large and long. A small, elongate depression is in front of the umbones. Concentric sculpture of numerous wavy, sharp threads. Colour greyish white. Abundant in rock crevices and wharf pilings from northern California to Mexico.

Bark Semele
2.5 in (6.5 cm)

Bark Semele,
Semele decisa **(Conrad, 1837).**
Shell strong, heavy, oval in outline, with coarse, wide, irregular concentric folds on the outer surface, resembling rotting bark. Colour yellowish grey; interior glossy white, with a purple tinge, especially prominent on the hinge and margins. Commonly found in rocky rubble in shallow water from northern California to north-west Mexico.

Oxheart Clams
(Families Glossidae and Arcticidae)

Popular as a food and desired by shell collectors, the Oxheart Clam is the only member of this strange family of bivalves in the northern hemisphere. The beaks are strongly curled in, and there is no lunule nor any pallial sinus scar.

Oxheart Clam
3 in (7.5 cm)

Oxheart Clam,
Glossus humanus (Linnaeus, 1758). Shell medium-sized, solid, globular, without any gape, and with strongly enrolled, swollen beaks. Ligament brown and external. Sculpture of fine concentric and radial lines. Exterior tan, sometimes with reddish streaks. Periostracum greenish brown. A common offshore species ranging from Iceland and Norway to the Mediterranean.

Ocean Quahog,
Arctica islandica (Linnaeus, 1767). Oval in outline, moderately inflated. Colour yellowish to brown; periostracum thick and chestnut-brown. No pallial sinus. A common edible hard-shell clam ranging from Iceland to France; Labrador to off North Carolina. This offshore clam is commercially fished in New England. In the family Arcticidae.

Ocean Quahog
4 in (10 cm)

False Mussels
(Family Dreissenidae)

Among the advanced families of bivalves, such as the tellin and venus clams, are found the curious false mussels that secondarily have taken on the shape and habits of the more primitive Mytilidae mussels. However, the interior of the shell is not nacreous and there are two well-developed siphons. The beak cavity is bridged by a shelf, or myophore. The posterior adductor muscle scar is long. Members of this family may live in salt, brackish or fresh water. Some species have spread throughout various parts of the world and have become a nuisance by clogging drainage pipes and water purification plants.

Zebra Mussel
1 in (2.5 cm)

Zebra Mussel,
Dreissena polymorpha (Pallas, 1771). Shell shaped like a *Mytilus* mussel. Anterior muscle attached to a shelf-like platform in the apical region. Byssus strong. Colour tan with dark zebra stripes. Common in freshwater bodies in Europe and now in the Great Lakes of United States where it is becoming a nuisance by clogging drainage pipes.

Conrad's False Mussel,
Mytilopsis leucophaeata (Conrad, 1831).
Superficially resembling a small *Mytilus* mussel because of its shape. The small shelly shelf at the small beak end has a tiny, downwardly projecting, triangular tooth on the side facing the long internal ligament. The hinge has a long thin bar under the ligament. Exterior bluish brown to tan with a thin somewhat glossy periostracum. Interior a dirty bluish-tan. This common bivalve attaches itself by its short byssus to rocks and twigs in clumps which resemble colonies of mussels. It is found in brackish to freshwater near river from New York to Texas and east Mexico.

Conrad's False Mussel
0.8 in (2 cm)

Venus Clams
(Family Veneridae)

This is a large and diverse family used extensively for food in many parts of the world. Many have colourful patterns and intricate sculpturing. The strong ovate shells have beaks that curl forward. There are usually three cardinal teeth in each valve and one or two laterals. The pallial sinus is usually large.

Chicken Venus
1.5 in (4 cm)

Warty Venus
2.5 in (6.5 cm)

Chamber Venus
2 in (5 cm)

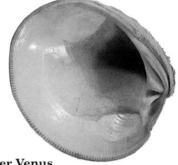

Chicken Venus,
Chamelea gallina (Linnaeus, 1758).
Shell solid, oval, similar in outline to the Warty Venus. Exterior has numerous, crowded, concentric cords or threads, but with no radial sculpture. Cardinal teeth not bifid. Colour cream with numerous, fine, brownish, V-shaped markings and three or four faint radial rays of tan. Interior white with purple blotches at the posterior end. Pallial sinus very short. A warm-water species mainly limited to the Mediterranean and Black Sea in shallow, sandy areas.

Chamber Venus
Circomphalus casinus (Linnaeus, 1758)
Circular in outline and with numerous, smooth, raised concentric ridges. Colour whitish tan, sometimes with reddish-brown rays. Inner margin of valves crenulate. Pallial sinus short and triangular. A common offshore species ranging from Norway to Senegal.

Warty Venus
Venus verrucosa Linnaeus, 1758.
Circular in outline and rather swollen. Colour greyish white to brownish cream. Periostracum brown but usually worn away. Lunules broad, heart-shaped, brown, with fine radiating threads. Eschutcheon prominent in the left valve. Pallial sinus small and triangular. A common edible clam found in shallow water from the British Isles to the Mediterranean and Canary Islands.

Northern Quahog
4 in (10 cm)

Northern Quahog or **Hardshell Clam,**
Mercenaria mercenaria (Linnaeus, 1758).
Ovate-trigonal, inflated. Exterior grey with fine growth threads. Centre of valves are smoothish. Interior white with purple stains. A common edible clam found in shallow water from Quebec to Texas. Introduced to California and England.

Common Pacific Littleneck,
Protothaca staminea (Conrad, 1837)
Solid, subovate, laterally compressed,
beaks nearer the anterior end.
Sculpture of fine concentric and radial
riblets which form beads at the anterior
end of the shell. Radial riblets stronger
on the middle of the valves. Lunule
feeble; eschutcheon absent. Colour
rusty brown with a purplish cast. This
common, edible, shallow-water clam is
quite variable in sculpturing and
colouring. Ranges from the Aleutians to
Mexico.

Common Pacific Littleneck
2 in (5 cm)

Filipino Venus
2 in (5 cm)

Decussate Venus
2 in (5 cm)

Rhomboidal Venus
1.5 in (4 cm)

Filipino Venus or **Japanese
Littleneck,**
Ruditapes philippinarum (Adams and
Reeve, 1850).
Subovate, laterally compressed, with
beaks nearer the anterior end. Lunule
smooth and incised. Eschutcheon
smooth and bordered by a low ridge.
With radial threads, those at posterior
end beaded. Interior purplish. This
eastern Asian species was introduced to
Puget Sound and California.

Decussate Venus or **Carpet-shell,**
Venerupis decussata (Linnaeus, 1758)
Broadly oval, with numerous radial
riblets crossed by fine concentric
growth lines. Colours of greys, yellows
and browns, sometimes with rays and
streaks. Interior glossy white with an
orange tinge, rarely purplish. Pallial
sinus deep. Margin smooth. Common
in shallow water from Norway to
Mediterranean.

Rhomboidal Venus,
Venerupis rhomboides (Pennant, 1777).
Shell ovate-elliptical with the beaks
nearer the rounded, anterior end. Both
cardinal teeth are bifid. Lateral teeth
absent. Sculpture of numerous, fine,
rounded, concentric threads. Colour
cream with a profusion of light-brown
freckles and rays. Pallial sinus one-
third the length of the shell. Common
offshore from Norway to the
Mediterranean.

Chione Venus,
Callista chione (Linnaeus, 1758).
Shell solid, polished, broadly ovate in
outline. Beaks nearer the anterior end.
Ligament prominent, reaching halfway
to the posterior end of the shell. Lunule
clearly defined, heart-shaped and with
a slightly elevated centre. Eschutcheon
absent. Exterior smoothish, except for
weak growth lines. Three cardinal
teeth in each valve, with a strong
anterior lateral in the left valve. Inside
of shell whitish; adductor muscle scars
are highly polished. Pallial sinus broad
and deep. An attractive clam found just
offshore in clean sand, from the British
Isles to the Mediterranean.

Chione Venus
3.5 in (9 cm)

Morrhua Venus
1 in (2.5 cm)

Smooth Washington Clam
3 in (7.5 cm)

Morrhua Venus,
Pitar morrhuanus Linsley, 1848.
Shell small, obese, oval-elongate, with
a large, elongate lunule. Beaks large
and towards the anterior end. Anterior
left lateral fits into a well-developed
socket in the right valve. Middle left
cardinal large; posterior right cardinal
bifid. Exterior dull grey to brownish
red, with numerous heavy lines of
growth. This is a fairly common
offshore clam ranging from the Gulf of
St Lawrence to off North Carolina
where it serves as an important food
for bottom fish.

Smooth Washington Clam,
Saxidomus gigantea (Deshayes, 1839).
Solid, oblong, heavy, with fairly coarse,
crowded concentric threads and fine
growth stoppages. Valves gape slightly
at the back end. Hinge with four or five
cardinal teeth in the right valve, four
in the left. Pallial sinus long and fairly
narrow. No lunule. Ligament large.
Colour greyish white. A common food
clam in Alaska. Extends southwards to
northern California.

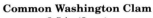

Common Washington Clam
3.5 in (9 cm)

Pismo Clam
4 in (10 cm)

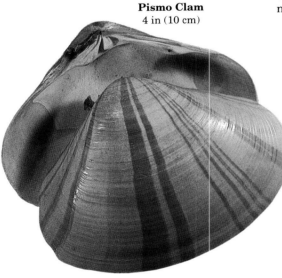

Wolf Dosinia
1.5 in (4 cm)

Pismo Clam,
Tivela stultorum (Mawe, 1823).
Shell heavy, ovate, moderately inflated,
glossy-smooth except for weak lines of
growth. Ligament large and strong.
Four cardinal teeth in each valve.
Colour brownish cream with wide,
mauve radial rays. Periostracum glossy
and thin. Lunule lanceolate and with
vertical scratches. A common, edible
shore species mainly found from
California to Mexico.

Wolf Dosinia,
Dosinia lupinus (Poli, 1791).
Shell solid, circular in outline,
moderately compressed. Beaks in front
of the mid-line. Ligament deeply inset.
Lunule short, heart-shaped and with
fine radial ridges. Sculpture of fine
concentric ridges crossed by faint
radiating lines. Three cardinal teeth in
each valve. Pallial sinus triangular,
deep. Margin smooth. Lives in sand
and silty mud offshore from Iceland to
the Mediterranean.

Common Washington Clam,
Saxidomus nuttalli (Conrad, 1837).
Shell solid, oblong, with the beaks
nearer the anterior end. Exterior with
coarse, crowded, concentric riblets.
Colour a dull, dirty, reddish brown to
grey with rust stains. Interior glossy
white, commonly with a flush of purple
at the posterior margins. No lunule.
Ligament large. Valves slightly gaping
posteriorly. A very common, edible
species, also called the 'butter clam'.
Ranges in shallow water from northern
California to Baja California.

Mature Dosinia,
Dosinia exoleta (Linnaeus, 1758).
Shell circular and laterally compressed.
Similar to the Wolf Dosinia, but the lunule is flatter, the valves are flatter, the pallial sinus is larger and broader and the exterior is not as glossy. The colour is light brown, with numerous fine, radial, reddish-brown streaks, usually accumulating at former growth stoppages. The clam occurs from the intertidal zone down to about 230 ft (70 m) of water. It has a wide range, from Norway to Portugal, and the Mediterranean, south to Senegal.

Mature Dosinia
2 in (5 cm)

Milky Pacific Venus
1.5 in (4 cm)

Kennerley's Venus,
Humilaria kennerleyi (Reeve, 1863).
Shell fairly large, elongate-oval, laterally compressed. Beaks near the smaller anterior end. Exterior with sharp, neatly spaced, concentric ribs whose edges are bent upwards. Colour and texture resembles grey Portland cement. Margin of shell finely crenulate. A fairly common collectors' item occurring offshore from 20–98 ft (6–30 m) from Alaska to northern California.

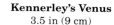

Kennerley's Venus
3.5 in (9 cm)

Milky Pacific Venus,
Compsomyax subdiaphana (Carpenter, 1864).
Shell small, thin-shelled, but strong, elongate-oval and moderately inflated. Beaks anterior and pointing forward. Colour chalky white. Sculpture of fine, irregular concentric lines of growth. Three cardinal teeth in each valve, the most posterior one in the right valve being deeply split. Dredged in soft mud from 32–164 ft (10–50 m). Ranges from Alaska to Mexico.

Wavy Mysia Clam
1.5 in (4 cm)

Wavy Mysia Clam,
Mysia undata (Pennant, 1777).
Shell roundish in outline, thin, fragile, with beaks near the mid-line. Colour light yellow. Periostracum transparent. Pallial sinus deep, extending two-thirds of the way towards the beaks. Exterior with fine, irregular concentric growth lines. Burrows in sandy mud and gravel offshore from Norway to the Mediterranean and the Canary Islands.

Amethyst Gem Clam
0.2 in (5 mm)

Amethyst Gem Clam,
Gemma gemma (Totten, 1834).
Shell very small, subtrigonal, moderately inflated and rather thin-shelled. Exterior whitish tan and purplish, and with numerous fine concentric furrows. This common, sand-dwelling, shallow-water clam may be sieved in large quantities in sheltered bays. It is a major food of aquatic birds and small fish. It ranges from Nova Scotia to Texas and the Bahamas.

Rock-borers
(Family Petricolidae)

This family is very diverse in shape, and usually white and elongate. They bore into peat, clay, wood and rocks. The confined habitats often cause malformed individuals. There is no lunule or escutcheon, and the hinge is without lateral teeth. There are three cardinal teeth in the left valve and two in the right. The pallial sinus is well developed.

Rock-eater Clam,
Petricola lithophaga (Retzius, 1786). Shell thick, oblong-oval, chalky white with coarse, raised, wavy radial ribs especially pronounced at the posterior end. Pallial sinus short. Bores completely within soft chalky rock. Moderately common from the English Channel south into the Mediterranean and Black Sea.

Rock-eater Clam
1 in (2.5 cm)

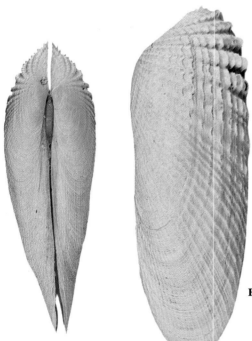

False Angel Wing
2 in (5 cm)

False Angel Wing, or American Piddock,
Petricola pholadiformis (Lamarck, 1818).
Shell elongate, rather fragile and chalky white. Has numerous radial ribs; the anterior ten or so are larger and bear prominent scales. Ligament external and located just posterior to the beaks. Cardinal teeth quite long and pointed. Siphons translucent grey, large, tubular and separated from each other almost to their bases. A very common clay and peat-moss borer. Rarely in limestone in Europe. Frequents estuaries. Ranges from the Gulf of St Lawrence to Texas and south to Uruguay; introduced to western Europe.

Hearty Rupellaria,
Rupellaria carditoides (Conrad, 1837). Oblong-ovate, obese, solid, pure white. Variable in shape because it bores into hard rock. Exterior chalky greyish-white with coarse, irregular, concentric growth lines. Radial sculpture of peculiar, fine, scratched lines crowded together. No lunule or escutcheon. Hinge without lateral teeth. Three cardinals in the left valve; two in right valve. Pallial sinus well developed. Nepionic shell at beak is oblong. Common in rocks in shallow water from Vancouver Island to Baja California, Mexico.

Hearty Rupellaria
1.5 in (4 cm)

Saxicave Clams
(Family Hiatellidae)

These misshapen, unattractive clams vary from the large, foot-long (30 cm) *Panopea* clams to the small quadrate Arctic Saxicave clams which have the habit of nestling or burrowing into constricted crevices. The shells are usually dirty-white and with one or two weak teeth in the hinge. The pallial sinus is well developed. Most live in temperate or Arctic waters. Large members of the genus *Panopea* occur on both sides of the Atlantic, the Mediterranean and New Zealand. Some are used extensively for food, and in north-west United States they are called 'gooeyducks'.

Arctic Saxicave
2 in (5 cm)

Arctic Saxicave,
Hiatella arctica (Linnaeus, 1767).
Shell chalky white, oblong, usually somewhat misshapen because it bores into rocks and small boulders. No definite teeth in the thickened hinge of adults. Pallial line discontinuous. Periostracum grey and thin. Sometimes has a radial rib at the posterior end, which may bear scales. Common also in kelp holdfasts and rock crevices subtidally. Arctic Seas to California; Labrador to Uruguay; Norway to the Mediterranean and Azores.

Northern Propeller Clam
2.5 in (6.5 cm)

Northern Propeller Clam,
Cyrtodaria siliqua (Spengler, 1793).
Oblong, gapes at both ends, chalky white with a thick flaky periostracum. Strong wide ligament is external. Hinge is a simple bar with a fairly bulbous swelling under the ligament. Moderately common offshore and often found in fish stomachs. Ranges from Labrador to Rhode Island.

Arctic Panomya,
Panomya arctica (Lamarck, 1818).
Squarish in outline; looks like a
misshapen *Mya* clam, but lacks teeth
and a chondrophore in the hinge, and
has a coarse, flaky, light-brown
periostracum. Characterized by oblong
or oval, sunk-in muscle and pallial line
scars. Common in mud in cold waters
offshore. Lives in Arctic seas to Alaska
and off Maryland.

Arctic Panomya
2.5 (6.5 cm)

Ample Rough Mya,
Panomya ampla Dall, 1898.
Shell fairly large, oblong, heavy and
peculiarly distorted with wide gaping
at both ends. Anterior end somewhat
pointed; posterior broadly truncate,
with three to six depressed scars on the
white interior. Exterior concentrically
roughened, ash-white, with a border of
thick, irregular, black periostracum.
Hinge without teeth. Uncommon
offshore from the Aleutian Islands to
Point Barrow, Alaska.

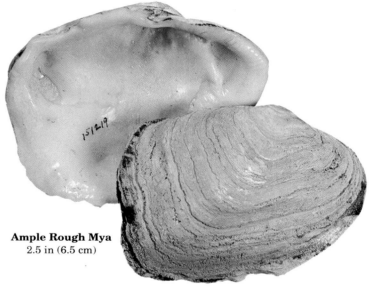

Ample Rough Mya
2.5 in (6.5 cm)

Geoduck
9 in (22 cm)

Geoduck (goo-ee-duck),
Panopea abrupta (Conrad, 1849).
Shell large, inflated, elongate, thick-
shelled and gaping at both ends.
Coarse, concentric wavy lines
especially noticeable near the small,
central, depressed beaks. Periostracum
thin and yellowish. Exterior dirty white
to cream; interior semi-glossy white.
Hinge with a single, large, horizontal
thickening. The two long, grey, united
siphons of the animal are half the
weight of the entire clam. Common in
mud 2–3 feet (60–90 cm) deep. An
edible species, raw or cooked. Ranges
from Alaska to the Gulf of California,
but commercially fished in Washington
and Oregon.

Sand-gapers or Soft-shell Clams

(Family Myidae)

California Softshell Clam
1.2 in (3 cm)

The gapers, or soft-shell clams, are popular seafood in the northern hemisphere, both in the New World and Old World. The chalky white shells are easily broken. The valves gape at the posterior end where a long, fused pair of siphons extend. The resilium is internal and rests upon a horizontally projecting chondrophore in the left valve.

California Softshell Clam,
Cryptomya californica (Conrad, 1837).
Shell small, fragile, oval, moderately obese. Right valve fatter. Right beak crowds slightly over that of the left valve. Posterior gape very small. Chondrophore in left valve is large and tucks against a small concave shelf under the right beak. Exterior chalky white. Periostracum grey and radially striped at the posterior end. Common in sand. Sometimes its siphons protrude into the water-filled burrows of other marine animals. Ranges from Alaska to Northern Peru.

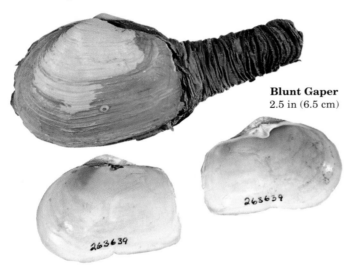

Blunt Gaper
2.5 in (6.5 cm)

263639

263639

Boring Softshell Clam,
Platyodon cancellatus (Conrad, 1837).
Shell solid, oblong and obese. Posterior gapes widely. Exterior chalky white, with a thin, brownish to rusty periostracum, and numerous clapboard-like, concentric growth lines. Chondrophore in left valve quite thick and arched. Lives in hard-packed clay or soft sandstone. Ranges from central British Columbia to southern California.

Blunt Gaper, or **Truncate Soft-shell Clam,**
Mya truncata Linnaeus, 1758.
Shell similar to the Sand-gaper, but smaller, abruptly truncate at the posterior siphonal end. A common Arctic species found offshore south to Massachusetts, Portugal, Washington State and Japan.

Sand-gaper
4 in (10 cm)

Sand-gaper, or **Soft-shell Clam,**
Mya arenaria Linnaeus, 1758.
Shell chalky, brittle, elliptical, oblong, and gaping at the posterior end. Colour white to greyish, with a thin grey to straw periostracum. Chondrophore in left valve is long, spoon-shaped and shallow. An abundant, intertidal, mud- or sand-flat species. It has a wide range from southern Labrador to off North Carolina; from Norway to France and from Alaska to California.

Boring Softshell Clam
2.5 in (6.5 cm)

Corbula or Basket Clams
(Family Corbulidae)

These small sturdy clams are unusual in that the left valve is much flatter and smaller than the right one. The centre of the hinge bears a small black resilifer which sits inside a projecting, tooth-like chondrophore. Most species have concentric sculpturing. They live from shallow to deep water where the bottom is sandy or muddy.

Swift's Corbula 0.3 in (7 mm)

Common Basket-shell
0.5 in (1 cm)

Common Basket-shell, or Fat Corbula,
Corbula gibba (Olivi, 1792).
Shell small, solid, with the right valve deeper and larger than the left one which fits into it. Left valve with chondrophore and a deep triangular pit. Pallial sinus absent. Colour cream, with a brownish periostracum. An abundant shallow-water species ranging from Norway to the Mediterranean and to West Africa.

Swift's Corbula,
Corbula swiftiana C. B. Adams, 1852.
Shell, small, strong, oblong, moderately obese; right valve larger, more obese and overlapping the left valve at the ventral posterior region. Posterior slope in the right valve bounded by two radial ridges, one of which is close to the margin of the valve. The left valve has only one ridge. Exterior of valves with irregular, concentric ridges. Colour whitish with a thin yhellow periostracum. Common offshore from about 32–3937 ft (10–1200 m) from New England to Texas and the West Indies.

Piddocks
(Family Pholadidae)

Angel Wing
6 in (15 cm)

This is a large and diversified family of wood- and mud-boring clams found throughout the world. Many large species live in soft mud or peat, while the smaller *Martesia* clams do great damage to wooden wharf pilings and boats. The siphons are long and usually welded together and encased in a single muscular tube. Most have white, delicate shells without hinge teeth, but may have several accessory shelly plates. Inside the valves may be one or two apophyses, or finger-like shelly projections, extending from beneath the beaks to which the foot muscles are attached.

Wart-necked Piddock
3 in (7.5 cm)

Wart-necked Piddock,
Chaceia ovoidea (Gould, 1851).
Shell oblong, very obese, divided by an oblique sulcus in the middle of each valve with the anterior half bearing the beaks and internal, shelly apophysis, with its anterior gape partially closed by a smooth shelly callum. Periostracum thin, yellowish. Siphons very large, warty and with elongate, brownish-orange chitinous patches. Lives in soft shale rock below low tide mark. Ranges from California to Mexico.

Angel Wing,
Cyrtopleura costata (Linnaeus, 1758).
Shell elongate, thin-shelled but strong, pure-white with a thin grey periostracum. Has about 30 well-developed, beaded axial ribs which bear scales at the anterior end of the valve. A thin, external, chitinous triangular pad or 'protoplax' fits over the beaks, as well as a heavy, calcareous, butterfly-shaped 'mesoplax'. Inside and under each beak is a shelly, spoon-shaped 'apophysis'. The siphons are long and united. This mud-dweller is rare north of Virginia, but common in shallow water in south-eastern United States.

Paper Piddock,
Pholadidea loscombiana Turton, 1819.
Shell fragile, elongate-oval, divided into two regions by the umbonal-ventral sulcus. Cup-shaped siphonoplax thin, chitinous. Gaping anterior end may be sealed over by a smooth bulbous callum. Tooth-like apophyses are small, fragile and project from beneath the umbones. Large chondrophore in left valve, smaller one in right valve. Two mesoplax plates small, triangular. Edge of wide gape is serrated. Pallial sinus broad and deep. Common in clay, peat and sandstone in British Isles and coast of France.

Paper Piddock
1 in (2.5 cm)

European Piddock,
Pholas dactylus Linnaeus, 1758.
Shell brittle, elongate, gaping at both
ends; umbones near the anterior end
and covered with two elongate,
separate, calcareous protoplax plates.
On the back edge is the small central
mesoplax, and behind that is the long,
narrow, calcareous metaplax plate.
Within the valve and under the
umbonal reflection is the long, narrow,
projecting apophysis. Anterior end of
valve has about 40 spined radiating
ribs. Remainder of valve has concentric
ridges. Pallial sinus scar wide and
shallow. Bores into many subtidal
substrates, including peat, wood, shale
and sandstone. Ranges from Norway to
the Black Sea and from Labrador to
Delaware.

European Piddock
5 in (13 cm)

Gabb's Piddock
2 in (5 cm)

Striate Martesia,
Martesia striata (Linnaeus, 1758).
Variable in shape, usually pear-shaped,
producing a round, smooth callum over
the wide foot-gape in the adult.
Posterior end compressed and rounded
in outline. Anterior to the oblique
external furrow there are numerous
finely denticulate riblets. The almost
circular, soft mesoplax above the
umbones has irregular wrinkles. White
in colour, with a tan periostracum.
Sculpture of fine concentric parallel
threads. Apophyses long, thin. Pallial
sinus deep. Common in floating or
submerged wood from North Carolina
south to Brazil. Introduced to the
British Isles.

Striate Martesia
1 in (2.5 cm)

Gabb's Piddock,
Penitella gabbi (Tryon, 1863).
Shell thin but strong, elongate-oval,
with an oblique external sulcus, in
front of which is the wide oblique gape
for the foot. Anterior end has numerous
beaded radial ribs. Mesoplax plate in
the adult has broad lateral wings.
Siphonoplax absent. Siphons fused, two
times the length of the shell, without
periostracum, white in colour and
strongly pustulose. Moderately common
in clay and sandstone. Ranges from
Drier Bay, Alaska, to San Pedro,
California.

Smith's Martesia
0.3 in (7 mm)

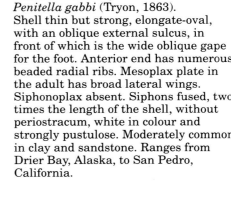

Flat-tipped Piddock
3.5 in (9 cm)

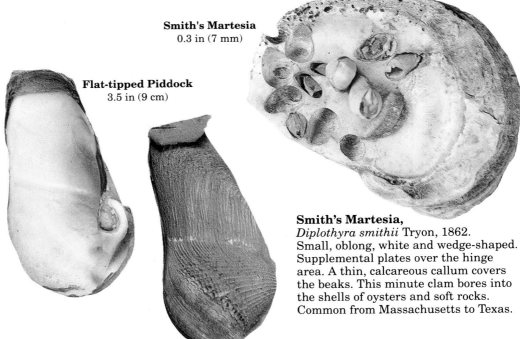

Flat-tipped Piddock,
Penitella penita (Conrad, 1837).
Oval-elongate; adults have a callum
which protrudes beyond the beaks.
Mesoplax plate sharply pointed
posteriorly, truncate anteriorly with
short, pointed lateral wings. Plates on
the siphon composed of two heavy,
flexible chitinous flaps. Siphons
smooth. This is the most common
pholad along the Pacific coast. It bores
into stiff blue clay, sandstone and
cement. It ranges from Alaska to
Mexico.

Smith's Martesia,
Diplothyra smithii Tryon, 1862.
Small, oblong, white and wedge-shaped.
Supplemental plates over the hinge
area. A thin, calcareous callum covers
the beaks. This minute clam bores into
the shells of oysters and soft rocks.
Common from Massachusetts to Texas.

Shipworms
(Family Teredinidae)

Several dozen species of so-called shipworms have for centuries plagued the world of wooden ships. These clams burrow into wood as they grow, leaving a long, white shell-lined tunnel connected with the open sea. Living specimens are common in floating logs and wharf pilings. The shells are of little use in the identification of the teredinid clams, the main useful characters being in the pair of plume-like or club-shaped pallets found at the siphonal end of the worm-like body. Boring is done by the shell. Identification usually requires careful dissection and by consulting an advanced monographic work on the subject.

Gould's Shipworm
8 in (20 cm)

Gould's Shipworm,
Bankia gouldi Bartsch, 1908.
There are many species of *Teredo* and *Bankia* shipworms throughout the northern hemisphere, and a scientific monograph must be consulted in order properly to identify them. The drilling is done by a pair of cup-like shelly valves. The soft parts of the bivalve are encased in long, shelly, white tunnels. The exit to the water is protected by a pair of 'feathery' pallets. The latter are used in identifying species. Great destruction to wooden ships and wharf pilings are done by shipworms and by the crustacean, *Limnoria*.

Lyonsia Clams
(Family Lyonsiidae)

These fragile clams are usually distorted in shape because they are nestlers in peat, sponges and rock crevices. The hinge is without teeth, the ligament is internal, and the resilium rests in a long narrow slot under the dorsal margin. The shell material is usually nacreous, and many species have the habit of cementing sand grains to the shell.

Glassy Lyonsia
0.5 in (1 cm)

California Lyonsia
1 in (2.5 cm)

Glassy Lyonsia,
Lyonsia hyalina Conrad, 1831.
Shell small, fragile, thin and quite elongate, with the anterior end somewhat obese and the posterior end tapering and laterally compressed. Without teeth in the weak hinge, but with a small, free, elongate, calcareous ossicle inside just under the small, inflated, anteriorly pointing beaks. Colour semi-translucent tan. Periostracum very thin, with numerous raised radial lines. Commonly has tiny sand grains attached. Common in shallow sandy areas from Nova Scotia to South Carolina.

California Lyonsia,
Lyonsia californica Conrad, 1837.
Shell very thin, fragile, almost transparent. Quite elongate and moderately obese. Beaks are swollen. Outer surface opalescent-white, commonly with numerous weak, dark radial lines of periostracum. Ossicle inside under the hinge is opaque white. Common in sandy mud bottoms of many Californian sloughs and bays.

Sanded Lyonsia,
Lyonsia arenosa Moller, 1842.
Resembles the Glassy Lyonsia, but much less obese, and more oblong in shape. The periostracum is heavy and often has a dusting of attached sand grains. The dorsal margin of the right valve behind the beak overlaps that of the left valve. There is no posterior gape, as in the Glassy Lyonsia. Moderately common from the low-tide mark to 39 ft (12 m). Ranges from Arctic Seas from Greenland to Maine and from Alaska to Vancouver, British Columbia, and occurs in Scandinavia.

Sanded Lyonsia
0.5 in (1 cm)

Northwest Rock Clam,
Entodesma saxicolum Baird, 1863.
Shell fairly large, ugly, and misshapen;
found along the shore burrowing into
rocks. Usually oblong in shape with the
posterior end flaring and gaping.
Covered with a thick, rough, brown
periostracum which flakes off when
dry. Interior brownish with a slight
opalescence. Hinge without teeth, but
with a rather large, oblong, whitish
ossicle lying under the internally
placed ligament. Moderately common
from southwest Alaska to Washingon.

Northwest Rock Clam
4 in (10 cm)

Pearly Lyonsia
0.5 in (1 cm)

Pearly Lyonsia,
Entodesma beana (Orbigny, 1842).
Shell small, fragile, irregular in shape,
oblong, with a squarish anterior end
where the beaks are located. Pearly
within and outside. Periostracum thin,
tannish. Valves gape slightly at both
ends. Found living in sponges, usually
in shallow water. Rare in the north-
east United States, but moderately
common from North Carolina
southwards to Brazil.

Norwegian Lyonsia,
Lyonsia norvegica (Gmelin, 1791).
Shell elongate-oblong with the
posterior end rosatrate and turned
slightly upwards. Anterior third
swollen. Surface irregular with weak
lines of growth. Periostracum thin,
brownish, opaque, with numerous
microscopic, wavy radial threads.
Rarely reaches 2 in (5 cm) in length.
Common offshore from 64–410 ft
(20–125 m). Ranges from Scandinavia
to the Adriatic Sea.

Norwegian Lyonsia
1.2 in (3 cm)

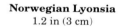

Nuttall's Bladder Clam
2 in (5 cm)

Nuttall's Bladder Clam,
Mytilimeria nuttalli Conrad, 1837.
Shell fragile, obliquely oval, opaque
white with a thin, brownish
periostracum. Beaks small and spiral.
Hinge toothless; a small, calcareous
ossicle is located under the beaks.
Common under rocks at low-tide mark
to 64 ft (20 m), always embedded in
compound ascidians or sea squirts.
Ranges from Alaska to Mexico.

Pandora Clams
(Family Pandoridae)

These are cold-water clams characteristically compressed laterally and with a nacreous shell. Hinge without true teeth, but reinforced by short buttresses or denticles. The black, chitinous resilium is narrow, obliquely set internally. Ligament and pallial sinus absent. The right valve is usually flatter than the left one. Anterior end rounded and the posterior end sometimes rostrate. There are several dozen species in the northern hemisphere, mostly in cold, deep water.

Great Pandora
2 in (5 cm)

Punctate Pandora
1 in (2.5 cm)

Great Pandora,
Pandora grandis Dall, 1877.
Shell white, flat, oval, with the dorsal margin angulated on the more convex valve. Convex valve externally smooth, except for fine lines of growth. An incised line runs from the umbo to the ventral margin of the valve. Interior of valves bright pearly, sparsely punctuated, and with fine grooves radiating from the hinge teeth. Surface chalky white with a thin periostracum with faint, radial incised lines. Uncommon offshore from the Bering Sea to Oregon.

Gould's Pandora
1 in (2.5 cm)

Common European Pandora
1 in (2.5 cm)

Punctate Pandora,
Pandora punctata Conrad, 1837.
Compressed laterally, crescent-shaped with the posterior dorsal margin quite concave, and with small distinct punctations on the inner surface of the valves. This is an abundant species living in sandy mud from the low-tide mark to 128 ft (40 m). It ranges from Vancouver Island to Baja California, Mexico.

Common European Pandora,
Pandora inaequivalvis (Linnaeus, 1758).
Shell thin, oblong, right valve flat, left valve convex. Posterior dorsal margin straight. Anterior end short and evenly rounded. Interior pearly white. Exterior chalky white, usually somewhat eroded. Periostracum thin and greyish. Common offshore from England to the Mediterranean and Canary Islands. *Pandora albida* (Röding, 1798) is a small elongate form of this species.

Gould's Pandora,
Pandora gouldiana Dall, 1886.
Compressed and half-moon-shaped in outline, thick-shelled. The white shell is opaque, chalky and commonly eroded away, showing the pearly underlayers. The posterior rostrum on the hinge line is very short, stubby and turned up. Margin of valves bordered with brownish periostracum. Common from the intertidal area to a depth of 656 ft (200 m). Ranges from the Gulf of St Lawrence to off North Carolina.

Thracia Clams
(Family Thraciidae)

T hese are cold-water clams rarely over 3 inches (8 cm) long, with fragile, white, porcelaneous shells. The surface in most species is microscopically granular. The hinge is without teeth. There is a narrow, spoon-shaped chondrophore directed obliquely toward the posterior end. The pallial sinus is well developed.

Conrad's Thracia,
Thracia conradi Couthouy, 1838. Shell fairly large, oval-oblong. Valves obese and chalky white. Hinge without teeth, but thickened considerably behind the beak and below the large, wide external ligament. Right beak always punctured by the beak in the left valve. Pallial sinus U-shaped, but not very deep. Posterior end of valves slightly rostrate and with a weak radial ridge. Rarely washed ashore. Not uncommon offshore down to 984 ft (300 m). Ranges from Nova Scotia to Long Island Sound, New York.

Conrad's Thracia
4 in (10 cm)

Common Pacific Thracia,
Thracia trapezoides Conrad, 1849. Thin-shelled, but strong, chalky white and with the posterior end broadly rostrate. The beak of the right valve has a hole punctured in it by that of the left valve. Colour drab, greyish white. Commonly dredged offshore from Alaska to central California.

Common Pacific Thracia
2 in (5 cm)

Convex Thracia,
Thracia convexa (Wood, 1815).
Shell oval-elongate, obese, with the
beaks near the centre. Right valve
larger and more convex than the left.
The beak of the left valve sits in a hole
in the beak of the right valve. Colour
white to cream. Periostracum greenish
yellow. Ligament external and internal.
Sculpture of irregular concentric lines
and undulations on a finely granular
surface. Pallial sinus shallow. Lives in
sandy mud offshore from the
Norwegian Sea south to the
Mediterranean.

Convex Thracia
2 in (5 cm)

Paper Thracia
1.5 in (4 cm)

Paper Thracia,
Thracia phaseolina (Lamarck, 1818).
Shell oblong, thin-shelled, but strong;
beaks slightly nearer the posterior end.
Right valve more convex than the left.
Posterior margin truncate and slightly
gaping. Colour white with a brownish
periostracum. Ligament external and
internal, the external part being wide
and small and set immediately behind
the small beaks. The internal portion is
set in a triangular resilifer immediately
below it. Sculpture of smooth concentric
lines and ridges on a very finely
granulated surface. Ranges offshore in
sand and gravel from Norway to the
Mediterranean and Black Sea. Also
known as *papyracea* Poli.

Youthful Thracia
2.7 in (7 cm)

Youthful Thracia,
Thracia pubescens (Pulteney, 1799).
Shell oblong-oval, strong, brittle,
inflated, right valve slightly larger and
more convex than the left. Beaks near
the centre. White or cream in colour.
Periostracum light yellow. Sculpture of
uneven concentric undulations on a fine
granulated surface. Hinge line without
teeth. Interior of shell white with a low
ridge running from the posterior
adductor muscle scar to below the
resilifer. Pallial sinus shallow. Occurs
in sand in shallow water from the
British Isles to the Mediterranean,
West Africa and the Canary Islands.

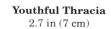

Fleshy Thracia,
Thracia myopsis Möller, 1842.
Shell oval-elongate, evenly rounded at
both ends, brittle, white with a flesh-
coloured periostracum. Exterior
smoothish, with numerous concentric,
irregular lines of growth. Beak in left
valve is punctured by that in the right
valve. Ligament large and prominent.
A common offshore Arctic species
found from Norway to Greenland,
Canada and the north Pacific.

Fleshy Thracia
1 in (2.5 cm)

Spoon Clams
(Family Periplomatidae)

Shell small, oval, right valve fatter than the left, and with a slightly pearly sheen. Hinge has a narrow, oblique spoon and a small free triangular lithodesma. Ligament absent. An internal rib extends from under the hinge to the posterior margin. There are fewer than a dozen North American offshore species and none in north-west Europe.

Lea's Spoon Clam
1 in (2.5 cm)

Lea's Spoon Clam,
Periploma leanum (Conrad, 1831). Thin-shelled and brittle, oval-elongate, moderately compressed, dull white with a thin, yellowish-grey periostracum. Beaks slit or broken by a short radial break. Spoon-like chondrophore faces downwards and is reinforced by a sharp curved rib. Sculpture of fine concentric growth lines. A weak radial groove runs from the beak to the anterior part of the ventral margin. Moderately common from shallow water to 164 ft (50 m). Ranges from Nova Scotia to off North Carolina.

Cusdpidaria Clams
(Family Cuspidariidae)

Small white shells with a swollen, globular anterior half, and a narrow, handle-like posterior half. Hinge without a lateral tooth in the right valve. External ligament elongate. Resilium in a small, spoon-shaped fossette. Lithodesma distinct and semi-circular. These small cold-water species live in large colonies usually at considerable depths.

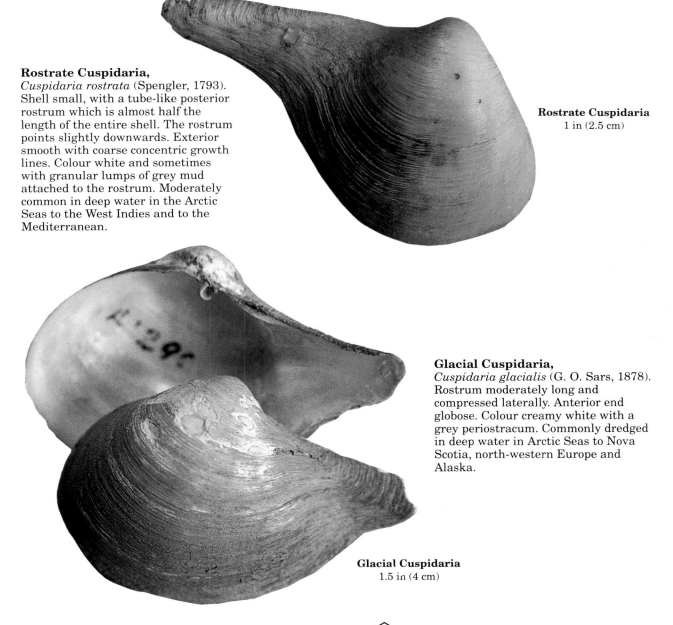

Rostrate Cuspidaria,
Cuspidaria rostrata (Spengler, 1793). Shell small, with a tube-like posterior rostrum which is almost half the length of the entire shell. The rostrum points slightly downwards. Exterior smooth with coarse concentric growth lines. Colour white and sometimes with granular lumps of grey mud attached to the rostrum. Moderately common in deep water in the Arctic Seas to the West Indies and to the Mediterranean.

Rostrate Cuspidaria
1 in (2.5 cm)

Glacial Cuspidaria,
Cuspidaria glacialis (G. O. Sars, 1878). Rostrum moderately long and compressed laterally. Anterior end globose. Colour creamy white with a grey periostracum. Commonly dredged in deep water in Arctic Seas to Nova Scotia, north-western Europe and Alaska.

Glacial Cuspidaria
1.5 in (4 cm)

Glossary of Shell Terms

While many unfamiliar nouns and adjectives used in conchology may be found in dictionaries, for convenience, a glossary of the most frequently used words in our shell descriptions is included here.

Adductor muscle
 (in bivalves) Large muscle inside the shell that closes the two valves.

Anterior end Front end in univalves, the head or siphonal end; in bivalves, where the foot usually protrudes.

Aperture
 The opening in the last whorl, providing an outlet for the head and foot of a snail.

Apex
 The first-formed, narrow end of a snail shell, usually of several whorls.

Axial
 Parallel to the lengthwise axis of a shell; suture to suture features.

Base
 The lower siphonal end of the body or last whorl; opposite the apex.

Beak (or umbo)
 The first formed part of a bivalve's valve, usually above the hinge.

Bivalve
 A member of the class Bivalvia (or Pelecypoda), such as a clam or oyster.

Body whorl
 The largest and most recently formed whorl.

Byssus
 A clump of horny threads spun by the foot of a bivalve and used for attachment.

Callus
 A thickening, usually of shelly material.

Chitinous
 Horny or corneous, usually soft and flexible material making up an operculum.

Chondrophore
 Spoon-shaped shelf in the hinge of a bivalve.

Circumpolar
 Found around either the North or South Pole.

Columella
 The solid pillar at the axis of the univalve shell, around which the whorls grow.

Concentric
 Sculpturing of ridges, ribs or threads, or colour markings, running parallel to the margins of a bivalve or operculum.

Dextral

Right-handed or of whorls growing clockwise. Aperture at right if apex is held uppermost.

Escutcheon

A smooth, long surface on the upper margin of the valve of a bivalve behind the ligament.

Fimbriated

Having thin, wavy, rough, fringed borders.

Fusiform

Shaped like a spindle, swollen in the centre, narrow as each end.

Gape

Opening between the margins of the valves when the bivalve is shut.

Globular

Bulbous, or shaped like a round globe.

Hinge

Top margin of a bivalve where shelly teeth interlock.

Inner lip

The wall on the body whorl opposite the outer lip of the aperture.

Intertidal

Area between high- and low-tide mark.

Ligament

An internal or external horny band, usually behind the beaks, holding the clam's valves together or ajar.

Lira(ae)

Fine, raised lines or teeth, usually spiral in nature.

Lunule

A long or heart-shaped impression on the upper margin of the valves in front of the clam's beaks, one half being in each valve.

Multispiral

Of many whorls, as in some opercula.

Nuclear whorl

The first and smallest whorl in the apex.

Nucleus

The centre or beginning point, usually in an operculum or spire.

Operculum (opercula)

A 'trapdoor' attached to the foot of a snail that, when withdrawn, helps to seal the aperture.

Outer lip

Final edge of the body whorl, often thickened in adults.

Pallial line

A scar line on the inside of a clam's shell, where the mantle muscles are attached.

Pallial sinus

An embayment in the pallial line indicating where the siphon-retracting muscles are attached to the shell.

Parietal wall

The area on the body whorl on the columella side of the aperture (or inner lip).

Paucispiral

Having few whorls, as in *Littorina* opercula.

Periostracum

The chitinous layer covering the outer shell, sometimes thin, thick or hairy.

Plankton

Small animals and plants normally floating in the open ocean.

Prodissoconch

Minute, first-formed shell on the clam's beak.

Radial

Sculpturing or color rays (in bivalves) or (in univalves) ribs running parallel to the main axis, from suture to suture.

Resilium

A horny, pad-like cushion located on the bivalve's chondrophore.

Reticulations

Squarish pattern formed by the crossing of concentric and axial sculpturing.

Sculpture

Relief pattern on the shell surface; ribs, spines.

Sinistral

'Left-handed' or of whorls growing counter-clockwise.

Spiral

Sculpturing or colouring encircling the whorls parallel to the sutures.

Spire

The whorls at the apical end, exclusive of the last whorl.

Substrate

The bottom or supporting surface.

Suture

Continuous line on the shell surface where whorls adjoin.

Teeth, cardinal

The largest two or three teeth just under the beak of a clam.

Teeth, lateral

Smaller, narrow and longer teeth in front or back of the cardinal teeth.

Umbilicus

A central cavity at the base of the shell, around which the whorls coil.

Umbo (umbones)

The beak or beginning part of a bivalve.

Valve

One of the main shelly halves of a bivalve.

Varix

An axial rib or swelling made during a major growth stoppage.

Veliger

Larval form of a mollusc, usually free-swimming and propelled by cilia.

Whorls

A turn or coil of a snail shell.

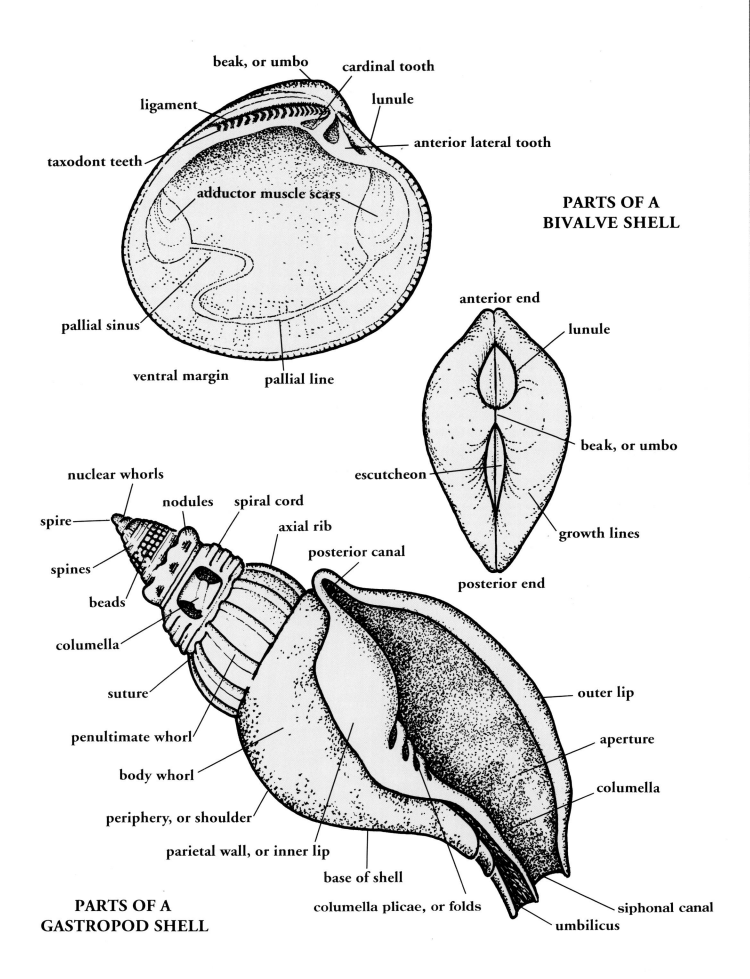

beak, or umbo

cardinal tooth

ligament

lunule

taxodont teeth

anterior lateral tooth

adductor muscle scars

**PARTS OF A
BIVALVE SHELL**

pallial sinus

ventral margin

pallial line

anterior end

lunule

beak, or umbo

escutcheon

growth lines

posterior end

nuclear whorls

nodules

spiral cord

spire

axial rib

spines

posterior canal

beads

columella

suture

penultimate whorl

outer lip

body whorl

aperture

periphery, or shoulder

columella

parietal wall, or inner lip

base of shell

columella plicae, or folds

siphonal canal

umbilicus

**PARTS OF A
GASTROPOD SHELL**

Bibliography

This bibliography will lead you to major reference books and specialized monographs that deal with certain families. Annual listings of the world's literature on molluscs is cross-referenced by subject matter in *The Zoological Record*, section 9 on Mollusca, London and Philadelphia.

Northeastern Pacific

Abbott, R. Tucker 1974, *American Seashells.* 2nd ed., 663 pp., (about 3000 figs), Van Nostrand Reinhold, New York.

Bernard, F. R. 1979, *Bivalve Mollusks of the Western Beaufort Sea [Alaska].* In Sci. Nat. Hist. Mus. Los Angeles Co., no. 313, pp. 1-80, (109 figs).

Bernard, F. R. 1983, *Catalogue of the Living Bivalvia of the Eastern Pacific Ocean*: Bering Strait to Cape Horn. Canadian Special Publ. Fish. Aquat. Sci., vol. 61, 102 pp.

MacGinitie, N. 1959, *Marine Mollusca of Point Barrow,* Alaska. Proc. U.S. Nat. Mus., vol. 109, pp. 59-208.

McLean, James H. 1969, *Marine Shells of Southern California.* 104 pp., (illus.), Los Angeles County Mus. Nat. Hist., Zoology no. 11, Los Angeles.

Rice, Thomas C. 1968, *A Checklist of the Marine Gastropods from the Puget Sound Region.* 169 pp. Of Sea and Shore Publ., Port Gamble, Washington.

Western Atlantic

Abbott, R. Tucker, 1974, *American Seashells.* 2nd ed., 663 pp., (24 pls, 3000 text figs), Van Nostrand Reinhold Co., New York.

Abbott, R. Tucker, 1986, *Seashells of North America.* Revised ed., 280 pp., (illus.), Golden Press, New York.

Bousefield, E. L. 1960, *Canadian Atlantic Shells.* 72 pp. National Mus. Ottawa, Canada.

Clench, William J., (ed.) 1941-74, *Johnsonia - Monographs of the Marine Mollusks of the Western Atlantic,* vols. 1-5, nos. 1-50. Harvard Univ., Cambridge, Massachusetts.

Eastern Atlantic

Ankel, W. E. 1936, *Prosobranchia. In Die Tierwelt der Nord- und Ostsee.* Vol, IX bl. Akadem. Verlagsgesell., Leipzig.

Bouchet, P, Danrigal, F. and Huyghens, C. 1978, *Coquillage des Côtes atlantiques et de la Manche.* Editions du Pacifique, Paris.

Fretter, V. and Graham. A. 1962, *British Prosobranch Molluscs.* 755 pp. Ray Society, London.

Graham, Alastair 1988, *Molluscs: Prosobranch and Pyramidellid Gastropods.* 2nd ed. 662 pp., (276 text figs). E. J. Brill/Dr. W. Backhuys, Leiden.

McMillan, Nora F. 1968, *British Shells.* 196 pp., (80 pls.-32 in colour, 144 illus.pgs). Frederick Warne & Co., London and New York.

Nordsieck, Fritz 1968-69, *Die europaischen Meeresmuscheln (vol. 1, Prosobranchia; vol. 2, Bivalvia; vol. 3, Opisthobranchia).* G. Fischer, Stuttgart.

Parenzan, Pietro 1970-76, *Carta d'identita delle conchiglie del Mediterraneo.* Vol. 1 Gastropodoi; vol. 2, pts 1 and 2, Bivalvi. Ed. Bios Taras, Taranto.

Tebble, Norman 1976, *British Bivalve Seashells.* 2nd ed. 212 pp., (12 pls, 110 text figs). Royal Scottish Mus., Edinburgh.

Thompson, T. E. and Brown, G. H. 1976, *British Opisthobranch Molluscs.* 203 pp. Synopses of the British Fauna (New Series), no. 8. Academic Press, London and New York.

van Benthem Jutting, W. S. S. 1959, *The Netherlands as an environment for molluscan life.* Basteria, vol. 23, supplement, 174 pp. Leiden.

General and Special Groups

Breisch, L. L. and Kennedy, V. S. 1980, *A Selected Bibliography of Worldwide Oyster Literature.* 309 pp. Univ. Maryland, Maryland.

Kaas, P. and Van Belle, R. A. 1980, *Catalogue of Living Chitons.* 144 pp. E. J. Brill/Dr. W. Backhuys, Leiden.

Kaas, P. and Van Belle, R. A. 1985-90, *Monograph of Living Chitons.* Vols. 1-4. E. J. Brill/ Dr. W. Backhuys, Leiden.

Lalli, Carol M. and Gilmer, Ronald W. 1989, *Pelagic Snails: The Biology of Holoplanktonic Gastropod Mollusks.* 259 pp., (76 text figs). Stanford University Press, California.

Moore, R. C. (ed.). 1960-69, *Treatise on Invertebrate Paleontology. Part I (Gastropoda), Part N, vols. 1 and 2 (Bivalvia).* Geol. Soc. America, Boulder, Colorado.

Morton, J. E. 1976, *Molluscs.* 4th ed. 244 pp., (41 text figs). Hutchinson & Co., London.

Thompson, T. E. 1976, *Biology of Opisthobranch Molluscs.* Vol. 1, 207 pp. Ray Society, London.

Thompson, T. E. and Brown, G. H. 1984, *Biology of Opisthobranch Molluscs.* Vol. 2, 229 pp. (41 coloured pls), Ray Society, London.

Turner, Ruth D. 1966, *A Survey and Illustrated Catalogue of the Teredinidae.* 265 pp., (64 pls), Mus. Comp. Zool., Harvard Univ., Cambridge, Massachusetts.

Yonge, C. M. and Thompson, T. E. 1976, *Living Marine Molluscs.* 288 pp., (16 pls, 162 text figs). Collins, London.

Index

Abalone (*Haliotis* spp.)
Black (*H. cracherodii*) 25
Japanese (*H. kamtschatkana*) 26
Northern Green (*H. walallensis*) 26
Red (*H. rufescens*) 25
Threaded (*H. kamtschatkana assimilis*) 26
Acteon, Lathe (*Acteon tornatilis*) 99
Admete (*Admete* spp.)
Greenish (*A. viridula*) 93
Northern (*A. couthouyi*) 93
Aforia, Goode's (*Aforia goodei*) 98
Akera, Bubble (*Akera bullata*) 100
Alvania, Bug (*Alvania cimex*) 48
Amphissa (*Amphissa* spp.)
Joseph's Coat (*A. versicolor*) 69
Columbian (*A. columbiana*) 69
Angel Wing (*Cyrtopleura costata*) 174
Angel Wing, False (*Petricola pholadiformis*) 169
Ark (*Anadara* spp.)
Blood (*A. ovalis*) 123
Transverse (*A. transversa*) 123
Ark, Four-sided (*Arca tetragona*) 123
Ark, Milky (*Arcopsis lactea*) 124
Ark, Nodulose (*Acar nodulosa*) 124
Ark, Ponderous (*Noetia ponderosa*) 124
Astarte (*Astarte* spp.)
Crenate (*A. crebricostata*) 144
Montagu's (*A. montagui*) 143
Smooth (*A. castanea*) 143
Sulcate (*A. sulcata*) 143
Waved (*A. undata*) 144

Baby's Ear, Common (*Sinum perspectivum*) 66
Basket-shell, Common (*Corbula gibba*) 173
Bittersweet (*Glycymeris* spp.)
European (*G. glycymeris*) 125
West Coast (*G. subobsoleta*) 125
Bonnet (*Galeodea* spp.)
Rugose (*G. rugosa*) 62
Spiny (*G. echinophora*) 62
Bonnet, Mediterranean (*Phalium granulatum*) 62
Buccinum (*Buccinum* spp.)
Angulate (*B. angulosum*) 76
Baer's (*B. baeri*) 77
Common Northern (*B. undatum*) 76
Finely-striate (*B. striatissimum*) 78
Finmark (*B. finmarkianum*) 77
Flaky (*B. hydrophanum*) 77
Glacial (*B. glaciale*) 76
Humphreys' (*B. humphreysianum*) 77
Plectrum (*B. plectrum*) 76
Polar (*B. polare*) 77
Silky (*B. scalariforme*) 77
Totten's (*B. totteni*) 76
Buccinum (*Volutharpa* spp.)
Ample Fragile (*V. ampullacea*) 85
Perry's Fragile (*V. ampullacea perryi*) 85
Buccinum, Chestnut (*Volutopsius castaneus*) 78
Buckie *see* Buccinum, Common Northern

Cadulus, Carolina (*Cadulus carolinensis*) 107
Canoe-bubble (*Scaphander* spp.) Giant
(*S. punctostriatus*) 99
Wooden (*S. lignarius*) 99
Cardita (*Cyclocardia* spp.)
Fine-ribbed (*C. crebricostata*) 142
Northern (*C. borealis*) 142
Stout (*C. ventricosa*) 142
Carpet-shell *see* Venus, Decussate
Cavoline, Three-spined (*Diacria trispinosa*) 101
Cavoline, Uncinate (*Cavolinia uncinata*) 102
Chinese Hat (*Calyptraea* spp.)
European (*C. chinensis*) 55
Pacific (*C. fastigiata*) 55
Chiton (*Tonicella* spp.)
Lined Red (*T. lineata*) 111
Mottled Red (*T. marmorea*) 110
Northern Red (*T. rubra*) 110
Chiton, Eastern American (*Chaetopleura apiculata*) 112
Chiton, Giant Pacific (*Cryptochiton stelleri*) 113
Chiton, Magdalena (*Stenoplax magdalenensis*) 112
Chiton, Mertens' (*Lepidozona mertensii*) 111

Chiton, Smooth European (*Callochiton septemvalvis*) 113
Cingulas (*Cingula* spp.)
Pointed (*C. aculeus*) 48
Striate (*C. semistriata*) 48
Clam (*Donax* spp.)
Banded Wedge- (*D. vittatus*) 158
Truncate Wedge- (*D. trunculus*) 158
Clam (*Ensis* spp.)
Atlantic Jackknife (*E. directus*) 152
Giant Razor (*E. siliqua*) 153
Narrow Jackknife (*E. ensis*) 153
Clam (*Gari* spp.) Californian Sunset (*G. californica*) 159
Depressed Sunset (*G. depressa*) 159
Faroes Sunset (*G. fervensis*) 159
Tellin-like Sunset (*G. tellinella*) 159
Clam (*Limaria* spp.)
Hians File (*L. hians*) 136
Inflated File (*L. inflata*) 136
Loscomb's File (*L. loscombi*) 136
Clam (*Lutraria* spp.)
European Otter (*L. lutraria*) 150
Oblong Otter (*L. magna*) 150
Clam (*Nucula* spp.)
Atlantic Nut (*N. proxima*) 118
Nuclear Nut (*N. nucleus*) 119
Smooth Nut (*N. tenuis*) 118
Sulcate Nut (*N. sulcata*) 119
Turgid Nut (*N. turgida*) 119
Clam (*Nuculana* spp.)
Fossa Nut (*N. fossa*) 120
Pitcher Nut (*N. pella*) 121
Pointed Nut (*N. acuta*) 120
Taphria Nut (*N. taphria*) 121
Clam (*Saxidomus* spp.)
Common Washington (*S. nuttalli*) 167
Smooth Washington (*S. gigantea*) 167
Clam (*Siliqua* spp.)
Atlantic Razor (*S. costata*) 152
Pacific Razor (*S. patula*) 152
Squamate Razor (*S. squamata*) 152
Clam (*Solemya* spp.)
Atlantic Awning (*S. velum*) 117
Boreal Awning (*S. borealis*) 117
Toga Awning (*S. togata*) 117
Clam (*Solen* spp.)
Blunt Jackknife (*S. sicarius*) 153
European Razor (*S. vagina*) 153
Clam (*Spisula* spp.)
Atlantic Surf (*S. solidissima*) 149
Catilliform Surf (*S. catilliformis*) 148
Elliptical Trough (*S. elliptica*) 150
Hooked Surf (*S. falcata*) 148
Solid Trough (*S. solida*) 149
Stimpson's Surf (*S. polynyma*) 148
Subtruncate Trough (*S. subtruncata*) 149
Clam (*Thyasira* spp.)
Atlantic Cleft (*T. trisinuata*) 139
Pacific Cleft (*T. bisecta*) 139
Clam, Amethyst Gem (*Gemma gemma*) 168
Clam, Arctic Wedge (*Mesodesma arctatum*) 151
Clam, Bean Razor (*Pharus legumen*) 160
Clam, Boring Softshell (*Platyodon cancellatus*) 172
Clam, California Softshell (*Cryptomya californica*)172
Clam, Flat Furrow (*Scrobicularia plana*) 161
Clam, Giant European File (*Acesta excavata*) 136
Clam, Hardshell *see* Quahog, Northern
Clam, Lea's Spoon (*Periploma leanum*) 182
Clam, Northern Propeller (*Cyrtodaria siliqua*) 170
Clam, Northwest Rock (*Entodesma saxicolum*) 178
Clam, Nuttall's Bladder (*Mytilimeria nuttalli*) 178
Clam, Oxheart (*Glossus humanus*) 163
Clam, Pellucid Razor (*Cultellus pellucidus*) 153
Clam, Pismo (*Tivela stultorum*) 167
Clam, Rayed Trough (*Mactra corallina*) 149
Clam, Rock-eater (*Petricola lithophaga*) 169
Clam, Soft-shell *see* Sand-gaper
Clam, Strigate Razor (*Solecurtus strigillatus*) 160
Clam, Truncate Soft-shell *see* Gaper, Blunt
Clam, Wavy Mysia (*Mysia undata*) 168
Clam, White Abra (*Abra alba*) 161
Clio, Pyramid (*Clio pyramidata*) 101

Cockle (*Acanthocardia* spp.)
European Spiny (*A. aculeata*) 145
Sand (*A. spinosa*) 145
Tuberculate (*A. tuberculata*) 145
Cockle (*Cerastoderma* spp.)
Common European (*C. edule*) 147
Northern Dwarf (*C. pinnulatum*) 147
Cockle (*Clinocardium* spp.)
Iceland (*C. ciliatum*) 147
Nuttall's (*C. nuttallii*) 147
Cockle (*Laevicardium* spp.)
Heavy Egg (*L. crassum*) 146
Morton's Egg (*L. mortoni*) 146
Cockle, Greenland (*Serripes groenlandicus*) 146
Cockle, Hians (*Ringicardium hians*) 146
Colus (*Colus* spp.)
Fat (*C. ventricosus*) 81
Herendeen's (*C. herendeenii*) 81
Iceland (*C. islandicus*) 81
Jeffreys' (*C. jeffreysianus*) 80
Pygmy (*C. pygmaeus*) 79
Simple (*C. gracilis*) 80
Spitzbergen (*C. spitzbergeni*) 80
Stimpson's (*C. stimpsoni*) 81
Twisted (*C. tortuosus*) 80
Colus (*Siphonorbis* spp.)
Fenestrate (*S. fenestratus*) 84
Howse's (*S. howsei*) 84
Ivory (*S. ebur*) 84
Colus, Destiny (*Turrisipho lachesis*) 84
Colus, Kroyer's (*Plicifusus kroyeri*) 84
Cone, Mediterranean (*Conus ventricosus*) 96
Coquina (*Donax variabilis*) 158
Corbula, Fat *see* Basket-shell, Common Corbula, Swift's (*Corbula swiftiana*) 173
Cowrie, Agate (*Cypraea achatidea*) 62
Crenella, Glandular (*Crenella glandula*) 129
Cumingia, Californian (*Cumingia californica*) 162
Cup-and-saucer, Striate (*Crucibulum striatum*) 57
Cuspidaria (*Cuspidaria* spp.)
Glacial (*C. glacialis*) 183
Rostrate (*C. rostrata*) 183

Diplodont (*Diplodonta* spp.)
Pacific Orb (*D. orbellus*) 140
Rotund (*D. rotundata*) 140
Dogwinkle (*Nucella* spp.)
Atlantic (*N. lapillus*) 73
Channeled (*N. canaliculata*) 73
Emarginate (*N. emarginata*) 73
File (*N. lima*) 73
Frilled (*N. lamellosa*) 72
Dosinia (*Dosinia* spp.)
Mature (*D. exoleta*) 168
Wolf (*D. lupinus*) 167
Dove-shell (*Astyris* spp.)
Lunar (*A. lunata*) 68
Rosy Northern (*A. rosacea*) 68
Variegated (*A. tuberosa*) 68
Dove-shell (*Nitidella* spp.)
Carinate (*N. carinata*) 69
Gould's (*N. gouldi*) 69
Drill, Atlantic Oyster (*Urosalpinx cinerea*) 71
Drill, Thick-lipped (*Eupleura caudata*) 72
Drillia, Incised (*Ophiodermella incisa*) 98
Drupe (*Acanthina* spp.)
Checkered Thorn (*A. paucilirata*) 72
Spotted Thorn (*A. spirata*) 72

Emarginula (*Emarginula* spp.)
Crass (*E. crassa*) 27
Sicilian (*E. sicula*) 27

Fan-mussel *see* Pen Shell, Fragile
Flask, Spotted (*Ampulla priamus*) 95

Gaper, Alaskan (*Tresus capax*) 149
Gaper, Blunt (*Mya truncata*) 172
Geoduck (*Panopea abrupta*) 171
Gibbula (*Gibbula* spp.)
Ashen (*G. cineraria*) 41
Magical (*G. magus*) 40
Umbilicate (*G. umbilicalis*) 41

Hairy-shell (*Trichotropis* spp.)
Cancellate (*T. cancellatus*) 54
Grey (*T. insignis*) 54
Two-keeled (*T. bicarinatus*) 54
Half-slipper, Pacific (*Crepipatella lingulata*) 57
Hoof-shell, White (*Hipponix antiquatus*) 58

Jewel Box, Clear (*Chama arcana*) 141
Jewel Box, Pacific Left-handed (*Pseudochama exogyra*) 141
Jingle, False Pacific (*Pododesmus macroschisma*) 135
Jingle Shell (*Anomia* spp.)
Common (*A. simplex*) 135
Prickly (*A. squamula*) 135
Saddle (*A. ephippium*) 135

Lacuna (*Lacuna* spp.)
Common Northern (*L. vincta*) 47
Variegated (*L. variegata*) 47
Lamellaria, Transparent (*Lamellaria perspicua*) 59
Limopsis, Sulcate (*Limopsis sulcata*) 124
Limpet (*Diodora* spp.)
Graecian Keyhole (*D. graeca*) 29
Italian Keyhole (*D. italica*) 29
Rough Keyhole (*D. aspera*) 30
Tanner's Keyhole (*D. tanneri*) 30
Limpet (*Fissurella* spp.)
Cloudy Keyhole (*F. nubecula*) 29
Volcano (*F. volcano*) 29
Limpet (*Lottia* spp.)
File (*L. limatula*) 33
Fingered (*L. digitalis*) 34
Shield (*L. pelta*) 33
Unstable (*L. instabilis*) 34
Limpet (*Patella* spp.)
Common European (*P. vulgata*) 31
European China (*P. aspera*) 32
Rayed Mediterranean (*P. caerulea*) 32
Ribbed Mediterranean (*P. ferruginea*) 32
Rustic (*P. rustica*) 32
Limpet (*Tectura* spp.)
Atlantic Plate (*T. testudinalis*) 35
Fenestrate (*T. fenestrata*) 35
Mask (*T. persona*) 34
Pacific Plate (*T. scutum*) 35
Rough Pacific (*T. scabra*) 34
Limpet, Blue-rayed (*Helcion pellucidum*) 31
Limpet, Fool's Cap (*Capulus ungaricus*) 55
Limpet, Seaweed (*Discurria insessa*) 34
Limpet, Two-spotted Keyhole (*Megatebennus bimaculatus*) 30
Limpet, White-cap (*Acmaea mitra*) 33
Littleneck, Common Pacific (*Protothaca staminea*) 166
Littleneck, Japanese *see* Venus, Filipino
Lora, Elegant (*Oenopota elegans*) 97
Lucina (*Lucinoma* spp.)
Boreal (*L. borealis*) 138
Northeast (*L. filosa*) 138
Western Ringed (*L. annulata*) 138
Lyonsia (*Lyonsia* spp.)
California (*L. californica*) 177
Glassy (*L. hyalina*) 177
Norwegian (*L. norvegica*) 178
Sanded (*L. arenosa*) 177
Lyonsia, Pearly (*Entodesma beana*) 178

Macoma (*Macoma* spp.)
Balthica (*M. balthica*) 155
Bent-nose (*M. nasuta*) 156
Brota (*M. brota*) 157
Chalky (*M. calcarea*) 155
Doleful (*M. moesta*) 156
Fouled (*M. inquinata*) 156
Queen Charlotte (*M. carlottensis*) 156
Tenta (*M. tenta*) 156
White Sand (*M. secta*) 157
Yoldia-shaped (*M. yoldiformis*) 157
Macron, Livid (*Macron lividus*) 85
Mactra (*Mactra* spp.)
California (*M. californica*) 148
Gould's Pacific (*M. nasuta*) 150
Malletia, Obtuse (*Malletia obtusa*) 122
Mangelia (*Mangelia* spp.)
Attenuated (*M. attenuata*) 97
Slender (*M. gracilis*) 97
Margarite (*Lischkeia* spp.)
Adams' Spiny (*L. cidaris*) 37
Baird's Spiny (*L. bairdii*) 36
Otto's Spiny (*L. ottoi*) 37
Regular Spiny (*L. regularis*) 37

Margarite (*Margarites* spp.)
Greenland (*M. groenlandicus*) 36
Northern Rosy (*M. costalis*) 36
Puppet (*M. pupillus*) 37
Sordid (*M. sordidus*) 36
Marginella, Boreal (*Marginella roscida*) 94
Martesia, Smith's (*Diplothyra smithii*) 175
Martesia, Striate (*Martesia striata*) 175
Melampus, Eastern (*Melampus bidentatus*) 103
Melampus, Mouse (*Ovatella myosotis*) 103
Mitre (*Mitra* spp.)
Ebony (*M. ebenus*) 92
Little Trumpet (*M. cornicula*) 92
Mitre (*Volutomitra* spp.)
Alaskan False (*V. alaskana*) 92
False Greenland (*V. groenlandica*) 92
Monodont (*Monodonta* spp.)
Articulate (*M. articulata*) 42
Lined (*M. lineata*) 41
Turbinate (*M. turbinata*) 42
Mopalia (*Mopalia* spp.)
Hinds' (*M. hindsii*) 112
Mossy (*M. muscosa*) 111
Murex, Festive (*Pteropurpura festiva*) 71
Murex, Purple Dye (*Bolinus brandaris*) 70
Murex, Trunculus (*Hexaplex trunculus*) 70
Musculus (*Musculus* spp.)
Black (*M. niger*) 129
Discord (*M. discors*) 129
Mussel (*Adula* spp.)
Californian Date (*A. californiensis*) 127
Falcate Date (*A. falcata*) 127
Non-boring Date (*A. diegoensis*) 127
Mussel (*Modiolus* spp.)
Adriatic Horse (*M. adriaticus*) 129
Bearded Horse (*M. barbatus*) 129
False Tulip (*M. modiolus squamosus*) 128
Fan-shaped Horse (*M. rectus*) 128
Northern Horse (*M. modiolus*) 128
Tulip (*M. americanus*) 128
Mussel (*Mytilus* spp.)
Blue (*M. edulis*) 126
Californian (*M. californianus*) 126
Mediterranean Blue (*M. galloprovincialis*) 126
Mussel, Atlantic Ribbed (*Geukensia demissa*) 128
Mussel, Conrad's False (*Mytilopsis leucophaeata*) 164
Mussel, European Date (*Lithophaga lithophaga*) 126
Mussel, Hooked (*Ischadium recurvum*) 127
Mussel, Senhouse's (*Muscilista senhousei*) 127
Mussel, Zebra (*Dreissena polymorpha*) 164
Mya, Ample Rough (*Panomya ampla*) 171

Nassa (*Nassarius* spp.)
Clathrate (*N. clathratus*) 90
Common Eastern (*N. vibex*) 89
Giant Western (*N. fossatus*) 88
Little Horn (*N. corniculum*) 90
New England (*N. trivittatus*) 89
Pygmy (*N. pygmaeus*) 89
Reticulated (*N. reticulatus*) 90
Thickened (*N. incrassatus*) 90
Western Fat (*N. perpinguis*) 89
Western Lean (*N. mendicus*) 88
Western Mud (*N. tegula*) 90
Natica (*Naticarius* spp.)
Dillwyn's (*N. dillwyni*) 66
Flamed (*N. filosus*) 66
Fly-specked (*N. sterncusmuscarum*) 66
Natica, Arctic (*Natica clausa*) 66
Necklace Shell, European (*Lunatia catena*) 64
Neptune (*Beringion* spp.)
Behring's (*B. behringi*) 79
Kennicott's (*B. kennicottii*) 79
Marshall's (*B. marshalli*) 79
Neptune (*Neptunea* spp.)
Ancient (*N. antiqua*) 82
Clench's (*N. despecta clenchi*) 82
Common Northwest (*N. lyrata*) 81
Contrary (*N. contraria*) 83
Disreputable (*N. despecta*) 82
Double-sculptured (*N. intersculpta*) 80
Heros (*N. heros*) 83
New England (*N. lyrata decemcostata*) 82
Phoenician (*N. lyrata phoenicia*) 82
Smirnia (*N. smirnia*) 83
Stiles (*N. stilesi*) 83
Tabled (*N. tabulata*) 83
Upright (*N. ithia*) 80
Ventricose (*N. ventricosa*) 82
Neptune, Turton's (*Neoberingius turtoni*) 79

Olive (*Olivella* spp.)
Beatic Dwarf (*O. baetica*) 91
Purple Dwarf (*O. biplicata*) 91
San Pedro Dwarf (*O. pedroana*) 91
Ormer, European (*Haliotis tuberculata*) 26
Oyster (*Crassostrea* spp.)
Eastern American (*C. virginica*) 137
Giant Pacific (*C. gigas*) 137
Oyster (*Ostrea* spp.)
Common European (*O. edulis*) 137
Crested (*O. equestris*) 137

Pandora (*Pandora* spp.)
Common European (*P. inaequivalvis*) 179
Gould's (*P. gouldiana*) 179
Great (*P. grandis*) 179
Punctate (*P. punctata*) 179
Panomya, Arctic (*Panomya arctica*) 171
Paper-bubble (*Haminoea* spp.)
Gould's (*H. vesicula*) 100
Solitary (*H. solitaria*) 100
Sowerby's (*H. virescens*) 100
Watery (*H. hydatis*) 100
Paper-bubble, Open (*Philine aperta*) 99
Pelican's Foot (*Aporrhais* spp.)
American (*A. occidentalis*) 60
Common (*A. pespelecani*) 60
MacAndrew's (*A. serresianus*) 60
Pen Shell, Fragile (*Pinna fragilis*) 130
Periwinkle (*Littorina* spp.)
Checkered (*L. scutulata*) 46
Common (*L. littorea*) 45
Eroded (*L. keenae*) 46
Marsh (*L. irrorata*) 45
Northern Rough (*L. saxatilis*) 46
Northern Yellow (*L. obtusata*) 45
Sitka (*L. sitkana*) 46
Pheasant Shell (*Tricolia* spp.)
Baby (*T. pullus*) 44
Beautiful (*T. speciosa*) 44
Piddock (*Penitella* spp.)
Flat-tipped (*P. penita*) 175
Gabb's (*P. gabbi*) 175
Piddock, American *see* Angel Wing, False
Piddock, European (*Pholas dactylus*) 175
Piddock, Paper (*Pholadidea loscombiana*) 174
Piddock, Wart-necked (*Chaceia ovoidea*) 174
Pteropod, Cigar (*Cuvierina columnella*) 102
Puncturella (*Puncturella* spp.)
Helmet (*P. galeata*) 28
Hooded (*P. cucullata*) 28
Noah's (*P. noachina*) 28
Purpura (*Ceratostoma* spp.)
Foliated Thorn (*C. foliatum*) 70
Nuttall's Thorn (*C. nuttalli*) 70

Quahog, Northern (*Mercenaria mercenaria*) 165
Quahog, Ocean (*Arctica islandica*) 163

Rissoa, Parchment (*Rissostomia membranacea*) 48
Rupellaria, Hearty (*Rupellaria carditoides*) 169

Sand-gaper (*Mya arenaria*) 172
Saxicave, Arctic (*Hiatella arctica*) 170
Scallop (*Chlamys* spp.)
Hinds' (*C. rubida*) 134
Iceland (*C. islandica*) 132
Pacific Spear (*C. hastata hastata*) 133
Snow (*C. nivea*) 133
Sulcate (*C. sulcata*) 133
Variable (*C. varia*) 133
Scallop (*Hinnites* spp.)
Giant Rock (*H. giganteus*) 134
Hunchback (*H. distortus*) 134
Scallop (*Pecten* spp.)
Giant Pacific (*P. caurinus*) 132
Great (*P. maximus*) 131
St James' (*P. jacobaeus*) 131
Scallop, Atlantic Bay (*Argopecten irradians*) 134
Scallop, Atlantic Deepsea (*Placopecten magellanicus*) 131
Scallop, Bald (*Proteopecten glaber*) 132
Scallop, Kitten (*Camptonectes tigerinus*) 133
Scallop, Queen (*Aequipecten opercularis*) 134
Scallop, Seven-rayed (*Pseudamussium septemradiatum*) 132
Semele (*Semele* spp.)
Bark (*S. decisa*) 162
Rose Petal (*S. rubropicta*) 162
Shark Eye (*Neverita duplicata*) 63
Shipworm, Gould's (*Bankia gouldi*) 176

Slipper-shell (*Crepidula* spp.)
Common Atlantic (*C. fornicata*) 58
Convex (*C. convexa*) 58
Eastern White (*C. plana*) 58
European White (*C. unguiformes*) 57
Hooked (*C. adunca*) 57
Western White (*C. nummaria*) 58
Slipper-shell, False Arctic
(*Capulacmaea commodum*) 59
Snail (*Amauropsis* spp.)
Iceland Moon (*A. islandicus*) 65
Purplish Moon (*A. purpurea*) 65
Snail (*Janthina* spp.)
Common Purple Sea- (*J. janthina*) 49
Dwarf Purple Sea- (*J. exigua*) 49
Elongate Purple Sea- (*J. globosa*) 49
Pallid Sea- (*J. pallida*) 49
Snail (*Lunatia* spp.)
Alder's Moon (*L. alderi*) 64
Common Northern Moon (*L. heros*) 64
Dusky Moon (*L. fusca*) 65
Guillemin's Moon (*L. guillemini*) 64
Lewis' Moon (*L. lewisi*) 64
Pale Northern Moon (*L. pallida*) 64
Spotted Northern Moon (*L. triseriata*) 63
Snail (*Neverita* spp.)
Drake's Moon (*N. draconis*) 63
Josephine's Moon (*N. josephinia*) 63
Snail, Eastern Mud (*Ilyanassa obsoleta*) 88
Snail, Oldroyd's Fragile Moon (*Calinaticina oldroydii*) 65
Snail, Smith's Moon (*Bulbus smithi*) 65
Solarelle (*Solariella* spp.)
Lovely Pacific (*S. permabilis*) 37
Obscure (*S. obscura*) 37
Spindle (*Fusinus* spp.)
Harford's (*F. harfordi*) 87
Syracuse (*F. syracusanus*) 87

Tagelus (*Tagelus* spp.)
Purplish (*T. divisus*) 160
Stout (*T. plebeius*) 160
Tegula (*Tegula* spp.)
Black (*T. funebralis*) 40
Brown (*T. brunnea*) 41
Tellin (*Angulus* spp.)
European White (*A. albicans*) 157
Flat (*A. planatus*) 157
Fleshy (*A. incarnatus*) 155
Tellin (*Tellina* spp.)
Bodegas (*T. bodegensis*) 154
Donax (*T. donacina*) 155
Great Alaskan (*T. lutea*) 154
Modest (*T. modesta*) 154
Salmon (*T. nuculoides*) 154
Story (*T. fabula*) 155
Tellin, Thick (*Arcopagia crassa*) 156

Thracia (*Thracia* spp.)
Common Pacific (*T. trapezoides*) 180
Conrad's (*T. conradi*) 180
Convex (*T. convexa*) 181
Fleshy (*T. myopsis*) 181
Paper (*T. phaseolina*) 181
Youthful (*T. pubescens*) 181
Top-shell (*Calliostoma* spp.)
Baird's (*C. bairdii*) 38
Channeled (*C. canaliculatum*) 39
European Granular (*C. granulatum*) 40
European Painted (*C. zizyphinus*) 39
Gualteri's (*C. gualterianum*) 40
Horn (*C. conulum*) 39
Northern (*C. occidentale*) 38
Ringed (*C. annulatum*) 38
Variable (*C. variegatum*) 39
Western Ribbed (*C. ligatum*) 39
Top-shell, Exasperating (*Jujubinus exasperatus*) 40
Triton (*Ocenebra* spp.)
Carpenter's Dwarf (*O. interfossa*) 74
Poulson's Dwarf (*O. poulsoni*) 74
Triton (*Urosalpinx* spp.)
Lurid Dwarf (*U. lurida*) 71
Spindle Dwarf (*U. fusulus*) 71
Triton, Crested Dwarf (*Muricopsis cristatus*) 72
Triton, Knobbed (*Charonia lampas*) 67
Triton, Oregon (*Fusitriton oregonensis*) 67
Trivia (*Trivia* spp.)
Arctic (*T. arctica*) 61
Flea (*T. pulex*) 61
Nun (*T. monacha*) 61
Trophon (*Boreotrophon* spp.)
Alaskan (*B. alaskanus*) 75
Clathrate (*B. clathratus*) 74
Latticed (*B. craticulatus*) 75
Northwest Pacific (*B. pacificus*) 74
Orpheus (*B. orpheus*) 75
Stuart's (*B. stuarti*) 74
Truncate (*B. truncatus*) 75
Trophon, Sandpaper (*Trophonopsis lasius*) 75
Turban (*Astraea* spp.)
Red (*A. gibberosa*) 43
Rugose (*A. rugosa*) 43
Turban, Carpenter's Dwarf (*Homalopoma carpenteri*) 43
Turret-shell, Common (*Turritella communis*) 50
Turret-shell, Eroded (*Tachyrhynchus erosus*) 50
Turrid, Perverse (*Antiplanes voyi*) 98
Tusk (*Antalis* spp.)
Common (*A. vulgaris*) 107
Entale (*A. entalis*) 106
Stimpson's (*A. entalis stimpsoni*) 107
Wampum (*A. pretiosum*) 106
Western Atlantic (*A. occidentale*) 106
Tusk, European (*Dentalium dentale*) 107

Tusk, Meridian (*Fissidentalium meridionale*) 107
Tusk, Western Straight (*Laevidentalium rectius*) 106

Velutina, Smooth (*Velutina velutina*) 59
Venus (*Venerupis* spp.)
Decussate (*V. decussata*) 166
Rhomboidal (*V. rhomboides*) 166
Venus, Chamber (*Circomphalus casinus*) 165
Venus, Chicken (*Chamelea gallina*) 165
Venus, Chione (*Callista chione*) 166
Venus, Filipino (*Ruditapes philippinarum*) 166
Venus, Kennerley's (*Humilaria kennerleyi*) 168
Venus, Milky Pacific (*Compsomyax subdiaphana*) 168
Venus, Morrhua (*Pitar morrhuanus*) 167
Venus, Warty (*Venus verrucosa*) 165
Volute, Stearns' (*Arctomelon stearnsi*) 95

Wentletrap, Wroblewski's (*Opalia wroblewskii*) 51
Wentletrap (*Acirsa* spp.)
Costate (*A. costulata*) 51
Northern White (*A. borealis*) 51
Wentletrap (*Epitonium* spp.)
Angulate (*E. angulatum*) 52
Brown-banded (*E. rupicola*) 52
Common European (*E. clathrus*) 53
Couthouy's (*E. novangliae*) 53
Greenland (*E. greenlandicum*) 52
Humphreys' (*E. humphreysi*) 52
Many-ribbed (*E. multistriatum*) 52
Money (*E. indianorum*) 52
Trevely's (*E. trevelyanum*) 53
Turton's (*E. turtonis*) 53
Whelk (*Volutopsius* spp.)
Melon Volute (*V. melonis*) 78
Middendorff's Volute (*V. middendorffi*) 78
Norwegian Volute (*V. norvegicus*) 78
Whelk, Channeled (*Busycotypus canaliculatus*) 86
Whelk, Dire (*Searlesia dira*) 85
Whelk, Kellet's (*Kelletia kelleti*) 85
Whelk, Knobbed (*Busycon carica*) 86
Whelk, Ovum Arctic (*Liomesus ovum*) 81
Whelk, Sinistral Arctic (*Pyrolofusus deformis*) 78
Winkle (*Ocinebrina* spp.)
Edwards' Dwarf (*O. edwardsii*) 71
Sharp Dwarf (*O. aciculata*) 72
Winkle, Sting (*Ocenebra erinacea*) 73
Worm-shell, Scaled (*Serpuloides squamigerus*) 56

Yoldia (*Yoldia* spp.)
Almond (*Y. amygdalea*) 121
Broad (*Y. thraciaeformis*) 122
Cooper's (*Y. cooperi*) 122
Cross-cut (*Y. scissurata*) 122
File (*Y. limatula*) 122

Acknowledgments

The author thanks the curators and staff of the Departments of Mollusks at the Museum of Comparative Zoology, Harvard University; the Academy of Natural Sciences of Philadelphia and the U.S. National Museum in Washington D.C., for their kindness in permitting him to study and photograph the molluscs under their care.

Photographers Acknowledgments

Title page - Heather Angel
Page
8   Heather Angel
10   TOP Coastline La Push, Washington USA – Robert A Jureit, Planet Earth Pictures
10   MIDDLE Sedge-marsh peat banks, Virginia – R. Tucker Abbott
10   BOTTOM Gower Peninsula, Wales – John Lythgoe, Planet Earth Pictures
11   TOP Intertidal rocks, UK coastline – Geoff du Feu, Planet Earth Pictures
11   BOTTOM Menai Straits, Wales – John D. Orr
14   TOP R. Tucker Abbott
14   BOTTOM David George, Planet Earth Pictures
16   TOP R. Tucker Abbott
16   BOTTOM RIGHT Robert Robertson
16   BOTTOM LEFT R. Tucker Abbott
17   TOP Robert Robertson
17   BOTTOM PETER Scoones, Planet Earth Pictures
18   TOP Sinclair Stammers, Science Photo Library
18   BOTTOM David Maitland, Planet Earth Pictures
19   TOP RIGHT R. Tucker Abbott
19   TOP LEFT David George, Planet Earth Pictures
19   BOTTOM RIGHT David George, Planet Earth Pictures
19   BOTTOM LEFT R. Tucker Abbott
20   TOP RIGHT John Lythgoe, Planet Earth Pictures
20   TOP LEFT R. Tucker Abbott
20   BOTTOM RIGHT R. Tucker Abbott
20   BOTTOM LEFT R. Tucker Abbott
21   R. Tucker Abbott
22   David George, Planet Earth Pictures
104/5   David George, Planet Earth Pictures
108/9   Mark Mattock, Planet Earth Pictures
114/5   David Woodfall/NHPA
184/5   R. Tucker Abbott